Foundation Chemistry

second edition

Bob McDuell

Thomas Nelson and Sons Ltd
Nelson House   Mayfield Road
Walton-on-Thames   Surrey KT12 5PL

51 York Place
Edinburgh EH1 3JD

Thomas Nelson (Hong Kong) Ltd
Toppan Building 10/F
22A Westlands Road
Quarry Bay   Hong Kong

Distributed in Australia by

Thomas Nelson Australia
480 La Trobe Street
Melbourne   Victoria 3000
and in Sydney, Brisbane, Adelaide and Perth

First published by Thomas Nelson and Sons Ltd 1976
Reprinted 5 times
Second edition 1983
Reprinted 1984 (twice), 1987

ISBN 0—17—438239—1
NCN 12—KSC—3442—04

Diagrams by Colin Rattray and Illustrated Arts
Printed in Hong Kong

The author and publishers are grateful to the following for permission
to use their photographs.

Aero Films Limited p 30 (both)
Alcan Aluminium pp 39 (both), 91
Berger Paints p 122
British Oxygen Company Limited p 24 (all)
British Rail p 50
British Steel Corporation p 43
The British Tourist Authority p 33
Bullers Limited p 86
Canadian Tourist Office p 57 (top)
J. Allan Cash p 56
Chubb Fire Security Limited p 29
Corning Limited (Laboratory Division) p 157 (below)
Courtaulds Limited pp 69 (both), 106
De Beers p 152 (both)
De Lorean p 60 (below)
Evode Limited p 128
Fisons Limited p 64 (below)
Glass Manufacturers' Federation p 157 (top)
Imperial Chemical Industries Limited pp 42, 64 (top), 67 (all), 105,
   126, 136
International Nickel p 93
Nalfloc Limited p 34
Nchanga Consolidated Mines Limited pp 1, 92
Pilkingtons Limited p 160 (both)
Rolls-Royce Limited pp 46, 60 (top)
Salisbury Photo Press p 7
Shell Photographic Services p 99
Science Museum, London pp 26, 53, 57 (below)
Stoe, Darmstadt p 82 (below)
United Kingdom Atomic Energy Authority pp 140, 142
United States Information Services p 37
All other photographs by Thomas Nelson and Sons Limited

Thanks are due to the East Anglian Examinations Board, The Joint
Matriculation Board, the Southern Regional Examinations Board, the
Welsh Joint Education Committee, and the West Midlands
Examinations Board for their kind permission to reproduce questions
from past examination papers.

Contents

Preface

It was my intention in writing this book to produce a simple text which included, in a concise form, the information needed for a modern C.S.E. Chemistry course. In addition I attempted to provide some interesting background reading and illustrations to enable students to realize the importance of Chemistry in industry and everyday life.

In order to keep the book simple and readable mathematical concepts and most chemical equations using symbols have been removed from the main text and are to be found in Appendices.

Questions have been included at the end of Chapters and throughout the appendices. The questions have been designed to assist the teacher in ensuring the student's understanding of the text. The examination questions are not intended to copy exactly the questions of any particular examination board.

This book can be used in a variety of ways. These include:

1 A background reader to follow up a practical session. Many students have difficulty in getting the essential conclusions from practical work. This book aims to emphasize these conclusions and clarify them.

2 A useful revision book containing the basic content of each section together with questions.

3 A book that is useful for pupils with difficulties due to absence or incomplete notes.

The book has been used with C.S.E. students and I am grateful for their suggestions. Teachers faced with classes containing both G.C.E. and C.S.E. students or preparing students for a common examination at 16+ should find this book useful.

In conclusion, I must thank the publishers for their assistance, also Mr Roy Williams, and especially my wife and family for their encouragement and tolerance as the project developed.

Preface to the second edition

The first edition has been very well received and, from letters and conversations I have had, has fulfilled a need for a modern Chemistry text for CSE pupils.

It was intended to be used by teachers following a Nuffield-type course, but it has also been adopted for use with O-level classes. The aims and structure of the new edition are very similar. I have, however, extended the scope of the contents to make the book more useful for non-Nuffield courses. The section on atomic structure has been enlarged and new sections on metals and sulphur have been included.

The first edition has had a significant effect on the development of several CSE Chemistry schemes and has been included in at least one suggested book list. In this edition I felt this should be reflected, and a number of past examination questions appear.

The book, in its new form, is even more suitable for use in preparation for the common examination at 16+.

I am confident that this new edition will form the basis of a Chemistry course at 16+ in the eighties.

Again, I wish to thank my wife and family for their encouragement, and the staff of Thomas Nelson and Sons Ltd.

1. Tools of the chemist

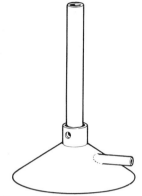

Figure 1.1a

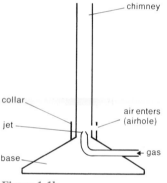

Figure 1.1b

The commonest heating apparatus used in the laboratory is the **bunsen burner** (figure 1.1). A bunsen burner uses **town gas, natural gas** or **bottled gas** as fuel.

The airhole enables different amounts of air to be mixed with the gas before burning. Different flames can be produced by opening and closing the airhole.

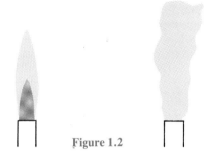

Figure 1.2

Table 1.1

Air hole open—non-luminous flame	Air hole closed—luminous flame
Very hot flame	Flame is not very hot
Regular shape	Irregular shape
Inner blue flame consists of unburnt gas	Soot is deposited in the flame
X is the hottest point in the flame	

One ring on a household **gas cooker** consists of about twenty small non-luminous flames.

Measuring temperature

Temperature is measured with a thermometer. There are two temperature scales used in chemistry. These are the **Celsius** (Centigrade) scale and **Kelvin** scale.

Table 1.2

	Celsius °C	Kelvin K
Lowest temperature possible	−273	0
Melting ice	0	273
Room temperature (approx.)	20	293
Boiling water	100	373
Boiling sulphur	444	717

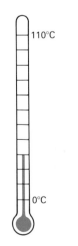

Figure 1.3 A thermometer. What temperature does the thermometer show?

Weighing

A balance is used for weighing. The units used for weighing are **grams** (g).

Measuring very small lengths

The unit used for measuring length is the **metre** (m). In chemistry we are often dealing with objects that are very small indeed. The unit used when measuring very small things is the **nanometre** (nm).

$$1 \text{ nm} = 10^{-9} \text{ m} = \frac{1}{1\,000\,000\,000} \text{ m}$$

A sewing needle has a diameter of about 500 000 nm.

Measuring volume

At a constant temperature the volume of a solid or a liquid remains unchanged. A gas, however, expands to fill all the available space inside a container. The volume of a gas is best measured using a gas syringe.
● The volume of a **gas** can be changed by varying both the temperature of the gas and the pressure exerted on the gas. It is usual to give the temperature and pressure when quoting the volume of a gas.
● The volume of a **liquid** can be measured using the apparatus in figure 1.5.
● The volume of a **solid** can be obtained by immersing the solid in a measuring cylinder half filled with water (or other suitable liquid). The change in reading on the measuring cylinder is the same as the volume of the solid. The volume of the solid in figure 1.6 is $60 \text{ cm}^3 - 50 \text{ cm}^3 = 10 \text{ cm}^3$.

The units frequently used to measure volume are:

cubic centimetres (cm^3—sometimes ml or cc are seen)
cubic decimetres (dm^3)
$1 \text{ dm}^3 = 1000 \text{ cm}^3$

The unit **litre** (l) is sometimes seen and this is the same as cubic decimetres.

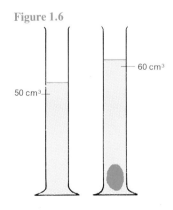

Microelectronics come to Chemistry! A top pan balance gives a direct read-out.

Figure 1.4

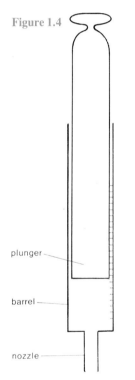

plunger

barrel

nozzle

Figure 1.5

graduated beaker (not very accurate)

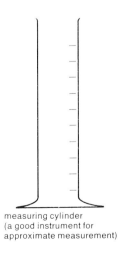

measuring cylinder (a good instrument for approximate measurement)

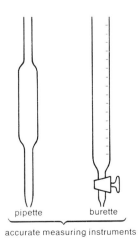

pipette   burette

accurate measuring instruments

Figure 1.6

50 cm³   60 cm³

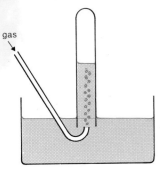

Figure 1.7

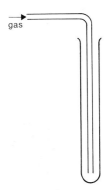

Figure 1.8

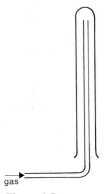

Figure 1.9

Methods of collecting a gas

Any gas can be collected in a gas syringe. There are three other methods of collecting a gas.

    a **over water** (figure 1.7): this cannot be used if the gas dissolves in water or if the gas is required dry.

    b **by downward delivery** (figure 1.8): this is used if the gas is much heavier than air, e.g. chlorine or sulphur dioxide.

    c **by upward delivery** (figure 1.9): this is used if the gas is much lighter than air, e.g. hydrogen.

Drawing chemical diagrams

Very often a clear diagram can be used instead of several sentences of explanation. The following points should be remembered when diagrams are drawn:

- Don't draw diagrams too small.
- Draw section diagrams, i.e. what you would see if the apparatus was cut in half. In figure 1.1, (b) should be drawn rather than (a).
- Try to ensure that no part of the diagram is too large or too small compared with the rest of the diagram.
- Don't attempt to draw all the stands, bosses and clamps used to support the apparatus. They only confuse the diagram.
- Don't forget to put in all bungs, corks and connecting tubes.
- Fully label the diagram.

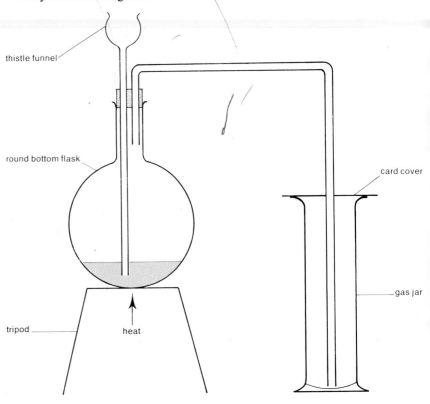

Figure 1.10

something to think about . . .

1 Figure 1.11 is a diagram that contains several mistakes. Look at it carefully and by comparing it with other diagrams in this book, list all the mistakes. You can then draw the diagram again correctly.

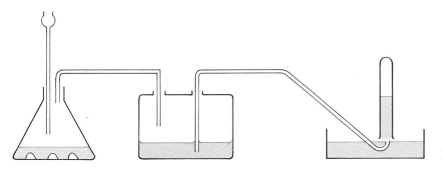

Figure 1.11

2 Copy and complete the following crossword (figure 1.12)

Across
1. A piece of apparatus used for measuring temperature. (11)
7. Found at the bottom of a burette. (3)
8. A top ____ balance is used for weighing in the laboratory. (3)
9. A container made of glass. (6)
11. A measuring ____ is used for measuring volume in the kitchen. (3)
12. Used to cool down steam in order to turn it to water. (9)
13. The abbreviation for a unit of length used for measuring the sizes of tiny particles. (2)

Down
1. A cheap piece of glass apparatus. (4, 4)
2. _____ basin. (11)
3. The abbreviation for one thousandth part of a litre. (2)
4. May be used for removing iron filings from a mixture of iron filings and salt crystals. (6)
5. May be used to support a flat bottomed vessel while heating. (6)
6. Used for collecting and measuring the volume of gases. (7)
8. A piece of apparatus used for measuring out an accurate volume of a liquid. (7)
10. You may think this piece of apparatus is in charge. (4)
11. A gas ____ is used for collecting gases. (3)

Figure 1.12

3 Figure 1.13 shows pieces of apparatus used frequently in chemistry. Copy the diagrams and label them correctly using the names in the following list:

conical flask   funnel   beaker   measuring cylinder
mortar and pestle   evaporating basin   crucible

Figure 1.13

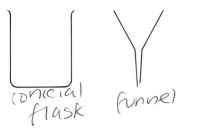
conical flask

funnel

mortar and pestle

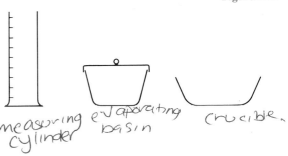
measuring cylinder   evaporating basin   crucible.

2. Separating things

When salt is added to water, it dissolves in the water. It is no longer possible to see the salt but it is, of course, still there. The substance which dissolves (salt in this case) is called the **solute**. The substance which does the dissolving (water in this case) is called the **solvent** and the resulting mixture is called a **solution**. Salt is said to be **soluble** in water.

Chalk is **insoluble** in water; in other words, it does not dissolve in water. If fine chalk powder is added to water and the mixture is stirred, the mixture is cloudy.

There are other common solvents, such as ethanol, hexane and xylene. If a solute dissolves in one solvent it does not necessarily dissolve in any other solvent.

There are other common solvents including ethanol, tetrachloromethane (sometimes called carbon tetrachloride), and xylene. If a substance dissolves in one solvent it does not necessarily dissolve in any other solvent.

Generally solids are more soluble in hot water than in cold water. Gases are more soluble in cold water than in hot water.

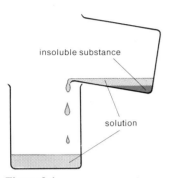

Figure 2.1

Separating an insoluble substance from a liquid

Examples could be chalk from a mixture of chalk and water, or sand from a mixture of sand and salt solution. There are three methods that can be used.

1 Decantation

If the insoluble substance is heavy (that is, if it has a high density) it may settle to the bottom and the solution can be poured off carefully; for example, in the cleaning of mercury, dilute nitric acid is added to the mercury. The dilute nitric acid reacts with the impurities in the mercury. The dilute nitric acid can be removed from the mercury by decantation (figure 2.1).

2 Filtration

The whole mixture is poured through a folded filter paper supported in a filter funnel (figure 2.2). The liquid passes through the small holes in the filter paper but the solid (or residue) is trapped on the filter paper. The liquid passing through the filter paper is called the filtrate.

In the purification of drinking water, solid impurities are removed by filtering the water through a bed of sand and gravel.

Filtration can be carried out more quickly by reducing the pressure to suck the filtrate through the filter paper (figure 2.3).

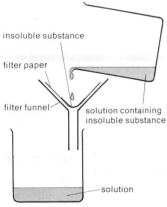

Figure 2.2

3 Centrifuging

This is usually used when there is only a small amount of material. The liquid containing undissolved solid is spun round very rapidly in a **centrifuge**. The solid collects at the bottom of the tube with the liquid above it. The liquid can be removed by decantation. Centrifuging is used when blood cells are being removed from a blood sample.

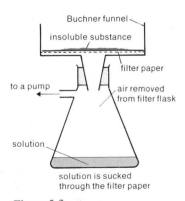

Figure 2.3

Separating the solute from a solution

An example of this might be separating **salt** from salt solution. The salt can be obtained by boiling away or evaporating away the water (figure 2.4). The salt remains in the evaporating basin. It is important to boil the solution carefully so that 'spitting' and loss of the salt is avoided. Slow evaporation of a solution can be achieved by putting the evaporating basin containing the solution under an infrared lamp.

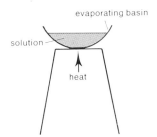

Figure 2.4

To obtain the solvent from a solution

In this case you could be separating pure (distilled) water from salt solution. When the solution is boiled, the water turns to **steam** and the solid impurities remain. If the steam is cooled down it condenses to form liquid water. The water is now pure as it has now been removed from its impurities. This process is called **distillation** (figure 2.5).

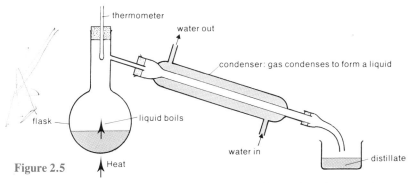

Figure 2.5

Heat is required to boil the water and heat is produced when the steam condenses. Cold water running through the condenser removes the heat evolved when the steam condenses.

Distillation can be used to produce drinking water from sea water in those countries where the sun can be used to boil the water.

Fractional distillation

Distillation is used to remove a liquid from solid impurities. If the impurities are also liquids, fractional distillation is used (figure 2.6).

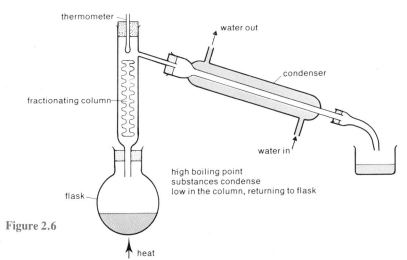

Figure 2.6

Simple distillation in progress.

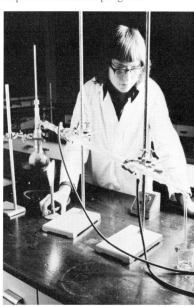

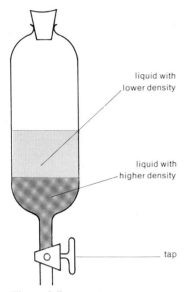

liquid with lower density

liquid with higher density

tap

Figure 2.7

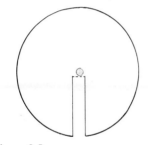

Figure 2.8a

spot of solution

filter paper

wick

solvent

Figure 2.8b

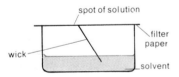

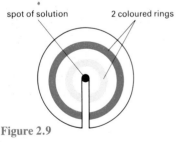

spot of solution   2 coloured rings

Figure 2.9

Fractional distillation is used to increase the strength of ethanol in whisky and other spirits. It is also used in the refining of crude oil into saleable products such as petrol, paraffin, and so on. Fractional distillation is also used to separate the gases in air. (They are turned into liquids first.)

Solvent extraction

Two solvents which dissolve in one another are said to be **miscible**. Water and ethanol are miscible and if they are mixed together only a single layer is produced.

Two solvents which do not dissolve in one another are water and hexane. They are said to be **immiscible**. If they are mixed together they form two separate layers (figure 2.7). Hexane, being less dense than water, forms the upper layer. These liquids can be separated by running the lower water layer through the tap until only the upper layer remains.

If solid iodine is added to the mixture of water and hexane, more of it dissolves in the hexane layer than in the water layer (called the **aqueous** layer). This is because iodine is more soluble in hexane than in water. This is called **partition**.

Two solvents which do not dissolve in one another are water and tetrachloromethane (carbon tetrachloride). They are said to be **immiscible**. If they are mixed together they form two separate layers (figure 2.7). They can be separated by running the lower layer off through the tap until only the upper layer remains.

If solid iodine is added to the mixture of water and tetrachloromethane, more of it dissolves in the tetrachloromethane layer than in the water layer (called the **aqueous** layer). This is because iodine is more soluble in tetrachloromethane than in water. This is called partition.

Radioactive protactinium 223 can be separated from uranium and its decay products by forming a complex protactinium compound which is very soluble in an organic solvent. This dissolves in an organic solvent while other substances remain in the aqueous layer.

Chromatography

Chromatography is a method of separating a mixture of substances in solution. Frequently the substances to be separated are coloured. Chromatography is based on the idea of partition.

When the solvent in the beaker travels up the wick it reaches the spot of solution to be separated. This spot spreads out on the piece of filter paper (figure 2.8a, b). Each substance in the mixture spreads out at a different rate depending on the relative liking of this substance for the solvent used and the paper. When dry, the chromatogram in figure 2.9 would show that the sample contained a mixture of two substances in solution.

In practice, a square sheet of paper is often used. The sample **spots** are put on a base line and the paper is allowed to dry thoroughly. The paper is then coiled into a cylinder and put into a tank with a lid. At the bottom of the tank there is a small amount of solvent. The position of the spots must be above the level of the **solvent**. The tank is then left until the solvent has travelled about three-quarters of the way up the paper. The paper is removed, the final position of the solvent is marked and the paper allowed to dry. This is called ascending paper chromatography (figure 2.10).

If the substances being used are colourless they must be developed (or coloured) in some way before the chromatogram can be used.

Chromatography can be used as a detective to solve problems. For instance food can be coloured only by certain water-soluble food dyes. These dyes are made from coal tar residues.

If the dye is extracted from a sample of orange squash, for example, the dyes present in the food can be found by paper chromatography. In this way the use of illegal or unsafe dyes in food can be controlled. This kind of work is done by the public analyst.

Chromatography can be used to diagnose certain medical conditions. **Amino acids** taken in as food by a person are used to build up proteins in the body. If a sick person is not able to use the amino acids correctly, excess of amino acids can be detected in a urine sample by paper chromatography.

Sublimation

Usually when a solid is heated it turns to a liquid and then on further heating to a gas. However, some substances change from a solid to a gas without becoming a liquid. On cooling the solid reforms. This is called sublimation. Examples of substances that sublime are ammonium chloride and iodine.

Iodine can be separated from substances that do not sublime using the apparatus in figure 2.11.

something to think about . . .

1 Which of the methods mentioned in this chapter would you use in order to separate
    a large pieces of glass from a solution?
    b ammonium chloride from a soluble fertiliser? ⁻f
    c pure (or distilled) water from river water?
    d the coloured dyes in a plant?

2 Copy and complete the following crossword.

Across
1. Change directly from a vapour to a solid. (7)
3. Abbreviation for a solution in which the solvent is water. (2)
6. This is done to prevent loss of heat in pipes etc. (3)
8. Used to remove an undissolved solid from a solution. (6)
9. Water will _____ if it is left exposed to the air. (9)
11. Often used for simple demonstrations of chromatography. (3)
12. A solute is said to be _____ in the solvent. (7)

Down
1. Water is a good _____ because it dissolves a wide range of substances. (7)
2. Formed when water is cooled below 0°C. (3)
4. Turn to vapour by heat, condense by cold, and recollect to remove impurities. (6)
5. Pour off a liquid slowly without disturbing the sediment. (6)
7. The material used to make most pieces of laboratory apparatus. (5)
10. Crude ___ is separated into fractions by fractional distillation. (3)

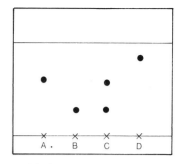

× original position of each substance
● final position of each substance

A and B have not separated
C is shown to be a mixture of A and B

Figure 2.10

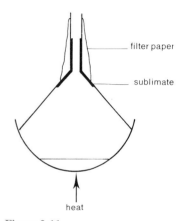

filter paper

sublimate

heat

Figure 2.11

Figure 2.12

3. Elements, mixtures, compounds

Table 3.1

Hydrogen	H
Oxygen	O
Sulphur	S
Calcium	Ca
Helium	He
Magnesium	Mg
Nitrogen	N
Chlorine	Cl
Silver	Ag
Copper	Cu
Iron	Fe
Mercury	Hg
Sodium	Na
Potassium	K

An **element** is a single pure substance which cannot be split up by chemical action. All substances we know are either elements or they are made up from several elements in different amounts.

There are approximately 105 different elements known. Some of these like gold, carbon and copper have been known for many thousands of years and some like einsteinium and nobelium have been man-made in the last thirty years of so. Each element is represented by one or two letters called a **symbol**. Some common elements and their symbols are shown in table 3.1. (A complete list of elements and their symbols will be found on pages 186–8.)

Elements are made up of **atoms**. Atoms are very small and it is impossible to see them even with a microscope. A piece of the element iron is made up from iron atoms and a piece of the element carbon is made from carbon atoms.

Dividing elements into groups

Elements can be divided into groups according to their state at room temperature and pressure (that is, whether they are solid, liquid or gas). At room temperature, there are only two liquids—mercury and bromine. Of the remainder, most are solids at room temperature. The only gases are hydrogen, helium, nitrogen, oxygen, fluorine, neon, chlorine, argon, krypton, xenon and radon.

The elements can also be divided into **metals** and **non-metals**. Table 3.2 shows the differences between metals and non-metals.

Unfortunately some elements do not clearly fit into either group. They are called **metalloids**.

As a guide, most elements ending in -ium are metals (exceptions include helium, selenium).

Mixtures and compounds

If two powdered elements are mixed together, the atoms of the two elements are mixed. They can still be easily separated.

However, it may be possible to combine these **elements** together to form a **compound**. This compound formation is usually accompanied by an **energy change**.

Examples of mixtures and compounds are described in Tables 3.4, 3.5 and 3.6.

Compound formation involves the joining together of atoms of different elements into groups of atoms called **molecules**. The molecules of a compound are all composed of the same number of each type of atom.

The elements iodine and aluminium reacting together to form the compound aluminium iodide. Much energy is evolved, and this is called an **exothermic** reaction.

Table 3.2

Metals	Non-metals
Physical Properties	
Solid at room temperature	Solid, liquid or gas at room temperature
Shiny	Dull
High density	Low density
Conducts heat and electricity	Does not conduct heat and electricity
Can be beaten into thin sheets and drawn into wires	Easily broken
Chemical Properties	
Forms a neutral or alkaline oxide	Forms acidic or neutral oxide
Forms positive ions	Forms negative ions
Sometimes produces hydrogen from dilute acid solutions	Never produces hydrogen from dilute acid solutions

Table 3.3

Mixture	Compound
Proportions of different elements can be altered.	Different elements have to be present in fixed proportions.
Elements can be separated by simple methods.	Difficult to separate into its constituent elements.
Properties of the mixture are the same as the properties of the elements making it up.	Properties of the compound are different from the properties of the elements making it up.
No energy change when a mixture is made.	Energy is usually evolved or absorbed when a compound is formed.

Examples of mixtures and compounds

Table 3.4

Elements	**Iron** is a grey, magnetic metal **Sulphur** is a yellow solid
Mixture of elements	Mixture is greenish in colour. Iron can be removed with a magnet. Sulphur can be removed by dissolving in a suitable solvent, e.g. carbon disulphide.
Forming the compound	Heat the mixture. Energy is evolved on compound formation.
Compound	Black solid lump called **iron sulphide**. Iron cannot be removed with a magnet. Sulphur cannot be removed by dissolving.

Table 3.5

Elements	**Aluminium** is a silvery metal which is insoluble in water. **Iodine** is a greyish black solid which is insoluble in water.
Mixture of elements	Greyish black mixture.
Forming the compound	Either heat the mixture gently or add a drop of water (acts as a catalyst). Energy is evolved and purple iodine vapour escapes from the hot mass.
Compound	White solid called **aluminium iodide**. Aluminium iodide is soluble in water.

Table 3.6

Elements	**Hydrogen** and **oxygen** are both colourless gases.
Mixture of elements	A colourless gas.
Forming the compound	Either apply a lighted splint (with care) or mix the elements in the presence of a platinum catalyst at room temperature.
Compound	Colourless liquid called **hydrogen oxide** (commonly called **water**).

Figure 3.1 shows what is happening in compound formation. (The diagrams are simplified. The arrangement of atoms in the original elements and the arrangement of molecules in the final compound may be more complex than shown. They are shown only in two dimensions and the atoms and molecules will be in constant motion.)

Figure 3.1

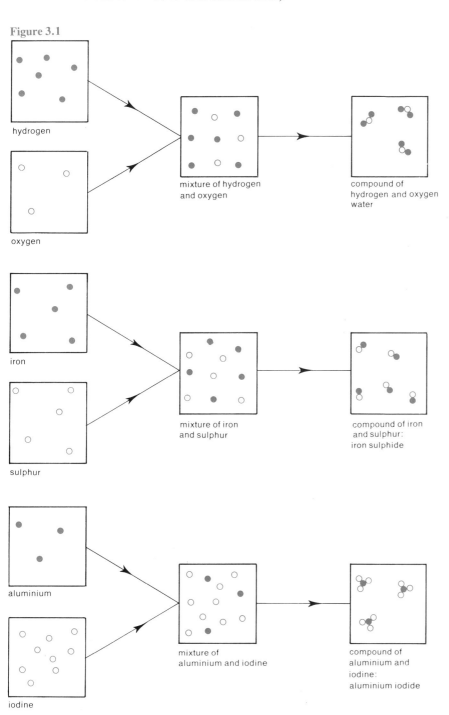

hydrogen

oxygen

mixture of hydrogen and oxygen

compound of hydrogen and oxygen water

iron

sulphur

mixture of iron and sulphur

compound of iron and sulphur: iron sulphide

aluminium

iodine

mixture of aluminium and iodine

compound of aluminium and iodine: aluminium iodide

something to think about . . .

1 The symbols of the elements are often the first letter of the name of the element, for example, carbon C or sulphur S. Sometimes the symbol is the first two letters of the name of the element, for example Ca for calcium or Co for cobalt. The first letter and one other letter in the name is used in some cases, for example Mg for magnesium or Cl for chlorine. A few elements have symbols that do not seem to come from their name. Find examples in Table 3.1 of elements with symbols that do not seem to come from their names. Can you explain how these elements got their symbols?

2 Which one of the diagrams in figure 3.2 represents
    a an element?
    b a pure compound?
    c a mixture of elements?
    d a mixture of compounds?
    e a reaction between two elements which is not completed?

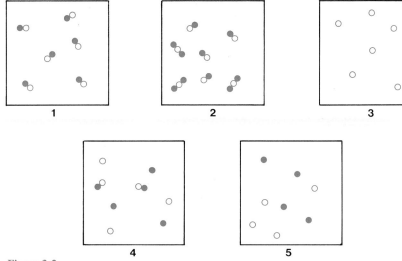

Figure 3.2

3   A a pure element
    B a mixture of elements
    C a pure compound
    D a mixture of compounds
    E a mixture of elements and compounds.
Into which of the above groups would you put (i) distilled water (ii) air (iii) petrol (iv) sugar (v) silicon (vi) iodine dissolved in hexane?

4 There are some interesting and exciting stories about the discovery of the elements. Find out what you can about the discovery of radium, caesium, sodium, helium, californium, oxygen.

5 One of the elements is called dysprosium. Using the letters in this name and the table on pages 186–8 write down as many symbols for known elements as possible. e.g. Po for polonium, and so on. You can find over thirty.

4. Action of heat

When a sample of a substance is heated in a test tube, in a crucible or by holding in tongs, one or more of the following changes may occur.

Change of state

There are three states of matter—solid, liquid and gas. A solid on heating may melt and change to a liquid. A liquid may boil and change to a gas. A solid may change directly to a gas or to a liquid and then to a gas. A change of state on heating can tell us something about the structure of the substance.

Change in colour

Since most chemicals are white in colour or colourless, any colour change may help in identification. Colours of common residues include:
black   carbon, copper(II) oxide, manganese(IV) oxide
reddish-brown   iron(III) oxide
white when cold but **yellow** when hot   zinc oxide
yellow powder on cooling (frequently cracks glass)   lead(II) oxide

A gas is produced

The gases commonly produced when substances are heated are shown in Table 4.1.

Table 4.1

Gas	Evolved from
Oxygen	Nitrates (often nitrogen dioxide also produced). Permanganates and other oxygen-rich compounds. Some metal oxides.
Carbon dioxide	Most carbonates and all hydrogencarbonates. Burning of carbon and carbon compounds.
Steam	Hydrated compounds. Burning of compounds containing hydrogen.
Nitrogen dioxide (brown gas)	With oxygen when some metal nitrates are heated.
Hydrogen chloride	Some hydrated chlorides.
Oxides of sulphur	Some sulphates.

Noticeable flame

Some substances when heated burn in a particular way. When magnesium burns it burns with a bright white flame.

Change in mass

If a substance is weighed before heating and again after heating (the substance must have cooled to room temperature) there may be an increase or decrease in mass. An increase in mass comes from the combination of

Table 4.2

Substance	Original appearance	Change on heating
Copper sulphate crystals	Blue crystals	On gentle heating, colourless gas produced which condenses to form colourless droplets on the cooler part of the tube.
Cobalt(II) chloride crystals	Purple-pink crystals	On gentle heating, colourless gas produced which condenses to form colourless droplets on the cooler part of the tube.
Ammonium chloride	White crystals	On gentle heating, solid turns directly to a gas. White solid collects on the cooler part of the tube. Avoid strong heating.
Iodine	Dark grey crystals	On gentle heating it readily vaporises forming a dark purple vapour. Dark grey crystals form on the cooler part of the tube. Avoid strong heating.
Zinc carbonate	White powder	On gentle heating, colourless gas is given off which turns limewater milky (carbon dioxide). Residue is yellow.
Magnesium ribbon	Silvery strip	No change on gentle heating. On strong heating it burns with a bright white flame producing dense white fumes.
Zinc oxide	White powder	Turns pale yellow on gentle heating.
Sulphur	Yellow solid	Melts on gentle heating to produce a yellow liquid. Further changes occur on further heating (Chapter 22). Avoid strong heating.
Copper foil	Reddish-brown solid	On heating it glows red.
Red lead	Reddish-orange powder	Darkens. Melts and produces a reddish-coloured liquid. Gives off oxygen which relights a glowing splint.
Potassium permanganate	Purple crystals	On gentle heating, mixture darkens. A fine black powder escapes and oxygen (which relights a glowing splint) is produced.
Silicon(IV) oxide	Yellowish powder	No change.

the substance with a gas from the surrounding air. A decrease in mass comes from the loss of part of the substance to the surroundings.

In Table 4.2 you can see what happens when some common substances are heated.

Change on cooling	Residue	Mass change
White residue remains	Anhydrous copper sulphate—water is lost.	Decrease
Pale blue residue remains	Anhydrous cobalt(II) chloride—water is lost.	Decrease
No residue at the bottom of the tube. White solid on the cooler part.	Ammonium chloride	No change unless gases escape
No residue at the bottom of the tube. Dark grey solid on the cooler part.	Iodine	No change unless gas escapes
White powder remains	Zinc oxide	Decreases
A white solid residue produced	Largely magnesium oxide	Increase in mass (providing fumes do not escape)
White powder	Zinc oxide	Nil
Yellow solid	Sulphur	Nil—unless heated strongly
Black coating on the foil	Copper(II) oxide coating	Small increase
Yellow powder	Lead(II) oxide	Decrease
Very dark green (looks black)	Potassium manganate and manganese(IV) oxide	Decrease
No change	Silicon(IV) dioxide	No change

Depending on the results of heating, substances can be divided into three groups:

1 Substances which **do not change** on heating, for example, sand (silicon(IV) oxide).

2 Substances which change **irreversibly** or permanently on heating (in other words, it is difficult or impossible to change the products back into the original substance). Examples of irreversible changes are the heating of red lead or the charring of wood on heating.

3 Substances which **change temporarily**. These changes are reversible, that is, the products either change back into the original substance on cooling (for example, zinc oxide or sulphur), or can be changed back simply (for example, addition of water to the residue from heating copper sulphate crystals reforms the original substance).

something to think about . . .

1 From the list of substances in Table 4.2 select
    (i) one substance which remains completely unchanged on heating.
    (ii) five substances which change irreversibly on heating.
    (iii) four substances which reform the original substances on cooling.

2 A white powder was heated in the apparatus in figure 4.1. A colourless gas was produced and collected in the gas syringe. The test tube and white powder were weighed before and after heating.
    Mass of test tube + white powder   = 23.19 g
    Mass of test tube + white powder after heating = 23.12 g
At the end of the experiment 40 cm³ of gas (at room temperature and pressure) were collected.
    a What mass change occured on heating?
    b What was the mass of 40 cm³ of the colourless gas?
    c Calculate the mass of (i) 1 cm³ of gas (at room temperature and pressure) (ii) 24 000 cm³ of gas (at room temperature and pressure).

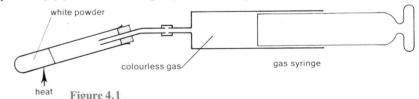

white powder

colourless gas

gas syringe

heat   **Figure 4.1**

Here are some values for the mass of 24 000 cm³ of different gases at room temperature and pressure.

hydrogen	2 g
nitrogen	28 g
oxygen	32 g
carbon dioxide	44 g
sulphur dioxide	64 g

    d Which one of these five gases is most likely to be lost when the white powder is heated?

5. Oxygen and the air

Air is a mixture of gases. Its composition varies from place to place because it is a mixture. Figure 5.1 shows the composition of a typical sample of air by volume.

The other gases present in air include

carbon dioxide	0.03 per cent	neon	0.002 per cent
water vapour	variable	krypton	0.0001 per cent
argon	0.9 per cent	xenon	0.00001 per cent
helium	0.0005 per cent		

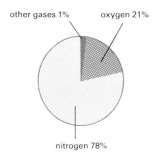

Figure 5.1

Separating air into its constituent gases

Air can be separated into its constituent gases by fractional distillation of liquid air.

Carbon dioxide and water are removed from the air first, by cooling until they freeze out. If this is not done these gases would freeze and block pipes during later stages.

The air is then compressed and cooled. When the air is then allowed to expand again it cools. These compression and expansion stages are carried out again and again until the temperature has cooled to about −200°C (73 K). At this temperature all gases apart from helium and neon have liquefied.

The liquid air is then allowed to warm up slowly. Nitrogen gas boils off before oxygen because nitrogen has a lower boiling point.

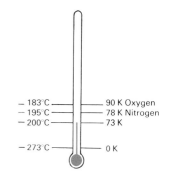

Figure 5.2

Uses of oxygen

1 Used for **breathing apparatus** in hospitals, high flying aeroplanes, diving etc.
2 Liquid oxygen is used to burn the fuel in a rocket.
3 **Steel making**. Oxygen is blown through molten iron to remove carbon, phosphorus and other impurities.
4 Oxy-acetylene cutting and **welding** equipment. Oxygen and acetylene (ethyne) produce high temperatures (about 3000 K) on combustion.

Uses of nitrogen

Nitrogen is not produced in such large amounts as oxygen because it has fewer uses.
1 Large quantities of nitrogen are used to produce **ammonia** (Chapter 19), **nitric acid** (Chapter 10) and explosives.
2 Nitrogen is used to provide an unreactive atmosphere in some chemical reactions.
3 Crisp bags are filled with nitrogen before sealing. This keeps oxygen out of the bag.

Uses of oxygen; BELOW cutting using a portable unit; RIGHT in the operating theatre.

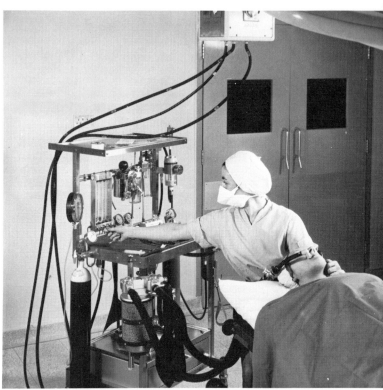

Uses of nitrogen; BELOW liquid nitrogen shrink fitting; RIGHT nitrogen freezing of ice cream.

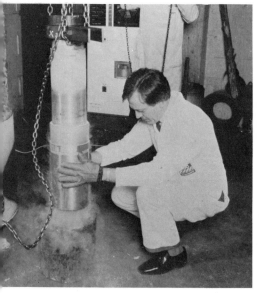

The percentage of oxygen in a sample of air

Oxygen is the active gas in the air. The other gases are inactive.

An approximate method

When a piece of phosphorus burns in air, phosphorus(V) oxide is produced. The phosphorus(V) oxide dissolves in water to form an acidic solution. If the piece of white phosphorus is set alight with a hot glass rod the phosphorus burns forming white fumes. After the burning the water level rises about one fifth.

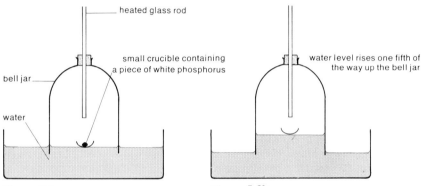

Figure 5.3a   Figure 5.3b

An accurate syringe method

Two gas syringes are connected to the opposite ends of a hard glass or silica tube packed with copper turnings. A sample of air (volume $100\,cm^3$) is trapped in one of the syringes and the other syringe contains no air. The apparatus is checked to ensure that no air can escape.

The hard glass tube is heated and the air passed from one syringe to the other so that it passes over the heated copper. Oxygen is removed from the air by the copper, and a black coating of copper(II) oxide forms on the surface of the copper.

The apparatus is allowed to cool again to room temperature so that the expanded gases can contract to the volume they occupy at room temperature and pressure. The volume of gas remaining will be about $80\,cm^3$ showing that about $20\,cm^3$ of oxygen was present in the $100\,cm^3$ sample of air.

During the experiment the hard glass tube and contents increase in mass by the same amount as the air decreases in mass.

Iron wool can be used instead of copper in the hard glass tube.

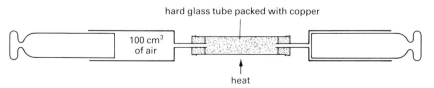

Figure 5.4

Table 5.1 Comparing oxygen, nitrogen and carbon dioxide

	Oxygen	Nitrogen	Carbon dioxide
	Colourless	Colourless	Colourless
Smell	No smell	No smell	No smell
Density At room temperature and pressure (g dm^{-3}).	1.33	1.17	1.83
Solubility in water	Almost insoluble	Almost insoluble	Slightly more soluble
pH of solution	7 (neutral)	7 (neutral)	5.5 (slightly acidic)
Test for gas	Glowing splint relights.	Lighted splint goes out. Limewater does not go milky.	Lighted splint goes out. Limewater turns milky.

Laboratory preparation of oxygen

Oxygen can be prepared by heating **red lead** or potassium permanganate in the apparatus in figure 5.5. The gas can be collected over cold water.

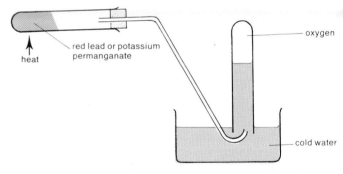

Joseph Priestly produced oxygen in 1774 by heating mercury (II) oxide.

Figure 5.5

A better method of preparing oxygen is the decomposition of hydrogen peroxide using a **catalyst** like manganese(IV) oxide (manganese dioxide).

hydrogen peroxide → water + oxygen

The apparatus in figure 5.6 can be used to prepare and collect oxygen.

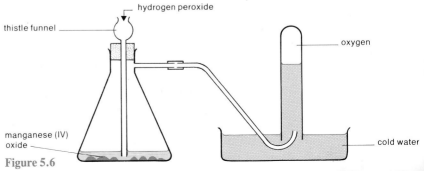

Figure 5.6

Burning or combustion

The burning or combustion of a substance is the combination of the substance with pure oxygen or the oxygen from the air. The loss of heat and/or light usually accompanies combustion.

The term combustion is occasionally used in reactions not involving oxygen. An example is the combustion of sodium in chlorine gas to form sodium chloride.

Burning elements in oxygen or air
From the results in Table 5.2 it can be concluded that
1 Elements burn better in oxygen than in air.

2 Metals burn in oxygen to produce **oxides** that are neutral or alkaline.

Acidic oxides are produced only when non-metals burn in oxygen.

Table 5.2

	Combustion in air	Combustion in oxygen	pH of residue	Name of residue
Magnesium	Burns brightly with a white flame	Burns brightly with a white flame	11 (strongly alkaline)	Magnesium oxide (a small amount of magnesium nitride is also formed when magnesium burns in air)
Sulphur	Burns with a very small blue flame	Burns with a bigger blue flame	4 (acidic)	Sulphur dioxide
Copper	No noticeable flame Copper glows red hot		7 (neutral)	Coating of copper(II) oxide
Carbon	Glows red	Glows brighter	5.5 (slightly acidic)	Carbon dioxide (mixed with carbon monoxide)
Iron wool	Glows red	Burns well	7 (neutral)	Iron oxide iron(II) diiron(III) oxide (ferrosoferric oxide) Fe_3O_4

Combustion of carbon compounds
Compounds of carbon like **petrol, paraffin**, or **sugar** burn in oxygen or air. If they burn in a large amount of oxygen or air, the products include **carbon dioxide** and **water**. When carbon compounds burn in air or oxygen the products include carbon monoxide and water.

Combustion of a candle
When a candle burns the heat from the flame turns the hydrocarbon wax

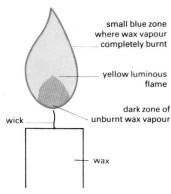

small blue zone
where wax vapour
completely burnt

yellow luminous
flame

dark zone of
unburnt wax vapour

wick

wax

Figure 5.7

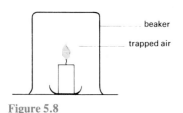

beaker

trapped air

Figure 5.8

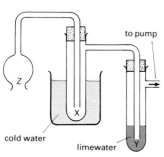

to pump

Z

X

cold water

limewater

Y

Figure 5.9

to a gas and it is this gas that burns. The flame (shown in figure 5.7) resembles a luminous bunsen burner flame because it is yellow and forms soot.

Combustion of a candle in a limited volume of air

If a burning candle is trapped under a beaker containing a volume of air the candle continues to burn for a while. After a while the flame goes smaller and then goes out.

The candle uses up the oxygen inside the beaker but the candle goes out before all the oxygen is used up. The burning candle produces a number of products including soot (or **carbon**), **carbon dioxide** and **water vapour** (which forms on the inside of the beaker as a mist).

To show that a burning candle produces carbon dioxide and water vapour

If a steady stream of air is drawn through the apparatus (figure 5.9) for a very long time water is collected in the side-arm test tube **X** and the limewater in the side-arm test tube **Y** turns milky. This shows that carbon dioxide, which turns the limewater milky, and water vapour are present in the air.

If a burning candle is placed at **Z** in the apparatus shown in figure 5.9, water is collected and the limewater turns milky within a couple of minutes. This shows that water and carbon dioxide must be produced when a candle burns.

Similar results are obtained with a spirit lamp or a small bunsen burner flame.

Fires and fire extinguishers

Fire causes much damage and loss of life each year. It is important for us to know how to control fires.

For a fire to burn three things are necessary. They are
- fuel
- air (or oxygen)
- heat

Methods of fire-fighting involve removing one or more of these essentials. During a forest fire a whole area may be cleared of trees to prevent the fire spreading by removing the fuel. A chip pan fire can be extinguished by covering the pan with a tight fitting lid or a damp cloth. In both cases the air supply is cut off.

Water is not suitable for putting out all types of fire. It only spreads an oil, paint or petrol fire because the burning oil floats on the water used. Also, it is dangerous to use water near electrical apparatus because water can conduct electricity.

A common type of fire extinguisher is the **soda-acid extinguisher** (figure 5.10). When the plunger is pushed in, the small bottle of sulphuric acid is broken and the sulphuric acid reacts with the sodium hydrogencarbonate solution to produce carbon dioxide. The mixture of carbon dioxide and aqueous solution can be directed at the fire.

A small cylinder of **carbon dioxide** is a very useful fire extinguisher. It produces no mess because the fire is smothered by the heavy carbon dioxide vapour. This is very useful for putting out small oil or electrical fires.

Foam fire extinguishers in use

Very effective **foam fire extinguishers** have been developed for dealing with aeroplane fires. A simple foam fire extinguisher consists of a solution of **aluminium sulphate** (which is acidic) and **sodium hydrogencarbonate** solution with detergent added. By a similar reaction to the reaction in the soda-acid fire extinguisher, bubbles of carbon dioxide are produced but they are trapped in a foam. The foam produces a layer over the fire and smothers the flames.

A **powder** fire extinguisher covers the fire with a layer of powder which does not burn. This prevents oxygen from reaching the fire and therefore puts it out.

A small fire extinguisher containing one of the liquids tetrachloromethane (carbon tetrachloride), bromomethane or bromochlorodifluoromethane (BCF) can be used to deal with a small fire. The heavy non-inflammable vapour produced by these liquids smothers the flames. However this type of extinguisher must be used carefully indoors because poisonous gases can be produced when the vapour comes in contact with the flames.

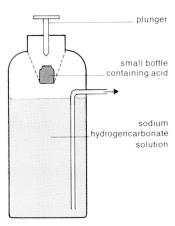

Figure 5.10 A soda-acid fire extinguisher

Air pollution

The presence of substances like sulphur dioxide, soot, carbon monoxide and nitrogen dioxide in the air causes **air pollution**.

Because these substances are in the air because of man's activities, air pollution is more serious in cities than in rural areas. About thirty years ago, a series of serious fogs produced by soot, ash and tar in city areas led to the Clean Air Act (1956). These fogs were nicknamed smogs and caused over four thousand extra deaths during one winter. Many of these deaths were caused by bronchitis and other breathing problems. The Act set up clean air zones in cities where smokeless fuel had to be burned rather than coal. The result of this Act, and other measures, has been to greatly improve the atmospheric conditions in our cities.

Sulphur dioxide in the air comes from the burning of sulphur present in most fuels. Coal, for example, contains about 1.6% sulphur. Sulphur dioxide reacts with water in the air to produce an acidic solution (sulphurous acid). Sulphurous acid can be changed into sulphuric acid in the presence of air. The presence of sulphur dioxide in the air increases the rate of corrosion of metals and stone buildings. Sulphur dioxide in the air also affects the growth of some plants like gladioli and peas, but it prevents the disease of black spot in roses.

LEFT London smog. RIGHT London now.

Smoke comes from the incomplete combustion of any fuel. The major source of smoke in the air is the inefficient burning of coal in household fires. About 3.5% of the fuel can be lost as smoke.

Carbon monoxide and **nitrogen dioxide** come from combustion in car engines. Lead is also emitted from car exhausts.

Rusting of iron

The rusting of iron is a slow reaction of iron with oxygen. The reddish-brown rust produced is a complex substance but it is basically an **iron oxide**.

Rusting of iron is an example of corrosion of metals. All metals, apart from noble metals such as platinum and gold, corrode when exposed to air. A more detailed account of corrosion will be found in Chapter 8 page 43.

Table 5.3 A summary of the processes involving the air

Components of the air	Combustion	Rusting	Breathing	Photosynthesis
Nitrogen	Usually not involved	Not involved	Not involved	Not involved
Oxygen	Usually necessary	Necessary	Necessary	Produced
Carbon dioxide	Formed if carbon or carbon compounds burn	Speeds up rusting but it is not necessary	Produced	Necessary
Noble gases	No effect			
Water vapour	Formed if hydrogen or hydrogen compounds burn	Necessary	Produced	Necessary

something to think about . . .

An experiment was carried out to investigate the composition of air. The apparatus in figure 5.11 was used.

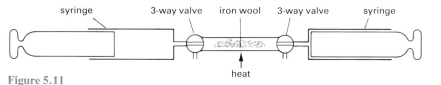

Figure 5.11

One of the gas syringes was filled with $100\,cm^3$ of air. The air was passed backwards and forwards over the heated iron wool in the hard glass tube. **The iron wool started to glow and the glow spread throughout the iron wool even when the flame was removed**. On cooling, the volume of air remaining was $80\,cm^3$ and a black solid residue remained in the hard glass tube.

a   (i) Name the metal more commonly used for this experiment.
  (ii) Name the gas removed from the air by the heated iron wool.
 (iii) Name the chief chemical constituent of the residue in the hard glass tube.
 (iv) Name two gases remaining in the syringe. One should be an element and one should be a compound.
b From the information in heavy type, what can be concluded about the reaction?
c Draw an energy level diagram for the reaction taking place when air is passed over heated iron wool.
d Why was the apparatus allowed to cool before the volume of gas remaining was measured?
e Why is the reaction faster with iron wool than with an iron nail of the same mass?
f How would the result have been different if exhaled air had been used? Give an explanation. (Exhaled air is air breathed out by a human or other animal.)

(*East Anglian Examinations Board*)

6. Water and hydrogen

Water is a most remarkable substance. Comparing it with similar compounds, you might expect water to be a gas at room temperature and pressure. Fortunately for life on this planet, water has a boiling point much higher than other similar compounds, making it a liquid at room temperature and pressure.

What does water consist of?

Water can be split up into the elements by electrolysis (that is, by passing an electric current through it). The volume of hydrogen produced is twice the volume of oxygen produced in the same experiment. This suggests that water is a compound of **hydrogen** and **oxygen** with twice as many hydrogen atoms as oxygen atoms. You have probably seen water written as H_2O. This electrolysis of water could be used as a source of hydrogen but it is not practical unless a very cheap supply of electricity is available. It has been suggested that if electricity from nuclear power stations could be produced cheaply, the hydrogen produced could be used to power cars and other vehicles. This would have the advantage of making the vehicles pollution free.

Water as a solvent

Water dissolves many substances including salt, sugars, etc. The amount dissolved, however, varies greatly from one substance to another, and also depends upon temperature.
    The number of grams of a particular solute dissolving in 100 g of water at a certain temperature is called the solubility. In figure 6.1, solubility curves show the variation of solubility of potassium nitrate and sodium chloride with temperature.
    Potassium nitrate is typical of many solutes. Its solubility increases dramatically with increasing temperature.
    Cooling of a hot, saturated solution of potassium nitrate produces crystals of potassium nitrate. This is because much of the potassium nitrate dissolved in the hot solution cannot remain dissolved when the solution is cooled. Rapid cooling of the solution produces small crystals and slow cooling will produce larger crystals.
    The solubility curve for sodium chloride is unusual. The solubility of sodium chloride is the same at all temperatures.

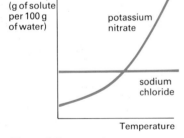

Figure 6.1

Hard and soft water

It is difficult to get a sample of completely pure water. This is because water is a very good **solvent**. Rain water is almost pure water but contains dissolved gases from the air, in particular carbon dioxide. When rain water trickles through the ground, some substances in the rocks dissolve in the water. The water may then be hard. Hard water does not readily lather with soap but first forms scum. **Hardness** in **water** is due to dissolved **calcium** and **magnesium** compounds.
    Table 6.1 summarises the results of a series of experiments with different samples of water. Soap solution was added from a burette to

Table 6.1 Amounts of soap required to form a lather.

Sample	Reading on the burette at the beginning (cm^3)	at the end (cm^3)	Volume of soap added (cm^3)
A Distilled water	0.0	1.0	1.0
B Rain water	1.0	2.0	1.0
C Tap water	2.0	13.0	11.0
D Boiled tap water	13.0	19.0	6.0
E Tap water with some washing soda added	19.0	20.0	1.0

water samples (100 cm^3). The results show how much soap was needed to produce a lasting lather. A lasting lather is a lather which lasts for at least thirty seconds.

From these results various conclusions can be drawn. **Distilled water** is pure water obtained by distillation of water. It contains no hardness and therefore only 1.0 cm^3 of soap solution was required to produce a lasting lather with pure water. **Rain water** also required only 1.0 cm^3 of soap solution to produce a lasting lather and so it also contains no hardness.

Tap water required 11.0 cm^3 of soap solution to produce a lasting lather, that is, 10 cm^3 more than completely soft water. The dissolved calcium and magnesium compounds used up 10 cm^3 of soap solution.

When the tap water had been boiled only 6.0 cm^3 of soap solution were required to produce a lasting lather, that is, 5.0 cm^3 more than completely soft water. Half of the hardness had been removed by boiling. Further boiling does not reduce the hardness further. There are two types of hardness in water and these are shown in Table 6.2.

Permanent hardness cannot be removed by boiling but only by a softening process. The sample of tap water contained half permanent and half temporary hardness.

Stalagmites (growing up from the floor) and stalactites (hanging from the ceiling) are formed inside limestone caves over millions of years. They are formed when water containing temporary hardness drips from the ceiling. As it drips, the calcium hydrogencarbonate decomposes to form solid calcium carbonate.

Table 6.2 Types of hard water

Type of hardness	Due to dissolved	Effect of boiling
Temporary hardness	Calcium hydrogencarbonate	Hardness destroyed
Permanent hardness	Calcium and magnesium sulphates or chlorides	Hardness not destroyed

Sample E was completely soft because the addition of sodium carbonate removed all hardness from the water. Sample E differed from samples A and B, however, because evaporation of A and B to dryness would produce no solid residue but the evaporation of softened sample of E would produce a solid residue. Adding sodium carbonate (washing soda) to tap water does not produce pure water but produces soft water which, like pure water, lathers readily with soap solution.

Ways of softening hard water

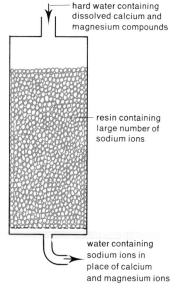

hard water containing dissolved calcium and magnesium compounds

resin containing large number of sodium ions

water containing sodium ions in place of calcium and magnesium ions

Figure 6.2 Ion exchange column

Boiling. Boiling softens temporary hard water but has no effect on permanent hard water.

Distillation. The water produced contains no hardness—permanent or temporary. It is, however, too expensive to consider on a large scale.

Addition of a softening agent. If water contains dissolved calcium compounds, addition of **sodium carbonate** (washing soda) precipitates solid calcium carbonate. The calcium compound is now removed from solution so the water is no longer hard. This is similar for magnesium compounds in solution. Both temporary and permanent hardness are removed by this method. There are other substances like 'Calgon' (sodium metaphosphate) which soften water when added.

Ion exchange columns. Complex resins called **zeolites** are used in softening water both at home and in industry. They are expensive but can be re-used many times. The hard water is allowed to trickle through a column packed with a suitable resin mixture (figure 6.2). The resin mixture contains an excess of free **sodium ions**. As the hard water passes through the column, calcium and magnesium ions in the hard water are exchanged for sodium ions in the column. The water leaving the column is soft because all the calcium and magnesium ions in the water have been removed and replaced by sodium ions which do not make the water hard.

When the column is exhausted (that is, when all the sodium ions have been removed from the column), the column can be regenerated by passing **sodium chloride** (salt) solution through the column.

Table 6.3 shows the advantages and disadvantages of hard water.

Table 6.3 Advantages and disadvantages of hard water

Advantages	Disadvantages
Supplies calcium compounds required by the body for bones and teeth.	Wastes soap because some of the soap forms scum with the impurities in the water.
Has a better taste than soft water.	Scum formed leaves marks on clothes and baths.
Better for brewing beer.	Causes a layer of 'fur' in kettles and scale in boilers and pipes. Scale in pipes may block pipes and radiators may be less efficient.
Lead compounds in the pipes are less soluble in hard water.	
	Spoils special finishes on fabrics.

Piece of pipe from a central heating system showing calcium carbonate deposited.

Household use of water softeners

The hardness of water in a particular area depends upon the geological character of the area from which the water is obtained. In general, water is hard in the south and east of England because of the calcium containing rocks such as chalk, limestone and gypsum. In the north and west of England and in Wales, the water is softer because rocks containing calcium are rarer.

In areas where the water is hard, a small domestic ion exchange column water softener may be worthwhile. This costs only a few pence a day to run and produces a supply of soft water.

Washing in hard water areas is less of a problem today because of the development of **soapless detergents**. These are included in washing-up liquids and many washing powders. A soapless detergent lathers when added to hard or soft water without producing scum.

Many bath preparations, such as **bath salts**, contain sodium sesquicarbonate (a mixture of sodium carbonate and sodium hydrogencarbonate which acts like sodium carbonate in softening water). Sodium sesquicarbonate is preferred to sodium carbonate because the solution produced is less alkaline.

Figure 6.3 Hard and soft water areas in England and Wales

Producing hydrogen in the laboratory

1 From water or steam

Hydrogen can be produced from **water** or steam using a **reactive metal** (Chapter 7). For example

calcium + water (liquid) → calcium hydroxide (solution) + hydrogen
magnesium + steam → magnesium oxide (solid) + hydrogen

Figure 6.4 shows a way of carrying out the reaction between magnesium and steam. It is not possible to collect the hydrogen as this reaction is too violent.

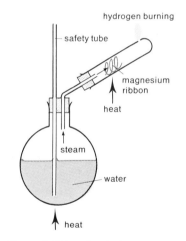

Figure 6.4 Reaction between magnesium and steam

2 From a dilute acid

Hydrogen can be made from the reaction of a **metal**, similar in reactivity to zinc, and dilute **sulphuric** or **hydrochloric acid**. For example

zinc + hydrochloric acid → zinc chloride + hydrogen
zinc + sulphuric acid → zinc sulphate + hydrogen

The apparatus in figure 6.5 could be used to prepare and collect a sample of hydrogen.

These reactions between zinc and acid are slow and can be speeded up if a little **copper(II) sulphate** solution is added.

3 From a cylinder

If hydrogen is required in the laboratory, it is best obtained from a cylinder. Hydrogen obtained in this way is dry and free from impurities.

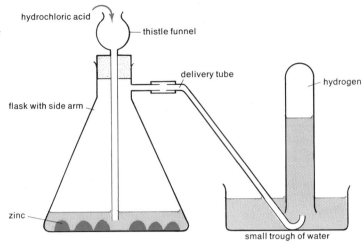

Figure 6.5 Preparation of hydrogen

Properties of hydrogen gas

Hydrogen is a colourless, odourless, tasteless gas. It is the lightest gas known and is neutral to indicators. It is practically insoluble in water but it is readily absorbed by certain metals.

When a lighted splint is put into a test tube of hydrogen, the hydrogen burns with a squeaky pop. If the test tube and hydrogen are dry, droplets of colourless liquid would be noticed afterwards. These are droplets of water produced when hydrogen burns. The apparatus in figure 6.6 can be used to show that water is produced when hydrogen burns.

If the experiment is carried out, a colourless liquid is collected in the U-tube. Table 6.4 shows the tests that can be used to prove this is pure water.

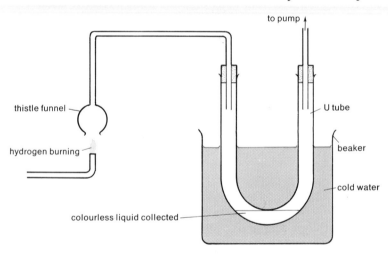

Figure 6.6 Burning of hydrogen

Reduction properties of hydrogen

Hydrogen can be used to **remove oxygen** from oxides of less reactive metals like lead and copper. Figure 6.7 shows a suitable apparatus for the reduction of a metal oxide.

For this experiment a hydrogen cylinder is usually used as the source of hydrogen. The excess hydrogen is burned safely at the jet. Before the jet is lit, a stream of hydrogen must pass through the apparatus for a while to remove all the air because mixtures of hydrogen and air can be explosive.

Table 6.4 Tests for water

Test	Observations	Conclusions
1 Add the colourless liquid to		
a Anhydrous copper(II) sulphate	Turns from white to blue.	Colourless liquid contains water but is not necessarily pure water.
b Cobalt(II) chloride paper	Turns from blue to pink.	
2 Boiling point	Boils at 100°C (373K)	Water.

If lead oxide is used the reaction is

lead oxide + hydrogen → lead + steam

The lead oxide decreases in mass during the experiment as oxygen is lost. When the reduction is complete the bunsen burner is removed and the apparatus allowed to cool before the flow of hydrogen is stopped. If this is not done the hot lead metal may react again with the oxygen of the air.

The launch of a Saturn rocket from Cape Kennedy.

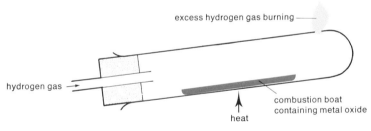

excess hydrogen gas burning

hydrogen gas

combustion boat containing metal oxide

heat

Figure 6.7 Reduction of a metal oxide

Uses of hydrogen

1 Hydrogen is used in the production of **margarine** (Chapter 15), **ammonia** (Chapter 19) and **methanol**.
2 **Airships** and balloons can be filled with hydrogen because it has the lowest density of all the gases. However, helium is frequently preferred, despite its higher cost and greater density, because it is not inflammable.
3 Hydrogen is used as a **fuel** for rockets. In the Saturn V rockets used by the Americans in the Apollo moon project, hydrogen was used as the fuel for the second and third stages. In the Space Shuttle the main rocket motors use hydrogen as fuel. The booster rockets which parachute back to earth are fuelled by a solid fuel. Liquid hydrogen and liquid oxygen carried in the rocket burn to produce water.
4 Because liquid hydrogen has a very low boiling point it is used in low-temperature **research** work.

something to think about . . .

1 Which of the following tests give the stated results if used with (i) distilled water (ii) salt solution?
   a Boils at exactly 100°C (373°K).
   b Turns anhydrous copper(II) sulphate blue.
   c Turns blue cobalt(II) chloride paper pink.
   d Evaporates away leaving no residue.

2 A similar experiment to the one whose results are shown in Table 6.1 was carried out. The samples used were 100 cm³ portions of solutions labelled W, X, Y and Z and the volume of a soap solution required to produce a lasting lather was found. The results are shown in Table 6.5.

Table 6.5

Sample	Reading on the burette		Volume of soap added (cm³)
	at the beginning (cm³)	at the end (cm³)	
Distilled water	0.0	0.5	0.5
W	0.5	7.0	6.5
X	7.0	18.5	11.5
Y	18.5	30.0	11.5
Z	30.0	30.5	0.5
W after boiling	30.5	34.0	3.5
X after boiling	34.0	45.5	11.5
Y after boiling	45.5	46.0	0.5
Z after boiling	46.0	46.5	0.5

   a How does the soap solution used in this experiment differ from the soap solution used in the original experiment?
   b Which of the four samples W, X, Y or Z could be (i) sodium carbonate solution (ii) calcium hydrogencarbonate solution (iii) tap water (iv) calcium chloride solution? Explain your choice in each case.

3 calcium carbonate   calcium sulphate   calcium hydrogencarbonate
sodium octadecanoate (sodium stearate)   calcium octadecanoate (calcium stearate)   sodium carbonate

   Use the names of the above chemicals to complete the following sentences:
   As rain water passes through rocks containing _____ a reaction occurs producing water containing _____ which causes temporary hardness in water. Permanent hardness is caused by dissolved _____ .
   The addition of soap containing _____ to water containing hardness causes a precipitate of _____ (sometimes called scum).

7. Chemicals from earth and sea

The earth and the sea are sources of chemicals. However these sources are limited and they must be used with care or they will soon be used up. Attempts are now being made to re-cycle metals; for example, copper is being reclaimed from scrap electrical wires.

Figure 7.1 shows the main elements found in the rocks of the earth.

In contrast, the rarest element in the rocks of the earth is astatine. It has been estimated that the total amount of astatine in the earth is sixty-nine thousandths of a gram (0.069 g).

Extraction of metals. How can we get at the metals?

The relative cost of a metal depends upon
- the **amount of the metal** present in the rocks of the earth
- **where the deposits are situated** in the world
- the **ease of extraction** of the metal.

Despite being the commonest metal in the earth, **aluminium** is not the cheapest because of the difficulties of extraction.

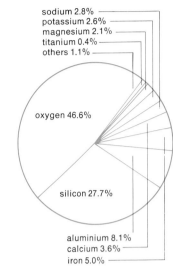

sodium 2.8%
potassium 2.6%
magnesium 2.1%
titanium 0.4%
others 1.1%

oxygen 46.6%

silicon 27.7%

aluminium 8.1%
calcium 3.6%
iron 5.0%

Figure 7.1 Elements from the rocks of the earth

Very few metals are found uncombined or native in the earth. The ones that are found uncombined are the ones at the bottom of the reactivity series. Copper, mercury, silver and gold have been found uncombined at some time.

Other metals are found in the form of an **ore**. This is a mixture of substances containing a **compound of the metal** considered. Iron ore consists of a mixture of substances including a compound of iron. The ore may be concentrated or purified before the extraction of the ore from the metal is tried.

LEFT Coal produced by the mine (top left) is conveyed to the power station (top centre); electricity from the power station is taken by cables to the smelter (centre). RIGHT Aluminium is mined as bauxite and then taken to the smelter where it is purified.

Table 7.1 Extraction of metals

Metal	Compound in the ore	Method of extraction
Potassium Sodium	Chloride	Electrolysis of the fused chloride.
Calcium Magnesium	Chloride or carbonate	
Aluminium	Oxide	Electrolysis of the fused oxide.
Zinc Iron	Oxides or sulphides	Reduction with carbon or other reducing agent.
Lead Copper	Sulphides or carbonates	
Mercury		Heating.

The method used to extract a metal from its ore depends on the position of the metal in the reactivity series. Table 7.1 shows the chief chemical constituents of the ores and the method of extraction.

Metals high in the reactivity series form stable compounds. Extraction of these metals requires much energy and is carried out by **electrolysis** (Chapter 14).

Metals in the middle of the reactivity series are present in less stable compounds. Extraction of these metals requires less energy and can be carried out by reduction with carbon, carbon monoxide or other suitable reducing agent.

If metals low in the reactivity series are found as compounds, these compounds are relatively unstable and can be split up simply by heating. **Cinnabar** is the ore containing mercury(II) sulphide. On heating mercury(II) sulphide decomposes to form mercury.

Table 7.2 summarises some of the useful minerals found in the earth.

Figure 7.2 Composition of sea water

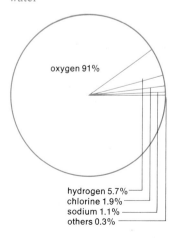

oxygen 91%

hydrogen 5.7%
chlorine 1.9%
sodium 1.1%
others 0.3%

Chemicals from the sea

Soluble substances from the rocks are washed into the sea by rivers. Since three quarters of the earth's surface is covered by sea, there are tremendous possibilities for extracting elements from the sea.

Figure 7.2 shows the composition of a typical sample of sea water.

Many elements are present in sea water in very small amounts. Some of these elements like **magnesium** and **bromine** are extracted economically at present but other elements may be obtained in the future. It has been estimated that one cubic mile of sea water contains £100 000 000 worth of **gold** dissolved in it. However, it is impossible to extract it economically because the dissolved gold compounds in one cubic mile of sea water are mixed with 150 000 000 tonnes of other mineral salts.

Sea water is a good source of the **halogen** family of elements (Chapter 10). Table 7.3 shows the availability and uses of the halogen elements.

Table 7.2 Important minerals in the earth

Mineral	Chemical composition	Origin	Uses
Salt	Sodium chloride	Evaporation of inland salty lakes.	Making chlorine, bleaches, pottery glazes, sodium carbonate (washing soda). Flavouring and preserving food.
Marble Limestone Chalk	Calcium carbonate	Shells of dead sea animals.	Making lime (calcium hydroxide), cement (roasting limestone with sand and aluminium oxide), glass (heating limestone with sand and sodium carbonate).
Coal	Largely carbon	Effect of pressure and temperature on trees and plants over millions of years.	Fuel and source of carbon chemicals.
Oil and natural gas	Largely a mixture of hydrocarbons	Effect of pressure and temperature on animal and vegetable material over millions of years.	Fuel and source of carbon chemicals.
Sulphur	Sulphur	Decomposition of calcium sulphate—volcanic gases.	Making sulphuric acid. Vulcanising (hardening) rubber.

Table 7.3 Availability and uses of halogen elements.

Halogen element	Amount dissolved in 1 cubic mile of sea water	Uses
Fluorine	7000 tonnes	Fluorides are added to tap water and toothpaste to reduce tooth decay.
Chlorine	100 000 000 tonnes	As a bleaching and germ-killing agent. For making a wide range of chlorine compounds including insecticides (DDT) and plastics (PVC).
Bromine	300 000 tonnes	For making dibromoethane (a petrol additive); BCF for fire extinguishers; bleaching and germ-killing.
Iodine	250 tonnes	For making quartz-iodine bulbs. Solution of iodine in ethanol used as an antiseptic.

something to think about . . .

The percentages of the common elements making up the rocks of the surface of the moon are shown in Table 7.4.

Table 7.4

Element	Percentage by mass
Oxygen	43
Silicon	21
Aluminium	7
Magnesium	5
Calcium	9
Iron	12
Titanium	2
Sodium	0.5
All other elements	0.5

  a Draw a 'cake' diagram (like figure 7.1) for the composition of moon rocks.
  b How does the composition of the moon differ from the composition of the earth?
  c There is little or no carbon or hydrogen in the surface rocks of the moon. What substances found in the rocks of the earth would you not expect to find on the moon?

Salt solution being pumped to the surface from underground salt deposits in Cheshire.

8. Metals

Metals are used today for a wide range of products. Table 3.2 (page 15) compares the properties of metals and non metals. Many of the uses of metals rely upon the strength, malleability, ductility or conductivity of metals.

In this chapter there is a detailed account of the extraction and uses of two important metals—iron and aluminium. Also there is a simple treatment of the arrangment of particles in metals and the study of simple alloys.

Iron

Iron is produced in large quantities by the reduction of iron ore in a blast furnace. A reduction process is used because iron is in the middle of the reactivity series (page 40).

The principal iron ore is haematite which consists largely of iron(III) oxide Fe_2O_3. Most of the good quality ore in Britain has been used up. Good quality ore is imported from Sweden and mixed with poorer quality ores or scrap iron.

The iron ore is loaded into the top of the furnace (figure 8.1) together with **coke (carbon)** and **limestone (calcium carbonate)**.

The furnace is heated with blasts of hot air which burn some of the carbon and produce carbon monoxide (CO). This is the active reducing agent which reduces the iron oxide by removing oxygen. The limestone decomposes in the furnace to produce calcium oxide. The calcium oxide reacts with **silica (silicon dioxide)**, which is an impurity in the ore, to produce **calcium silicate** (called **slag**). Removing the silica from the ore prevents the furnace from becoming 'clogged up'.

The reactions in the furnace can be summarised by the following word equations:

carbon + oxygen → carbon dioxide
carbon dioxide + carbon → carbon monoxide
iron(III) oxide + carbon monoxide → iron + carbon dioxide
calcium carbonate → calcium oxide + carbon dioxide
calcium oxide + silicon dioxide → calcium silicate.

The molten iron and molten slag are tapped from the furnace at intervals. The slag is used as a cheap phosphorus fertiliser as it also contains some calcium phosphate. It is also used for road chippings. The molten iron is cast into moulds and is then called pig iron or cast iron. Pig iron contains a wide range of impurities and as much as 4% carbon. It is very brittle and is of little use where strength is required. It can, however, be cast cheaply and is used for engine blocks in cars and manhole covers.

Wrought iron is pure iron containing no impurities. It can be produced by removing all the impurities by **puddling**. The pig iron is melted and then stirred to remove most of the carbon which oxidises to carbon dioxide. The remainder of the carbon is removed by passing the hot iron through heavy rollers. The carbon is removed as scale on the surface of the iron.

Wrought iron is used for ornamental iron work such as gates and railings. It is soft and can be easily worked without fear of breaking.

Most pig iron is converted to some form of steel. Steel consists of iron

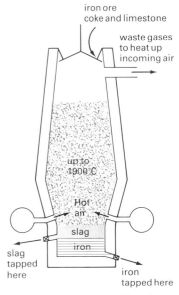

Figure 8.1 Extraction of iron in a blast furnace

Tapping a blast furnace.

(a)

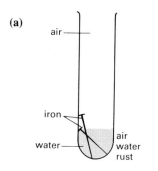

(b)

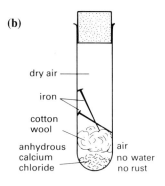

(c)

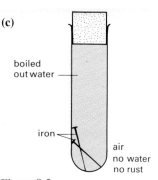

Figure 8.2
Rusting of iron

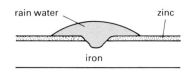

Figure 8.3 Scratch on galvanised iron—iron does not rust

with up to 1.5% carbon added. The properties of a particular sample of steel are dependant upon the percentage of carbon in it. Very hard steel, called tool steel because it is used to make metalworking tools, contains more carbon than very soft steels. Other elements may be added to improve particular properties of the steel. Stainless steel is more resistant to corrosion and contains added chromium and nickel.

Steel is made in a converter, which is a large furnace lined with brick. Oxygen is blown through molten iron to oxidise all the impurities. The carbon and phosphorus are lost as gaseous oxides. A small quantity of calcium oxide is added to remove any silica as slag, which is removed from the surface by skimming. The required amounts of carbon and other elements are added in the final stage.

Rusting of iron

In Chapter 5 it was seen that iron rusts when in contact with oxygen and water. A simple experiment to illustrate this is shown in figure 8.2.

Test tube **a** contains an iron nail in contact with air (containing oxygen) and water.

Test tube **b** contains dry air, but no water vapour. The water vapour is absorbed by the anhydrous calcium chloride.

Test tube **c** contains water which has been boiled before use to expel all dissolved oxygen. This tube therefore contains water but no oxygen.

Rusting takes place in **a** but not in **b** or **c**.

Methods of preventing rust

These methods involve excluding air, water or both air and water to prevent rusting. Before treatment by any process it is important to remove any loose rust which would flake off and expose fresh metal.

Buildings, bridges and similar iron structures are painted. The film of paint excludes air and water from the surface. Rusting will take place quickly if the film is damaged. Steel is often given a treatment with phosphoric acid before painting. This assists in slowing down the rusting process.

Machinery which cannot be painted may be coated in oil or grease to exclude air and water.

Iron can be **galvanised** to prevent corrosion. The iron is dipped in, or sprayed, with molten zinc so that the zinc forms a protective coating on the iron. Zinc is higher than iron in the reactivity series (Chapter 9) and should corrode faster than iron. As soon as a thick layer of zinc oxide forms on the zinc, this resistant oxide layer prevents corrosion. If the zinc coating is scratched deeply to expose fresh iron, an electrical cell is set up (figure 8.3) with water acting as the electrolyte. The zinc reacts in preference to iron because the zinc more readily loses electrons.

$$Zn \rightarrow Zn^{2+} + 2e^-$$

No rusting will take place while any zinc coating remains. Grey zinc-based primer paints are painted on bare metal surfaces during car body repairs. Aluminium also forms a very resistant surface oxide coating.

Iron can also be coated with a thin coating of tin to form **tin plate**. Tin plate is used to make food cans. Because tin is below iron in the reactivity series, iron will corrode in preference to tin if the plate is scratched to reveal iron.

The legs of an iron pier may dip into the sea at all times and we would expect very rapid corrosion. It would be impossible to oil or paint below the surface of the water and the legs would be extremely expensive to replace. The legs are protected by sacrificial anodes. Sheets of magnesium are lowered into the water to be in contact with the iron. Magnesium, being higher in the reactivity series, corrodes in preference to the iron which will not corrode while the magnesium remains. The magnesium anodes can easily be replaced.

Aluminium

Aluminium used to be far rarer than it is today. Napoleon impressed guests by using aluminium dishes rather than the gold dishes they replaced.

Aluminium is extracted by electrolysis (Chapter 14) because its ores are too stable to be split up by reduction. The common ore, bauxite (hydrated aluminium oxide $Al_2O_3.2H_2O$) is first purified and then dissolved in molten cryolite (Na_3AlF_6). The solution is then electrolysed in a cell (figure 8.4) using carbon anodes and the carbon lining of the cell as cathode.

The processes taking place at the anode and cathode are as follows:

$$\text{anode} \qquad 2O^{2-} \rightarrow O_2 + 4e^-$$

$$\text{cathode} \quad Al^{3+} + 3e^- \rightarrow Al$$

The aluminium is tapped off from the bottom of the furnace. The carbon anodes need to be replaced from time to time as they burn away in the oxygen produced.

This process is carried out in preference to the electrolysis of molten aluminium oxide because of the very high melting point of aluminium oxide.

Aluminium has a wide range of uses including electric overhead cables and cooking foil.

Arrangement of particles in metals

Metals can be considered as **regular arrangements** of **positive ions** held together by a 'sea' of free flowing electrons. The free flowing electrons explain the high electrical conductivity of metals.

Most metals, apart from the alkali metals, have arrangements of ions based on close packing. Figure 8.5 shows part of a close-packed layer of ions.

Each **ion** in the layer has **six** other **ions** touching it. These are arranged in a **regular hexagon**.

There are two alternative ways of stacking these close-packed layers in metals. Both of these are equally likely. Some metals have one type of stacking, some metals have the other type and some metals can exist in either depending on the conditions. The two ways of stacking these layers are:

a **ABA** or **hexagonal close packing** (figure 8.6): The ions in the third layer are immediately above ions in the first layer. The stacking of the layers will continue BABABAB. . . . **Magnesium** and **zinc** are examples of metals with this structure.

b **ABC** or **cubic close packing** (sometimes called face-centred cubic) (figure 8.7): The ions in the third layer are not immediately above the ions in the first layer. The stacking of the layers will continue ABCABCA. . . . Examples of metals with this structure are **calcium, aluminium, copper** and **lead**.

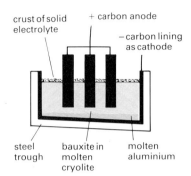

Figure 8.4 Extraction of aluminium

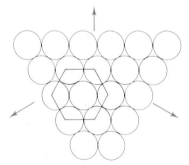

Figure 8.5 Close-packed layer of metallic ions

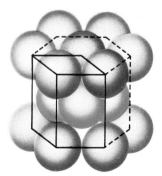

Figure 8.6 Hexagonal close packing

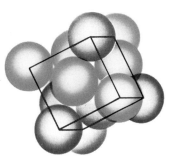

Figure 8.7 Cubic close packing

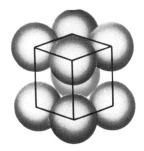

Figure 8.8 Body centred cubic packing

The stress patterns that caused this gear from a Rolls Royce engine to fracture through metal fatigue can be seen under magnification.

In both cases **any ion** in the structure has **twelve other ions** touching it—six in the same layer, three in the layer above and three in the layer below. The number of ions in contact with any ion in the structure is called the **co-ordination number**. The co-ordination number in both close-packed structures is **twelve**. In both structures about 75 per cent of the available space is filled by the ions.

Alkali metals and some other metals have a different arrangement of ions (figure 8.8). In this case the ions are not as closely packed (about 32 per cent of the space unfilled) and this explains the lower density of alkali metals. The co-ordination number is **eight** in this structure.

The description of metal structures above refers to ideal circumstances. In fact no metal sample will have a perfect arrangement of ions. When the molten metal cools and crystallizes, the crystals form around certain nuclei in the melt. When the individual crystals from the different nuclei meet up, there will be an imperfection. Each of the individual crystals is called a **grain** and the junction between two grains is called a **grain boundary**. The grain boundaries in a metal sample are not usually easy to see. Etching the metal sample with a suitable solution (2 per cent concentrated nitric acid in ethanol for iron and steel) causes the grain boundaries to show up.

The **strength** and **hardness** of a metal sample depends on **grain size**. As grain size decreases, the strength and hardness of the metal increases. Metallurgists (scientists who study metals and their structures) must pay attention to grain size in metal objects likely to suffer stress and strain.

Alloys

An alloy is composed of two or more metals mixed together. Sometimes a non-metal may be included, e.g. carbon in steel.

By mixing the metals in this way, the product may have more suitable properties than the pure metals. Alloys are usually less malleable and

Table 8.1 Examples of common alloys

Alloy	Constituent elements	Uses
Steel	Iron + between 0.15% and 1.5% carbon. The properties of steel depend on the percentage of carbon. Other metals may be present, e.g. chromium in stainless steel	Wide variety of uses including cars, ships, tools, reinforced concrete, tinplate (coated with tin)
Brass	Copper and zinc	Ornaments, buttons, screws
Duralumin	Aluminium, magnesium, copper and manganese	Lightweight uses e.g. aircraft, bicycles
Solder	Tin and lead	Joining metals (N.B. importance of low melting point)
Coinage bronze	Copper, zinc and tin	½p, 1p and 2p coins
Bronze	Copper and tin	Ornaments

ductile than pure metals. In a pure metal the layers of identical ions can slide over one another. In an alloy there are either small atoms of carbon in the holes between the ions which prevents sliding (figure 8.9a), or the ions are of different sizes, so the sliding is again reduced (figure 8.9b).

An alloy is usually made by weighing out the required amounts of the various metals in the correct proportions and then mixing them together and melting the mixture.

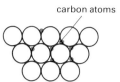

Figure 8.9a

Figure 8.9b

something to think about . . .

Study the diagrams (figures 8.10 and 8.11) which are concerned with the extraction of iron in a blast furnace and the extraction of aluminium by electrolysis.

a (i) Name the compound obtained when excess hot air is passed through coke. Why is this reaction important in reducing fuel costs for the process?
   (ii) Name the compound responsible for reducing iron(III) oxide in the blast furnace. How is this compound formed? Write an equation for the reduction of the iron(III) oxide (word and symbol equations).
   (iii) Calcium carbonate (limestone) will be decomposed in the blast furnace. Write an equation for the decomposition (word and symbol equations). Why is limestone added to the furnace?
   (iv) Give one use for the slag produced.
   (v) Give two differences in the composition of the iron obtained from the furnace and steel. Give one physical difference between blast furnace iron and steel.

b (i) What is the chemical name for alumina?
   (ii) Write an ionic equation for the discharge process occurring at the anodes. Why is it necessary to replace the anodes periodically?
   (iii) What material is used as the cathode of the cell?
   (iv) Why is aluminium not extracted in a blast furnace by a similar method to that used for producing iron?
   (v) Why is electrolysis not used for extracting all metals?

c (i) One of the following pairs of powdered substances will react when heated, the other pair will not.

iron(III) oxide and aluminium;   aluminium oxide and iron

Write an equation for the reaction which will occur (word and symbol equations)
   (ii) Metal window frames containing iron corrode quickly unless carefully protected but aluminium window frames seem resistant to corrosion even if unpainted. Give the chemical name of the substance formed when iron rusts. Why does aluminium not corrode as quickly as iron?
   (iii) Explain why galvanised iron is resistant to corrosion even when the protective surface of zinc is broken.
        (Joint Matriculation Board/West Midlands Examinations Board
        16+ Examination)

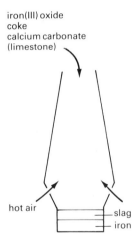

iron(III) oxide
coke
calcium carbonate
(limestone)

hot air

slag
iron

Figure 8.10

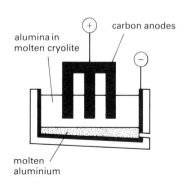

carbon anodes

alumina in
molten cryolite

molten
aluminium

Figure 8.11

9. Competition between metals

Any number of metals can be arranged in order by carrying out a series of reactions with the metals. By comparing the way in which they react, an **order of reactivity** (or reactivity series) can be drawn up. Metals at the top of the reactivity series are most reactive and the metals at the bottom are least reactive. Table 9.1 shows the reactions of a range of metals with air, water, and dilute hydrochloric acid.

A similar series can be drawn up by measuring the voltages of simple cells. Two pieces of metal rod or foil are dipped into a beaker containing salt solution as in figure 9.1. The voltage produced is measured on the voltmeter. The results of a series of experiments are shown in Table 9.2.

Table 9.1 Reactions of metals.

Metals in order of reactivity	Reaction with air	Reaction with water	Reaction with dilute hydrochloric acid
Potassium (most reactive)		Reacts violently with cold water to produce hydrogen. Hydrogen burns with a lilac flame.	Violent reaction producing hydrogen. (Dangerous)
Sodium		Reacts quickly with cold water to produce hydrogen. Hydrogen does not ignite.	
Calcium	Burn in air or oxygen to form an oxide	Reacts slowly with cold water to produce hydrogen.	
Magnesium		Reacts very slowly with cold water. Fairly fast with hot water. Violent with steam.	React with acid to produce a metal chloride and hydrogen. React more slowly down list.
Zinc		Fairly fast with steam.	
Iron		Reacts only reversibly with steam.	
Lead	Converted to the oxide by heating in air or oxygen but they do not burn.		Exceedingly slow reaction to produce hydrogen.
Copper		No reaction with water.	
Silver (least reactive)	Not affected by air or oxygen.		Hydrogen not produced. No reaction with dilute hydrochloric acid.

Table 9.2

Rod A	Rod B	Voltage produced (V)
Magnesium	Copper	1.00
Zinc	Copper	0.60
Iron	Copper	0.30
Lead	Copper	0.02
Copper	Copper	0.00
Silver	Copper	−0.05

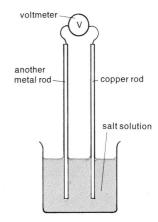

Figure 9.1 Measuring the voltage of a simple cell

You will notice that if the voltages are arranged in descending order, the metals in the first column are in the same order as the metals in the reactivity series. The reactivity series drawn up in this way is sometimes called the **electrochemical series**.

The reactivity series and the stability of compounds

Metals high in the reactivity series are most reactive. This means that when they react to form compounds, they produce the largest energy losses.

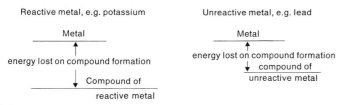

Figure 9.2

Compounds of metals high in the reactivity series are difficult to split up. The energy lost on compound formation must be returned if the compound is to be split up.

Studying Table 9.3 you will find that the stability of a compound of a metal is related to the position of the metal in the reactivity series.

Table 9.3 Stability of metallic compounds

Compound of	Carbonates	Nitrates
Potassium Sodium	Not decomposed even at temperatures of 1 million °C	On heating oxygen is lost at high temperatures—nitrite remains.
Calcium Magnesium Zinc Iron Lead Copper	Decomposed on heating into the oxide of the metal and carbon dioxide. Ease of decomposition increases down the list.	Decomposed on heating producing the oxide of the metal, brown nitrogen dioxide gas and oxygen gas.
Silver	Not stable.	Decomposed producing the metal, oxygen and nitrogen dioxide.

The reactivity series and replacement reactions

An old man carrying a large amount of money is liable to have it stolen by a robber. This is because the robber is more powerful.

If a security man is collecting money from a bank he is unlikely to have the money stolen by the old man.

Lengths of railway line are welded 'on the spot'.

Similarly, if a dry mixture of **magnesium powder** and **lead oxide** is heated, a violent reaction takes place. Magnesium is higher in the reactive series than lead; in other words, magnesium is more reactive than lead. On heating, the magnesium takes away the oxygen from the lead oxide.

magnesium + lead oxide → magnesium oxide + lead

This is called a **replacement** reaction. The lead oxide has lost oxygen. This loss of oxygen is called **reduction** and the 'robber' magnesium is called the **reducing agent**.

If a mixture of magnesium oxide and powdered lead are heated, no reaction takes place. Lead is not reactive enough to remove the oxygen.

Aluminium lies between magnesium and zinc in the reactivity series. If a mixture of **aluminium powder** and **iron oxide** are heated carefully, a violent reaction takes place. The aluminium removes the oxygen from the iron oxide. The iron oxide is reduced by the aluminium.

iron oxide + aluminium → iron + aluminium oxide

This reaction is called the **Thermit reaction** and can be used for 'on-the-spot' welding. For example, lengths of railway line are welded together by putting a mixture of iron oxide and aluminium between the two ends to be joined and setting light to the mixture with a magnesium fuse. The intense heat melts the iron and welds the two lengths together. This reaction was also used in incendiary bombs in World War II.

Replacement reactions for the extraction of metals

Another application of this kind of reaction is the extraction of metals.
Chromium metal can be extracted from chromium oxide by mixing the
powdered chromium oxide with powdered aluminium and igniting.
Chromium can be separated from the mixture.

chromium oxide + aluminium → chromium + aluminium oxide

Titanium is extracted from titanium(IV) oxide in two stages. Firstly, the
titanium(IV) oxide is converted to titanium(IV) chloride. The titanium(IV)
chloride is then heated with sodium. Sodium is more reactive than titanium
and so a replacement reaction takes place.

titanium(IV) chloride + sodium → titanium + sodium chloride

It is important that air is kept out of contact with the mixture otherwise
the sodium would burn to form sodium oxide.

Replacement reactions in solution

Replacement reactions also take place in solution. If iron nails are dipped
into copper sulphate solution, a reaction takes place because iron is more
reactive than copper. The iron nails become coated with copper and the
blue colour of the copper sulphate solution is gradually removed.

copper(II) sulphate solution + iron → iron sulphate solution + copper

something to think about . . .

1 Name a metal in each case that fits the statement given.
   a A reduces iron(III) oxide but not magnesium oxide.
   b B reacts reversibly with steam.
   c C is not affected at all by air, water or dilute hydrochloric acid.
   d D is more reactive than silver but less reactive than lead.

2 Which of the following pairs of substances undergo replacement
reactions?

    magnesium oxide and iron
    magnesium and copper oxide
    iron oxide and zinc
    silver nitrate solution and copper
    copper and lead nitrate solution.

In those cases where reaction takes place, write down the names of the
products.

3 What experiments would you carry out in order to find the correct place
in the reactivity series for the metal nickel?

It is possible to select **groups** or **families of elements** with similar properties from the list of all the elements (pages 186–8). The elements within each of these families are not identical but show certain similarities with other members of the same family. In the same way, if there are brothers in the same family they are not identical but they may show certain similarities and differences.

In this chapter we are going to look at three of these chemical families where the similarities between the elements can be clearly seen.

Alkali metal family

The members of this family are:

Lithium	Li
Sodium	Na
Potassium	K
Rubidium	Rb
Caesium	Cs
Francium	Fr

Of these elements lithium, sodium and potassium are the most common. Francium is very rare and differs from the others in being radioactive. Table 10.1 shows the melting points, boiling points and densities of the alkali metals.

Table 10.1 Properties of alkali metals.

Alkali metals	Atomic number	Melting point °C	Boiling point °C	Density g cm^{-3}
Lithium	3	181 (454 K)	1331 (1604 K)	0.54
Sodium	11	98 (371 K)	890 (1163 K)	0.97
Potassium	19	63 (336 K)	766 (1039 K)	0.86
Rubidium	37	39 (312 K)	701 (974 K)	1.53
Caesium	55	29 (302 K)	685 (958 K)	1.87

All of the elements in this family have **low melting** and **boiling points** compared with other metallic elements. For comparison the melting point and boiling point of iron are 1539°C (1812 K) and 2887°C (3160 K) respectively.

As the atomic number increases, the melting points and boiling points of the alkali metals decrease. The **density** of these alkali metals is low compared to other metals. For comparison, the densities of iron and water are approximately 8 g cm^{-3} and 1 g cm^{-3} at room temperature. The density of alkali metals increases as the atomic number increases. (The density of sodium is an exception to this.)

All of these elements are **metallic**. When cut, lumps of these elements show a shiny, silvery surface which rapidly corrodes. Because of this rapid corrosion, they are stored under paraffin oil which keeps them out of contact with air and water. They all **conduct electricity**. The oxides formed when they burn in air or oxygen are **alkaline**.

Reactions of alkali metals with cold water

The alkali metals all react with cold water to form hydrogen and leave an alkaline solution. The reaction of these metals with water gives an indication of the differing reactivities of these elements.

i) **Lithium.** When a small piece of lithium is put into a trough of cold water, the lithium floats on the surface and reacts steadily to produce hydrogen

lithium + water → lithium hydroxide + hydrogen
(alkaline solution)

The lithium on the surface of the water is solid and the hydrogen does not ignite.

ii) **Sodium** When a small piece of sodium is put into a trough of cold water, the sodium floats on the surface and reacts rapidly to produce hydrogen.

sodium + water → sodium hydroxide + hydrogen
(alkaline solution)

The sodium is molten when on the surface of the water and the hydrogen produced does not usually ignite.

iii) **Potassium.** When a small piece of potassium is put into a trough of cold water, the potassium floats on the surface of the water and reacts violently to produce hydrogen.

potassium + water → potassium hydroxide + hydrogen
(alkaline solution)

The potassium is molten when on the surface of the water and the hydrogen produced burns spontaneously with a **lilac flame**.

Rubidium and **caesium** react more violently with water. In the reactions with water, lithium is the least reactive and the reactivity increases in order of increasing atomic number:

Lithium—least reactive
Sodium
Potassium
Rubidium
Caesium—most reactive.

This order of reactivity applies not only to reactions with water but to all reactions of alkali metals.

Humphrey Davy who discovered sodium and potassium by electrolysis.

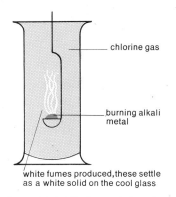

chlorine gas

burning alkali metal

white fumes produced, these settle as a white solid on the cool glass

Figure 10.1 Alkali metals burning in chlorine gas

Reactions of alkali metals with chlorine

All the alkali metals burn in chlorine gas to form a salt. For example

lithium + chlorine → lithium chloride
sodium + chlorine → sodium chloride
potassium + chlorine → potassium chloride

A small piece of alkali metal is heated in the bowl of a combustion spoon until it starts to burn. The spoon is then lowered into a gas jar of chlorine (figure 10.1).

The alkali metal continues to burn in the chlorine gas to produce white fumes of an alkali metal chloride that settle as a solid on the cool sides of the gas jar. In practice, however, the fumes are brownish in colour because the combustion spoon is made of iron and the heated iron reacts with the chlorine to form iron(III) chloride.

Formation of ions by alkali metals

All of the alkali metals form ions by losing electrons. Each atom loses a single electron to form a single positively charged ion. For example

$$Na \rightarrow Na^+ + e^-$$

The electron is lost more easily as the atomic number of the alkali metal increases.

Colour and solubility of alkali metal salts

Most alkali metal compounds are **colourless** and **soluble in water**.

The halogen family

The members of the halogen family are:

Fluorine   F (frequently mis-spelt Flourine)
Chlorine   Cl
Bromine   Br
Iodine   I
Astatine   At

The element astatine is formed as a product of radioactive decay. The melting points, boiling points and densities of the first four elements are shown in Table 10.2.

Table 10.2 Properties of the halogens.

Halogen	Atomic number	Melting point °C	Boiling point °C	Density at room temperature and pressure
Fluorine	9	−220 (53 K)	−188 (85 K)	1.58 g dm^{-3}
Chlorine	17	−101 (172 K)	−34 (239 K)	2.99 g dm^{-3}
Bromine	35	−7 (266 K)	58 (331 K)	3.12 g cm^{-3}
Iodine	53	114 (387 K)	183 (456 K)	4.94 g cm^{-3}

The melting points and boiling points of the halogen family increase with increasing atomic number. At room temperature (20°C), **fluorine** and **chlorine** are gases (melting and boiling points below 20°C), **bromine** is a liquid which boils easily (the melting point is below 20°C and the boiling point is above 20°C) and **iodine** is a solid (melting point and boiling point are above 20°C).

Table 10.3 Halogens at room temperature.

Halogen	Appearance
Fluorine	Colourless gas
Chlorine	Greenish-yellow gas
Bromine	Reddish-brown liquid
Iodine	Greyish-black solid

Solubility of the halogens in water and other solvents

The halogens do not readily dissolve in water, but they all react with water to a certain extent to form soluble products. Chlorine dissolves in water to form a solution called chlorine water, which consists of a mixture of hydrochloric acid and hypochlorous acid (chloric(I) acid). This solution is acidic and shows bleaching and germ-killing properties. On exposure to sunlight, the hypochlorous acid decomposes.

$$\text{hypochlorous acid} \rightarrow \text{hydrochloric acid} + \text{oxygen}$$

The extent of this reaction with water decreases with increasing atomic number.

The halogens dissolve readily in organic solvents. They produce coloured solutions. No reaction takes place between the solvent, for example hexane and a halogen.

Reactions of the halogens with metals

The halogens react with metals to form solid **salt compounds**. The name halogen means 'salt producer'.

Chlorine reacts with metals to form chlorides; bromine forms bromides; and iodine forms iodides.

Chlorine reacts with iron to form brown crystals of iron(III) chloride. Figure 10.2 shows the apparatus required to produce iron(III) chloride.

Bromine and iodine react to form similar products. Energy is evolved when iron reacts with chlorine, bromine and iodine.

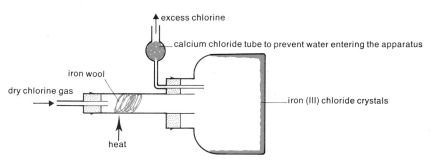

Figure 10.2 Preparation of iron(III) chloride

Reactions of the halogens with hydrogen

Chlorine, bromine and iodine react with hydrogen to produce hydrogen chloride, hydrogen bromide and hydrogen iodide, respectively.

hydrogen + chlorine → hydrogen chloride
hydrogen + bromine → hydrogen bromide
hydrogen + iodine ⇌ hydrogen iodide

The reaction between hydrogen and chlorine occurs slowly in the dark and explosively in sunlight. Hydrogen and bromine react when heated to about 200°C (473 K). Hydrogen and iodine do not react completely when heated to 500°C (773 K) in the presence of a catalyst.

From this and other reactions the following order or reactivity can be obtained.

Fluorine—most reactive
Chlorine
Bromine
Iodine—least reactive

Displacement reactions of halogens

If chlorine gas is passed into a colourless solution of potassium bromide, bromine is liberated because chlorine is more reactive and liberates the bromine.

chlorine + potassium bromide → bromine + potassium chloride
solution   solution

Uses of noble gases: helium and oxygen are used in breathing apparatus for deep sea diving.

The noble or inert gas family

The elements in the noble or inert gas family are shown in Table 10.4 together with their atomic numbers, melting points, boiling points and densities.

Table 10.4 Properties of noble gases.

Inert gas	Atomic number	Melting point K	Boiling point K	Density g dm^{-3}
Helium	2	3	4	0.17
Neon	10	24	27	0.84
Argon	18	83	88	1.66
Krypton	36	115	120	3.46
Xenon	54	161	164	5.45
Radon	86	201	211	8.9

All of these elements are **gases** at room temperature. Table 10.4 shows how the melting points, boiling points and densities are highest for the elements with largest atomic number.

These elements are very unreactive and until 1963 there was no reliable evidence that they formed stable compounds with other elements at all. It is now known that some compounds of noble gases can be made. An example of a noble gas compound is **xenon tetrafluoride** XeF_4 which can be prepared by heating a mixture of xenon and the halogen, fluorine, in contact with nickel at 300°C (573 K) and cooling rapidly. Xenon tetrafluoride is a colourless crystalline solid.

Uses of noble gases

i) **Helium.** Helium is being used in preference to hydrogen to fill **weather balloons** and **airships**. Although helium is denser than hydrogen and more expensive, it is widely used because it is not inflammable. It has been suggested that helium-filled airships could carry a cargo from England to Australia in four days using a route over the North Pole. This would be considerably faster than any ship and more economical than an aeroplane.

A deep sea diver uses a mixture of helium and oxygen in his breathing apparatus. Nitrogen is avoided because at depth under the sea nitrogen dissolves in the blood. On coming to the surface, the pressure is released and the nitrogen escapes producing a serious condition called 'divers bends'. One side effect of using this mixture of gases in breathing apparatus is it causes the diver to sound like Donald Duck.

ii) **Neon.** Neon lights are used for advertising signs and fog beacons. The light tubes are filled with neon at a low pressure and an electric spark is passed through the tube. The light tube glows with a red light.

iii) **Argon.** Argon and argon/nitrogen mixtures are used to fill electric light bulbs.

The **tungsten** filament is heated by the electric current passing through it. When it is very hot it glows. Tungsten is used because it is the metal with the highest melting point (3377°C or 3650 K). If oxygen is inside the bulb the filament will burn to form titanium oxide. If there is a vacuum (i.e. no gas at all) the tungsten filament vaporises.

iv) **Krypton** and **xenon.** These are used in special bulbs like photographic bulbs.

v) **Radon.** Radon differs from the other noble gases because it is **radioactive**. Radon is used to trace the progress of a gas through a gas pipe. It is added to the gas in small quantities and the movement of the gas is followed using a radioactivity counter. Radon is also used for treating some forms of cancer.

Neon lights are used for advertising signs.

In 1803 John Dalton (1766–1844) revived the Ancient Greek idea that matter is composed of fundamental particles, or atoms. He suggested these symbols for the atoms of the known elements. Note some of his 'elements' were later found to be compounds.

The periodic table

The modern periodic table is based on the work of the Russian chemist **Dmitri Mendeleef** in 1869. The periodic table, shown in Table 10.5, is an arrangement of the elements in order of increasing atomic number with elements having similar properties (i.e. in the same family) in the same vertical column or **group**. The horizontal rows are called **periods**. The elements in black are called the 'main block' elements. There are eight families or groups numbered 1–7 and 0. The three families considered earlier in this chapter were:

> **Group 1:** Alkali metals
> **Group 7:** Halogens
> **Group 0:** Noble or inert gases

In Chapter 23 the group 4 elements are compared.

Between groups 2 and 3 a block of '**heavy** or **transition metals**' are to be

ELEMENTS

⊙	Hydrogen	1	⊕ Strontian	46
⊖	Azote	5	⊕ Barytes	68
⬤	Carbon	54	① Iron	50
○	Oxygen	7	② Zinc	56
⊗	Phosphorus	9	© Copper	56
⊕	Sulphur	13	Ⓛ Lead	90
◉	Magnesia	20	Ⓢ Silver	190
⊖	Lime	24	Ⓖ Gold	190
⊕	Soda	28	℗ Platina	190
⊕	Potash	42	⊛ Mercury	167

Table 10.5 Modern Periodic Table of Elements

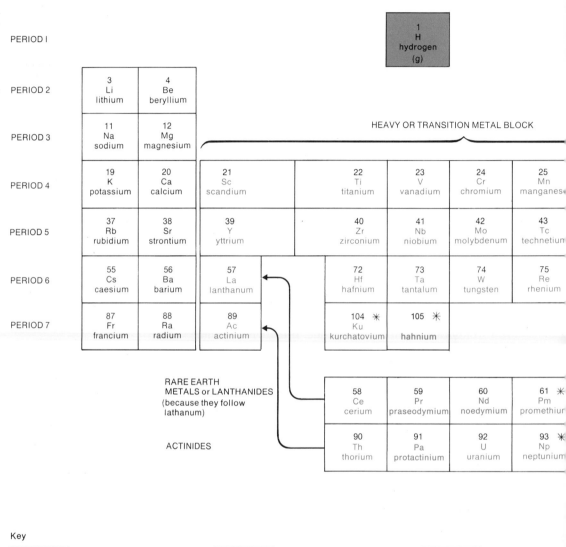

| | GROUP | 1 | 2 | | | | | | | |

PERIOD I								1 H hydrogen (g)	
PERIOD 2	3 Li lithium	4 Be beryllium							
PERIOD 3	11 Na sodium	12 Mg magnesium		HEAVY OR TRANSITION METAL BLOCK					
PERIOD 4	19 K potassium	20 Ca calcium	21 Sc scandium	22 Ti titanium	23 V vanadium	24 Cr chromium	25 Mn manganese
PERIOD 5	37 Rb rubidium	38 Sr strontium	39 Y yttrium	40 Zr zirconium	41 Nb niobium	42 Mo molybdenum	43 Tc technetium
PERIOD 6	55 Cs caesium	56 Ba barium	57 La lanthanum	72 Hf hafnium	73 Ta tantalum	74 W tungsten	75 Re rhenium
PERIOD 7	87 Fr francium	88 Ra radium	89 Ac actinium	104 ✳ Ku kurchatovium	105 ✳ hahnium

RARE EARTH
METALS or LANTHANIDES
(because they follow
lathanum)

| 58
Ce
cerium | 59
Pr
praseodymium | 60
Nd
noedymium | 61 ✳
Pm
promethiur |

ACTINIDES

| 90
Th
thorium | 91
Pa
protactinium | 92
U
uranium | 93 ✳
Np
neptunium |

Key

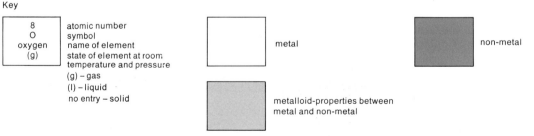

| 8
O
oxygen
(g) | atomic number
symbol
name of element
state of element at room
temperature and pressure
(g) – gas
(l) – liquid
no entry – solid |

metal

non-metal

metalloid-properties between
metal and non-metal

					0
					2 He helium (g)

3	4	5	6	7	0
5 B boron	6 C carbon	7 N nitrogen (g)	8 O oxygen (g)	9 F fluorine (g)	10 Ne neon (g)
13 Al aluminium	14 Si silicon	15 P phosphorus	16 S sulphur	17 Cl chlorine (g)	18 Ar argon (g)

					3	4	5	6	7	0
26 Fe iron	27 Co cobalt	28 Ni nickel	29 Cu copper	30 Zn zinc	31 Ga gallium	32 Ge germanium	33 As arsenic	34 Se selenium	35 Br bromine (e)	36 Kr krypton (g)
44 Ru ruthenium	45 Rh rhodium	46 Pd palladium	47 Ag silver	48 Cd cadmium	49 In indium	50 Sn tin	51 Sb antimony	52 Te tellurium	53 I iodine	54 Xe xenon (g)
76 Os osmium	77 Ir iridium	78 Pt platinum	79 Au gold	80 Hg mercury (l)	81 Tl thallium	82 Pb lead	83 Bi bismuth	84 Po polonium	85 At astatine ✳	86 Rn radon (g)

62 Sm samarium	63 Eu europium	64 Gd gadolinium	65 Tb terbium	66 Dy dysprosium	67 Ho holmium	68 Er erbium	69 Tm thulium	70 Yb ytterbium	71 Lu lutetium
94 ✳ Pu plutonium	95 ✳ Am americium	96 ✳ Cm curium	97 ✳ Bk berkelium	98 ✳ Cf californium	99 ✳ Es einsteinium	100 ✳ Fm fermium	101 ✳ Md mendelevium	102 ✳ No nobelium	103 ✳ Lw lawrencium

Elements in the main block of the Periodic table are in black.

✳ – element does not occur naturally
– man-made element

A fan blade from an RB211 engine is made of titanium alloy.

found. These elements are similar in many ways. Heavy or transition metals generally:

i) have **high melting points**, boiling points and densities. (An exception is mercury which has a low melting point.)

ii) are much **less reactive** than the alkali metals.

iii) form **coloured compounds**. (An exception is zinc.)

iv) form **more than one metal ion**. For example iron forms Fe^{2+} iron(II) ions (ferrous) by losing two electrons from each atom and Fe^{3+} iron(III) ions (ferric) by losing three electrons from each atom. Iron(II) compounds are often green in colour and iron(III) compounds are often yellow or brown.

The rare earth metals or lanthanides occur in very small quantities in monazite and other minerals. They have chemical properties similar to aluminium. The actinides are radioactive elements. Many of them have been man-made in small quantities.

Hydrogen has no obvious position in the periodic table. It has some similarities with the alkali metal family and the halogen family.

Points to remember about the periodic table

1 **Metals** are on the left-hand side of each period. The properties of the elements in a group become more metallic as the atomic number increases (that is, down each group).

2 Elements which are **gases** at room temperature and pressure are in the top right-hand corner of the periodic table.

3 In any group of the periodic table, the atoms of the different elements increase in size down the group. In any period, the atoms of the different elements decreases in size across the period from left to right.

4 **Metals** in groups 1, 2 or 3 form **positive ions** by losing electrons. The number of positive charges on the ion formed is the same as the group number of the metal. (Exception: thallium Tl in group 3 can form Tl^+ ions.)

5 **Non-metals** in groups 5, 6 or 7 form **negative ions** by gaining electrons. The number of charges on the ion formed is the same as the number of the group subtracted from eight. For example, oxygen in group 6 gains $8 - 6$ (i.e. 2) electrons to form O^{2-} ions.

6 The number of **electrons** in the **outer shell** of any element is the same as the group number of the group containing the element. The exception is the noble or inert gas family. These elements have eight electrons in the outer shell (neon, argon, krypton, xenon and radon) or two electrons (helium).

Stainless steel sports car from De Lorean

something to think about . . .

1 Write down the names of the substances produced when the following pairs react together.
   a Sodium and bromine.
   b Hydrogen and fluorine.
   c Chlorine and potassium iodide solution.
   d Bromine and potassium chloride solution. (Think carefully.)
   e Rubidium and water.

2 Here are five elements from the same period of the periodic table.
   A sodium (group 1)
   B chlorine (group 7)
   C magnesium (group 2)
   D aluminium (group 3)
   E phosphorus (group 5)

Which of the above elements
   a is an alkali metal?
   b is a halogen?
   c is a gas at room temperature and pressure?
   d is most likely to form ions with a 3+ charge?
   e is most likely to form ions with a 3− charge?
   f has the largest atomic number?
   g has atoms with the largest number of protons?
   h has the smallest atoms?
   i is a solid non-metal?

3 Table 10.6 shows a skeleton of the periodic table with some of the elements in their correct places in the table.
Choose from the elements given:
   a Three elements in the same period.
   b Three elements in the same group.
   c One heavy or transition metal.
   d Two elements usually stored under oil.
   e The element with the largest atomic number.
   f The element most likely to form 2+ ions.
   g The element most likely to form coloured ions.
   h The element that turns to a purple vapour on gentle heating.
   i Two metalloids.

Table 10.6

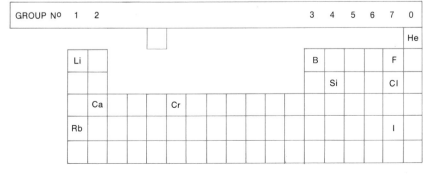

4 A section of the Periodic Table of Elements is shown below:

Table 10.7

I	II	III	IV	V	VI	VII	0
H 1							He 2
Li 3					O 8	F 9	Ne 10
Na 11	Mg 12	Al 13	Si 14	P 15	S 16	Cl 17	Ar 18
K 19						Br 35	Kr 36

a Using only the elements listed in this section of the Table write the symbol for
  (i) a non-metal which is solid at room temperature and pressure.
  (ii) a liquid at room temperature and pressure.
  (iii) an element which forms an ion with two positive charges.
  (iv) a gas consisting of separate atoms at room temperature and pressure.
  (v) an element which forms an oxide having a formula of the type X_2O_3.

b (i) Name one substance with which all the elements with atomic numbers 3, 11 and 19 will react.
  (ii) Name one product of the reaction of the element with atomic number 11 and the substance you have named in **b** (i).
  (iii) Explain in terms of electron structure why the elements with atomic numbers 3, 11 and 19 have similar chemical reactions.

c Elements with atomic numbers 20 and 34 are in the same period of the Table and both form white solid oxides. Give one test which can be used to distinguish between the two oxides.
What would be the result of this test with the oxide of element number 20?
What would be the result of this test with the oxide of element number 34?

(Joint Matriculation Board/West Midlands Examinations Board)

11. Ammonia and fertilisers

The world's population is growing rapidly. You can understand how quickly the population is growing if you remember that while your heart beats once, two more babies are born somewhere in the world. At the same time people are living longer. The growth of the world's population is shown in figure 11.1.

Figure 11.1

It is believed that there are more people alive today than have ever lived. In order to feed the increasing population an extra two-and-a-half square miles of farmland are required every hour.

Six main improvements can help to produce the food we need.

1 We can make the soil more suitable for growing plants by correct use of the soil and by adding the correct **fertilisers** to the soil. These will help in the growth of strong, healthy plants.

2 We can breed **new varieties of plant** and new strains of animal. These animals may, perhaps, be better at avoiding disease and so may produce more food.

3 We can prevent the loss of food by **pests**. It has been estimated that half of the food produced in some areas of the world is eaten by rats.

4 We can make **new kinds of food**.

5 We can manage the agricultural land better. It is important to prevent soil erosion by protecting exposed areas and growing suitable vegetation.

6 We can increase the area of land being cultivated. Unless new areas are reclaimed for agricultural use, the area of cultivated land will decrease as land is used for housing, factories, roads, etc. There have been dramatic examples of desert areas being converted to agricultural land by expensive irrigation.

Spreading nitrogen fertiliser in Spring.

Fertilisers and plant growth

Elements necessary for plant growth

Most soils contain natural plant foods. They have to be replaced by fertilisers and manures because they are used up by growing plants and are washed out of the soil by rain.

For good plant growth quantities of nitrogen, phosphorus, potassium, magnesium, calcium and sulphur are required. Iron, boron, zinc, manganese, copper and molybdenum are called trace elements because they are needed in the soil in small quantities. All these plant foods are absorbed in solution through the roots of the plants.

Table 11.1 shows the importance of the three elements nitrogen, phosphorus and potassium.

The effects of using a nitrogen fertiliser: the kale plants on the left have received no fertiliser but the plants on the right have been treated with a nitrogen fertiliser.

Table 11.1 The importance of nitrogen, phosphorus and potassium.

Element	Importance of the element to a growing plant	Natural sources	Artificial fertilisers
Nitrogen	Necessary for the growth of stems and leaves	Dried blood (14% N) Hoof and horn (14% N)	Sodium nitrate Calcium nitrate Ammonium sulphate Ammonium nitrate Urea
Phosphorus	Essential for root growth	Slag, bone meal, calcium superphosphate.	Ammonium phosphate
Potassium	For the production of flowers.	Wood ash	Potassium sulphate

When choosing a fertiliser the following points are important.

1 The percentage of the important **element** in the fertiliser (Appendix 4).
2 The **cost** of the fertiliser.
3 The **solubility** of the fertiliser. If a fertiliser is very soluble it will act quickly but will soon be washed out of the soil.

In Spring fields may need nitrogen fertiliser to help the growth of the grass for grazing, and a quick acting fertiliser like **ammonium nitrate** is often used. Only about half of the nitrogen applied to the soil as fertiliser benefits the plants. Some of the remainder finds its way into rivers and lakes and can pollute them. If ammonium compounds collect in a river or lake they remove oxygen dissolved in the water and are oxidised to nitrates. This is called **eutrophication** and can be recognised by the growth of a **green algae** or bloom on the water. The green algae prevent light entering the water and when it dies and decays it removes more oxygen from the water. The effects of nitrogen fertilisers getting into a river is similar to the pollution of a river by sewage.

Although urea (another nitrogen compound) is insoluble in water it can act as a good long-term nitrogen fertiliser. Urea reacts very slowly with water over a period of months to produce ammonium compounds.

The nitrogen cycle

Figure 11.2 shows the ways nitrogen is added to the soil and the ways it is removed. Since the air is composed of about 80 per cent of nitrogen, this is a good source of nitrogen for fertilisers. The trapping of this nitrogen in fertilisers is called the **fixation** of **nitrogen**.

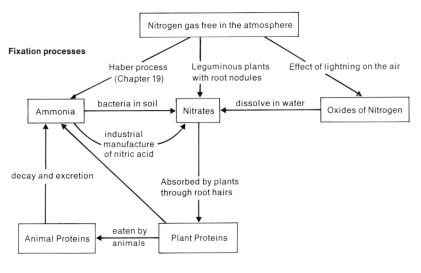

Figure 11.2 Nitrogen cycle

Making ammonia gas

Ammonia is a compound of **nitrogen** and **hydrogen** (NH_3). It is produced when a food containing protein is heated with sodium hydroxide or soda lime. The ammonia produced is mixed with a mixture of other gases.

To produce a pure, dry sample of **ammonia gas** an **ammonium compound** (such as ammonium sulphate) is heated with an **alkali** (such as sodium hydroxide).

ammonium sulphate + sodium hydroxide → ammonia gas + water + sodium sulphate.

The ammonia gas produced is dried with lumps of **calcium oxide**. Figure 11.3 shows the apparatus used to prepare and collect some ammonia gas.

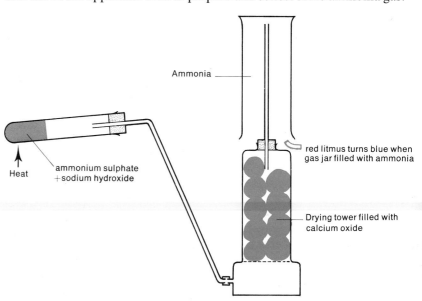

Figure label text:
Ammonia

Heat

ammonium sulphate + sodium hydroxide

red litmus turns blue when gas jar filled with ammonia

Drying tower filled with calcium oxide

Figure 11.3 Preparation of ammonia

Properties of ammonia gas

Ammonia gas is a colourless gas which is lighter than air. Ammonia dissolves very readily in cold water producing an alkaline solution sometimes called **ammonium hydroxide**. Ammonia gas turns red litmus paper blue.

Ammonia is used as a fertiliser. It is injected into the soil as liquid ammonia. It is quick-acting but is readily washed out of the soil.

Making ammonium sulphate in the laboratory

Ammonium sulphate is a soluble salt and is prepared in a similar way to the salts in Chapter 17. It can be prepared by the reaction between the alkali (ammonium hydroxide) and an acid (sulphuric acid).

Ammonium hydroxide + sulphuric acid → ammonium sulphate solution + water

Evaporation of the solution produces needle-like ammonium sulphate crystals. Addition of additives can change the crystal shape to make it easy to distribute the fertiliser over the ground. Small rice-like grains are easiest to use.

Making ammonium nitrate in industry

Ammonium nitrate is made by the neutralisation of **nitric acid** with **ammonia**. Ammonia is made from nitrogen and hydrogen by the **Haber process** (Chapter 19).

Ammonia is converted to nitric acid in three stages.

Stage 1: Ammonia gas is mixed with air and the mixture passed through a heated gauze made of a platinum alloy. The platinum gauze acts as a **catalyst**. Heat is given off during the reaction and the products are the gases **nitrogen monoxide** (NO) and steam.

Ammonia + oxygen → Nitrogen monoxide + steam

Stage 2: On cooling nitrogen monoxide reacts with more oxygen to form **nitrogen dioxide**.

Nitrogen monoxide + oxygen → nitrogen dioxide

Stage 3: The nitrogen dioxide is finally dissolved in water in the presence of oxygen to form **nitric acid**.

It is impossible to dissolve all the nitrogen dioxide and the undissolved nitrogen dioxide mixed with other waste gases escapes through a tall chimney. Nitrogen dioxide is a brown gas and, although it is only present in tiny amounts, the gas escaping looks brown.

Much of the nitric acid produced is used for making **ammonium nitrate**. It is important to avoid impurities in the ammonium nitrate because impurities can make it explode.

Fertilisers you can buy in the shops

Many fertilisers consist of mixtures of different compounds to provide a balanced fertiliser. The composition depends on what the fertiliser is going to be used for. A popular general purpose fertiliser contains:

Nitrogen (N) 16.5 per cent
Phosphoric acid (P_2O_5) soluble 5.0 per cent
                             insoluble 0.5 per cent
Potassium (K) 5.5 per cent

Adding a fertiliser to a soil can change the pH (acidity) of the soil. This can be important; for example, putting **lime** on the soil can reduce the acidity of the soil. Ammonium compounds and lime should not be used together otherwise free ammonia gas can be lost into the air.

Control of pests

Many chemicals have been used to control insect pests. Since the Second World War certain chlorine and phosphorus compounds have been used instead of chemicals like cyanide and nicotine in the control of insect pests. Although they are less poisonous to humans and other animals they cause problems because they remain unchanged in the soil.

Table 11.2 lists some of the chlorine and phosporus compounds used in the control of pests.

During the Second World War millions of lives were saved when DDT was used to stop the spread of disease. Soldiers and civilians were dusted with DDT to kill mosquitoes (carrying malaria) and lice (carrying typhus).

Dieldrin and Aldrin were removed from the list of pesticides when it

Preparation of nitric acid. TOP platinum gauze catalyst in place in the burner (top of the burner removed). CENTRE ammonia reacting with oxygen inside the burner. BELOW overall view of nitric acid plant.

was found that they were killing many forms of wildlife. Evidence was then found to show that DDT was reducing numbers of birds and fish. The problem was caused by the high solubility of DDT in fat, and its long-lasting effects. Birds of prey, like eagles, were particularly in danger. It was suggested that DDT causes birds to lay fewer eggs and those eggs had thinner shells. These effects reduced the numbers of birds in various places. There is also evidence that exposure to DDT in large quantities can lead to cancer in humans.

Constantly using a particular pesticide can make the pests resistant to the pesticide. There is evidence that species of insects were becoming resistant to DDT. DDT is now being replaced by safer chemicals. The chemical Warfarin has been used to control rats but constantly using it has produced a strain of super rats not killed by Warfarin.

Table 11.2 Chlorine and phosphorus compounds used to control pests.

Organophosphorus compounds (Compounds including carbon, hydrogen and phosphorus)	Organochlorine compounds (Compounds including carbon, hydrogen and chlorine)
Malathion	DDT **D**ichloro**d**iphenyl**t**richloroethane)
Parathion (pyrethum)	BHC (**B**enzene **h**exa**c**hloride)
	Dieldrin
	Aldrin
	Lindane

Chemicals in food

If you read the labels listing the ingredients in food packets or cans you will see many chemicals listed. These chemicals may be included for a variety of reasons including preserving, colouring, improving the flavour or sweetening. Some of the common chemicals are:

sulphur dioxide:	preservative
benzoic acid:	preservative
monosodium glutamate:	to bring out the flavour
lecithin:	emulsifier
saccharin:	sweetener
glyceryl monostearate:	emulsifier
sodium alginate:	whitener

Many new materials have been made by chemists that can be used as substitutes for other foods: for example, margarine (Chapter 15) is a substitute for butter. Chemists ensure that added vitamins make margarine a good substitute for butter.

Perhaps the most important man-made foods are the protein foods. A healthy adult needs to consume about 70 g of protein each day. Persistent shortage of protein can lead to kidney disease. Many of the people in poorer countries do not get sufficient protein. Protein is found in foods like meat (20 per cent), cheese (25 per cent), fish (15 per cent) and eggs (12 per cent).

Meat substitutes prepared from Kesp.

Meat substitutes are being made from **soya beans** or **field beans**. Both sorts of bean contain a high proportion of protein. The protein is extracted from the beans and the beany flavour is removed. The protein is then spun and knitted to give a product rich in protein which resembles chunks of meat in appearance. These chunks of 'meat' can be flavoured to taste like chicken or beef.

The manufacturers claim that these man-made meats contain protein and fat in the same ratio as stewing steak but 30 per cent more of each. In addition, they are easy to use, contain no waste like bone or gristle and they can be eaten by vegetarians. Courtaulds make a form of man-made meat called Kesp from field beans. Kesp can be bought dehydrated (i.e. with the water removed) or frozen.

Protein can also be produced from **yeasts** and **bacteria**. When fed to cattle the animals double their weight in two to four months. Chickens

LEFT Soya beans.
RIGHT protein extracted from soya beans.

take two to four weeks and plants one to two weeks to do the same. Yeasts and bacteria can double their weight in twenty minutes. A shallow lake the size of Essex could produce sufficient protein in the form of protein-rich bacteria to supply the whole world's need for protein. The bacteria used are short of some kinds of sulphur-containing amino acids but these can be added later.

Yeast can be grown on many industrial waste products. Methane (natural gas) can easily be converted into methanol. Yeasts and a wide range of bacteria grow on methanol.

It has also been found that certain types of yeast can grow on waste alkanes from crude oil distillation. A small factory can produce 100 000 tonnes of protein each year by this method. There are two objections to the use of alkanes for growing yeasts. There is a concern because alkane residues contain cancer producing substances. Also, poisonous metals in the wastes concentrate in the yeasts. Tests with yeasts do not suggest that either of these are serious problems.

It is not intended that this kind of yeast or bacteria will be used directly to feed people. In the United Kingdom fifteen million tonnes of protein-rich animal food is used each year. These yeasts and bacteria will be used for animal food.

something to think about . . .

1 Here is a list showing the percentages of fertiliser used in different parts of the world.

U.S.A. and Canada:	25 per cent
Western Europe:	25 per cent
Eastern Europe and U.S.S.R.:	25 per cent
Japan:	5 per cent
Rest of the world:	20 per cent

Draw a 'cake' diagram to show the use of fertilisers in different parts of the world.

How do you explain the unequal use of fertilisers in different parts of the world?

2 a Nitrogen is present in plants and animals. Plants take in nitrogen and these plants may be eaten by animals. Human beings eat both plants and animals. These processes are part of the nitrogen cycle.
  (i) Name the type of nitrogen-containing compound present in the tissues of plants and animals.
  (ii) Name a type of nitrogen-containing salt taken in by plants through their roots.
  (iii) State two ways in which nitrogen is returned naturally to the soil.
  (iv) State one way in which the nitrogen cycle is broken in a modern civilisation.
  b The reaction scheme in figure 11.4 outlines a method for the preparation of fertilisers

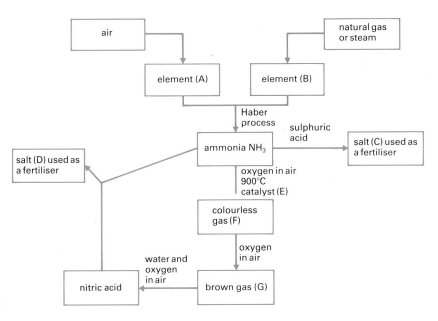

Figure 11.4

(i) The reaction scheme shows a process known as the fixation of atmospheric nitrogen. Explain the meaning of 'nitrogen fixation'.

(ii) Liquid ammonia has been used as a fertiliser in this country. Explain carefully why it should be injected down into wet soil to be successful.

(ii) Refer to the reaction scheme and name
    element (A)
    element (B)
    catalyst (E).

(iv) Refer to the reaction scheme and give the name and formula of
    salt (C)
    salt (D)
    colourless gas (F)
    brown gas (G).

(v) State two conditions used in making ammonia by the Haber process.

Sodium nitrate, $NaNO_3$, and calcium cyanamide, $CaCN_2$, are two nitrogenous fertilisers. (Relative atomic masses C = 12 N = 14 O = 16 Na = 23 Ca = 40)

c (i) Explain what is meant by 'nitrogenous fertilisers'.

(ii) Calculate the relative formula mass of
    sodium nitrate
    calcium cyanamide.
    Hence find the mass of nitrogen contained in
    100 tonnes of sodium nitrate
    100 tonnes of calcium cyanamide.

(Joint Matriculation Board/West Midlands Examinations Board 16+)

12. Solids, liquids and gases

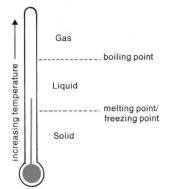

Figure 12.1

Any substance can be solid, liquid or a gas depending on the temperature and also the pressure. At 1 atmosphere pressure, water is in the form of **solid** ice below 0°C. Between 0°C and 100°C, it is **liquid** and above 100°C it is a **gas** called steam. The temperature 0°C (273 K) is called the **melting point** (or freezing point) and 100°C (373 K) is called the **boiling point**.

If the **pressure** is increased to 10 atmospheres water boils at 180°C (453 K).

As a result of these observations of solids, liquids and gases we can make some reasonable assumptions about the arrangement and the movement of **particles** in solids, liquids and gases (Table 12.1).

Table 12.1 Properties of a solid, liquid and gas.

	Solid	Liquid	Gas
Volume	Definite	Definite	Changes to fill the whole container.
Shape	Definite	Takes up the shape of the bottom of the container.	Takes up the shape of the whole container.
Density	High	Medium	Low
Expansion on heating	Low	Medium	High
Ease of compression	Very low	Low	High
Movement of particles	Very slow	Medium	Fast moving particles.

Solid

High density and the difficulty of compressing solids suggest that the **particles** are closely packed together. There are forces between the particles in the solid holding them together giving the solid a definite shape. The particles in the solid can be regularly arranged or irregularly arranged. A regular arrangement of particles in a solid leads to a regular **X-ray diffraction pattern** and the formation of **crystals**. The particles at room temperature are **vibrating** all the time.

Liquid

The **arrangement** of particles in a **liquid** is **irregular**. Again, there must be forces between the particles holding them together although the particles can move more freely than in a solid.

Figure 12.2 shows a simple two-dimensional representation of the arrangement of particles in a liquid.

Figure 12.2 Particles in a liquid

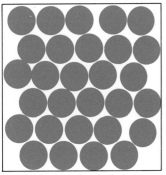

particles in random motion

Gas

When a given volume of boiling water is turned to steam, the number of particles is unchanged but they occupy about 1600 times the volume. The particles in a gas are, therefore, very widely spaced. There is no regularity in the arrangement of the particles or their movement in a gas. There should be no forces between the particles but, in practice, and particularly at high pressures, there is some attraction between the particles. Figure 12.3 shows a simple two-dimensional representation of the particles in a gas.

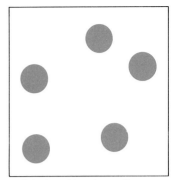

particles in rapid random motion

Figure 12.3

Movement of particles in solids, liquids and gases

If a gas jar of hydrogen gas is placed upside down over a gas jar of air so that the gases can mix, after some time, both gas jars contain a similar mixture of gases. This movement of particles of the different gases takes place despite the fact that hydrogen is a much lighter gas (that is, it has a lower density). This movement of particles of the gas to fill the whole apparatus, despite differences in density, is called **diffusion**. The rate of diffusion increases as temperature rises and small particles diffuse faster than larger particles.

Diffusion of particles also occurs, but more slowly, with liquids and, even more slowly, with solids.

Brownian motion

Individual particles of solids, liquids and gases are too small to be seen but the effects of their collisions with larger particles (called **Brownian motion** because it was first observed by Robert Brown in 1827) gives us evidence for the movement of the smaller particles.

If some very fine **pollen grains** (or small particles of carbon) are suspended in water, the movement of the pollen grains can be seen using a microscope. The pollen grains are much larger and heavier than the water particles. The pollen grains continue to move in all directions depending upon collisions between the pollen grains and the water particles. This is shown in a simplified form in figure 12.4.

Three points should be remembered from this:

1 The fact that the pollen grains move at all suggests that the much smaller water particles must be moving rapidly.

2 The direction of movement of the pollen grains depends on the collision of water particles.

3 The pollen grains and the water particles are moving randomly, that is, without any pattern.

Similar results can be obtained using a smoke cell. In a smoke cell the larger smoke particles are moved randomly by the collision of gas particles in the air.

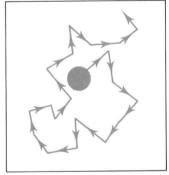

Tracing the movement of one pollen grain. Each change of direction is caused by a collision with a water molecule.

Figure 12.4

Converting from one state to another

Figure 11.5 summarizes the changes from one state to another.

Heating a liquid to boiling

If a liquid is heated to its boiling point with a heater that supplies the same amount of heat every minute, the temperature rises steadily providing there are no heat losses. The temperature remains unchanged while the liquid boils, that is, while it changes to a gas. While the liquid is changing to a gas, energy is still being supplied. The **change** of **state** from liquid to gas requires **energy**.

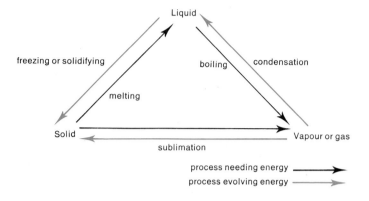

Figure 12.5 Converting from one state to another

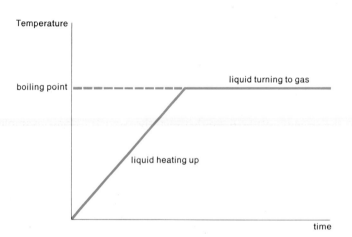

Figure 12.6 Converting from a liquid to a gas

Cooling a liquid to freeze it

If **water**, for example, is cooled in a suitable freezing mixture the temperature falls steadily to the **freezing point** where a change of state is going to take place. The temperature remains constant at the freezing point while the water turns to ice. It then cools further until it is nearly at the temperature of the freezing mixture. Ideally the graph obtained should be like the one in figure 12.7a but in practice a graph like the one in figure 12.7b is often obtained. This **supercooling** occurs when the water being frozen is not thoroughly stirred.

Molar heat of fusion

The change of state from solid to liquid involves the partial breakdown of the arrangement of particles in the solid. The energy required to **melt** one mole of a **solid** is called the **molar heat of fusion**.
Examples of molar heats of fusion:
Ethanol   5.0 kJ mole^{-1} (1.2 kcal mole^{-1})
Water   5.85 kJ mole^{-1} (1.4 kcal mole^{-1})

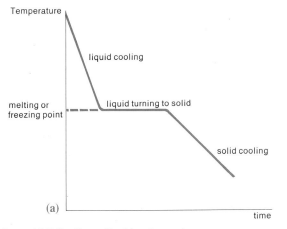

Figure 12.7 Cooling a liquid to freeze it

Molar heat of vaporisation

The change of state from a liquid to a gas involves the separation of the particles in the liquid and the speeding up of the particles. The **energy** required to change one mole of a **liquid to a gas** at the boiling point is called the **molar heat of vaporisation**. The molar heat of vaporisation of a substance depends upon:

1 the **masses** of the individual **particles**. Heavy particles require more energy to move them apart and more energy to speed them up.

2 the strength of the **forces** between the particles. Some examples of molar heats of vaporisation are shown in Table 12.2.

Table 12.2 Molar heats of vaporisation.

Substance	Boiling point °C	Molar heats of vaporisation	
		kJ mole^{-1}	kcal mole^{-1}
Hydrogen	− 253 (20 K)	0.8	0.2
Chlorine	− 35 (238 K)	20.5	4.9
Bromine	58 (331 K)	30.5	7.3
Sodium	890 (1163 K)	89.0	21.3
Sodium chloride	1400 (1673 K)	169.0	40.7
Copper	2500 (2773 K)	304.0	72.8

A graph of molar heat of vaporisation against boiling point for different substances is a straight line (figure 12.8).

A few liquids (including ethanol and water) have higher molar heats of vaporisation than expected from their boiling points. This is due to extra strong forces between the particles holding them together. These extra forces are called **hydrogen bonds**.

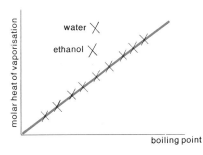

Figure 12.8 Molar heat of vaporisation relates directly to boiling point

Applications of change of state

1   A **refrigerator** contains a liquid which has a low boiling point. In the evaporator inside the food cabinet, the liquid turns to a gas. This requires energy and, in order to do this, heat is taken from the food. In the condenser outside the cabinet, heat is given out when the gas changes back to a liquid. A modern refrigerator contains a mixture of fluorine compounds called **freons**.

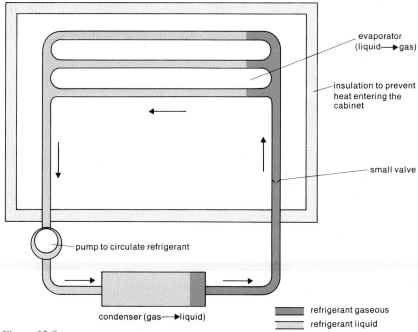

Figure 12.9

2   In many hot countries it can get very cold during the night. If a plastic container filled with a liquid with a freezing point of about 15°C (288 K) is put above the ceiling, the heat from the sun during the day warms up the liquid. During the night heat is lost from the liquid and if the temperature falls to 15°C the liquid starts to freeze. As it freezes it gives out heat which helps to keep the inside of the house warm. Next day heat from the sun will melt the solid.

something to think about . . .

A 90 cm long glass tube of diameter 2 cm was clamped horizontally. A pad of cotton wool soaked in concentrated hydrochloric acid (giving off hydrogen chloride fumes), and a pad of cotton wool soaked in concentrated ammonia solution (giving off ammonia fumes) were placed simultaneously at opposite ends of the glass tube.

After about five minutes a band of white solid formed inside the tube, as shown in figure 12.10.

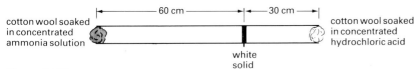

Figure 12.10

$$NH_3(g) + HCl(g) \rightarrow NH_4Cl(s)$$

a Name the white solid deposited in the tube.
b What is this movement of molecules called?
c The particles of ammonia and hydrogen chloride do not come into contact for about five minutes. Give a reason for this delay.
d The mass of 1 mole of ammonia molecules is 17 g and the mass of 1 mole of hydrogen chloride molecules is 36.5 g.
   From this information and the diagram, what connection is there between the mass of the molecules and the speed at which they travel?
In a similar experiment pads soaked in sulphur dioxide solution and hydrogen sulphide solution replaced the pads of concentrated hydrochloric acid and concentrated ammonia solution:

$$2H_2S(g) + SO_2(g) \rightarrow 3S(s) + 2H_2O(l)$$

e Name the solid deposited in this case.
f Calculate the mass of 1 mole of
   (i) hydrogen sulphide molecules H_2S.
   (ii) sulphur dioxide molecules SO_2.
        (H = 1, S = 32, O = 16)
g Where in the tube would the band of solid be deposited? Explain your answer.

                    (*Southern Regional Examinations Board CSE*)

An atom of an element is the smallest part of an element that can exist. Atoms are made up from three kinds of smaller or fundamental particles called protons, neutrons and electrons. The properties of these particles are shown in Table 13.1.

Table 13.1 Particles found in an atom.

Particle	Approximate mass*	Charge
Proton p	1 u	+1
Neutron n	1 u	0
Electron e	0	−1

*See Appendix 1.

As atoms are neutral, it follows that all atoms contain equal numbers of protons and electrons. If electrons have been gained or lost by an atom, the resulting particle is electrically charged and is called an **ion**.

The number of protons (or electrons) in an atom determines which element it is. Any atom with six protons (and also, of course, six electrons) must be an atom of carbon. The number of neutrons can be varied within limits. Atoms of the same element (containing identical numbers of protons and electrons) but containing different numbers of neutrons are called **isotopes**. Carbon can form various isotopes:

Carbon-12 6p 6e 6n
Carbon-13 6p 6e 7n
Carbon-14 6p 6e 8n

Any sample of carbon contains a mixture of these three isotopes. There is 98.9% carbon-12 and 1.1% carbon-13. Carbon-14 is present in small amounts in carbon in living things e.g. wood growing in a tree. When the tree is felled the carbon-14, which is radioactive (Chapter 20), decays. The decay of the carbon-14 can be used to date objects.

Most elements consist of a number of different isotopes. Tin, for example, consists of a mixture of ten stable isotopes.

In each atom the protons and neutrons are tightly packed together to form a positively charged nucleus. The electrons are in constant motion in the space around the nucleus (figure 13.1).

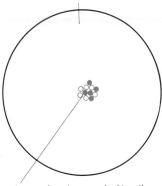

volume around the nucleus
containing electrons

protons and neutrons packed together
in the nucleus (positively charged)

Figure 13.1

Mass number and atomic number

The mass number (A) and the number (Z) are the two 'vital statistics for any atom. They enable you to work out the number of protons, neutrons and electrons in an atom.

Mass number. This is the sum of the number of protons and neutrons in an atom.

Atomic number. This is the number of protons in the atom.

This information may be recorded in a concise form. For example, $^{35}_{17}Cl$ represents a chlorine atom with mass number (shown at the top) of 35 and

Table 13.2

Atom	Atomic number	Mass number	Number of		
			protons	electrons	neutrons
$^{24}_{12}\text{Mg}$	12	24	12	12	12
$^{31}_{15}\text{P}$	15	31	15	15	16
$^{1}_{1}\text{H}$	1	1	1	1	0

atomic number (shown at the bottom) of 17. In this case the atom consists of 17 protons and 17 electrons. The number of neutrons is 35 − 17 i.e. 18. Table 13.2 shows the number of protons, neutrons and electrons in some atoms.

The relative atomic mass of an element can be regarded as an average of the mass numbers of the different isotopes of the element. Chlorine (relative atomic mass 35.5) is approximately 25% chlorine-37 and 75% chlorine-35.

Arrangement of electrons in an atom

The electrons move around the nucleus. It is impossible to trace the path of each electron around the nucleus. It is possible, however, to isolate certain possible **energy levels** for electrons. They are shown in a simple form in figure 13.2. In first energy level (shown by the circle marked 1 in figure 13.2) it is possible to put a maximum of two electrons. Eight electrons can be accommodated in the second energy level (marked 2) and a maximum

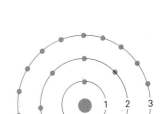

Figure 13.2

Table 13.3 Electronic structures of the first twenty elements.

Element	Atomic number	Arrangement of electrons
Hydrogen	1	1
Helium	2	2
Lithium	3	2,1
Beryllium	4	2,2
Boron	5	2,3
Carbon	6	2,4
Nitrogen	7	2,5
Oxygen	8	2,6
Fluorine	9	2,7
Neon	10	2,8
Sodium	11	2,8,1
Magnesium	12	2,8,2
Aluminium	13	2,8,3
Silicon	14	2,8,4
Phosphorus	15	2,8,5
Sulphur	16	2,8,6
Chlorine	17	2,8,7
Argon	18	2,8,8
Potassium	19	2,8,8,1
Calcium	20	2,8,8,2

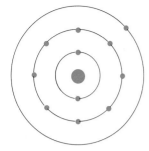

Figure 13.3

of 18 in the third energy level. There are other energy levels not shown in figure 13.2. These higher energy levels can accommodate larger numbers of electrons. The electrons in any atom occupy the lowest energy levels available.

A sodium atom contains 11 protons, 11 electrons and 12 neutrons. The protons and neutrons are in the nucleus and the eleven electrons are arranged in the energy levels around the nucleus. The first energy level holds two electrons, the second energy level holds eight electrons. The first two energy levels hold the maximum number of electrons. The one remaining electron enters the third energy level. This can be represented as an electronic structure of 2,8,1 or by a simple diagram (figure 13.3). Table 13.3 shows the electronic structures of the first twenty elements.

Relationship between electronic structure and chemical properties

Isotopes of the same element have identical chemical properties.

The alkali metal family (Chapter 10) is a family of similar elements. All of these elements have atoms with one electron in the outer energy level.

Lithium   2,1
Sodium   2,8,1
Potassium   2,8,8,1
etc.

In chemical reactions this one electron is lost and a positively charged ion is formed. Potassium loses its outer electron more easily than sodium making it more reactive than sodium.

Joining atoms together

Atoms can be joined together either in small groups called **molecules** or in a giant **network** or structure which extends indefinitely in either two or three dimensions. The atoms can be joined or bonded by two methods.

1 Covalent bonding or sharing

Two **hydrogen** atoms can be joined together to form a molecule of hydrogen gas. Each hydrogen atom gives its only electron to form a pair of electrons. The **pair of electrons** shared between the two hydrogen atoms holds them together.

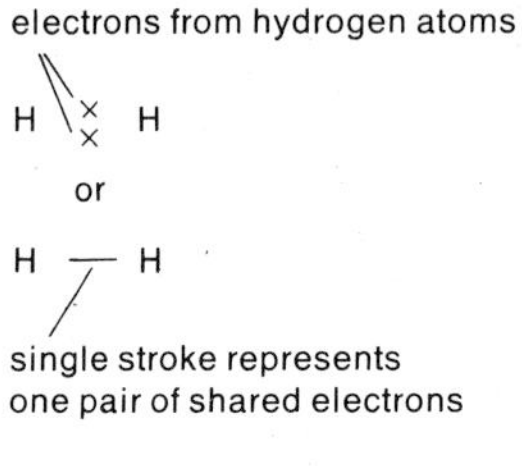

electrons from hydrogen atoms

H $\begin{smallmatrix} \times \\ \times \end{smallmatrix}$ H

or

H — H

single stroke represents
one pair of shared electrons

Figure 13.4

Similar sharing of electrons holds atoms together in chlorine (Cl_2), water (H_2O), ammonia (NH_3) and nearly all carbon compounds.

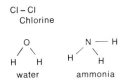

Figure 13.5

In a **double bond** two pairs of electrons are shared between the two atoms and in a **triple bond** three pairs of electrons are shared.

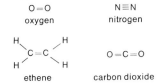

Figure 13.6

2 Ionic or electron transfer bonding

The arrangements of electrons in sodium and chlorine atoms are 2,8,1 and 2,8,7, respectively. The electronic arrangements of noble gases are particularly stable. A sodium atom has one more electron than the noble gas neon, and a chlorine atom has one less electron than argon. A complete transfer of an electron from a sodium atom to a chlorine atom would give each particle a stable electron arrangement. The resulting particles do not contain equal numbers of protons and electrons. They are therefore charged particles called ions. The ions are held together by strong electrostatic forces. The bonding process for sodium chloride is summarised in figure 13.7:

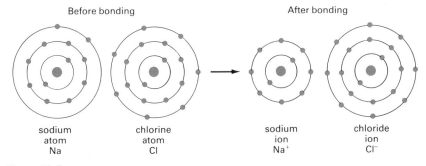

Figure 13.7

Magnesium oxide also contains ionic bonds but, in this case, two electrons are transferred. This is summarised in figure 13.8:

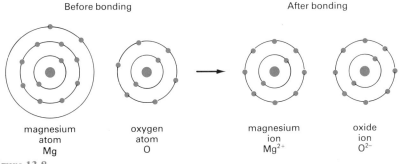

Figure 13.8

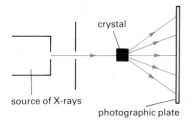

Figure 13.9 X-ray diffraction

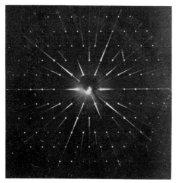

The developed photographic plate showing the X-ray diffraction pattern from a single crystal.

Apparatus used to investigate the structure of a single crystal using X-rays.

The forces between the ions in magnesium oxide are stronger than the forces in sodium chloride. Magnesium oxide has a very high melting point and is used as a refractory in furnaces.

In general, metal atoms lose electrons from higher energy levels to form positive ions. The number of electrons lost by each metal atom is generally the same as the group number of the group containing the metal in the periodic table. Non-metals gain electrons to form negatively charged ions.

The structure of compounds

The technique of X-ray diffraction can be used to find the arrangement of particles in a crystalline solid.

X-ray diffraction

If a beam of X-rays, similar to the X-rays used for X-raying hospital patients, is directed at a crystal, the X-rays are scattered by the particles in the crystal in certain directions. When the X-rays strike the photographic plate a spot is produced on examination of the plate.

From the spots on the developed photographic plate, it is possible for an expert to work out the arrangement of particles in the crystal. It is also possible to work out the distances between particles in the crystal.

A regular X-ray diffraction pattern is evidence for the regular arrangement of particles.

Sodium chloride structure

Sodium chloride forms **cube-shaped crystals**. Sodium chloride crystals consist of a regular arrangement of Na^+ (sodium ions) and Cl^- (chloride ions).

Solid carbon dioxide

Solid carbon dioxide is **crystalline** below $-78°C$ (195 K). It consists of a regular arrangement of CO_2 molecules. The forces within the molecules are strong but the forces between the molecules are weak. On gentle heating the forces between the molecules break down.

Naphthalene has a similar structure of $C_{10}H_8$ molecules.

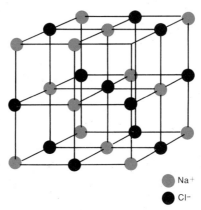

● Na+
● Cl-

Figure 13.10 Sodium chloride

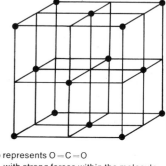

● represents O=C=O
with strong forces within the molecule

Forces between the molecules are weak

Figure 13.11 Carbon dioxide

Silicon(IV) oxide

The silicon atoms and the oxygen atoms are covalently bonded together to give a three-dimensional giant structure.
All the bonds between the atoms are strong and, therefore, silicon(IV) oxide has a high melting point.

Table 13.4 compares the properties of compounds and relates them to their type of structure.

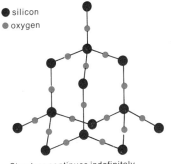

silicon
oxygen

Structure continues indefinitely
All bonds are strong bonds

Figure 13.12 Silicon (IV) oxide

Table 13.4

Property	Molecular structure	Giant structure of ions	Giant structure of atoms
	X – Y X – Y X – Y X – Y	$X^+Y^-X^+Y^-$ $Y^-X^+Y^-X^+$	Y Y —X—Y—X—Y— Y Y
	Solid carbon dioxide Naphthalene	Sodium chloride Magnesium oxide	Silicon(IV) oxide
Melting point	Low	High	High
Electrical conductivity of the melt	Nil	High	High
Boiling point	Low	High	High
Solubility in water	Low	Usually high, conducting solution produced	Low
Solubility in organic solvents	High	Low	Low

something to think about . . .

1 Draw diagrams similar to figure 13.3 to represent chlorine, magnesium and neon atoms.

2 Tetrabromomethane is a white crystalline solid. It does not dissolve in water but dissolves in organic solvents. Solutions in organic solvents do not conduct electricity. Tetrabromomethane melts at 90°C (363 K) and decomposes at 189°C (462 K). Molten tetrabromomethane does not conduct electricity.
    What can be concluded about the structure of this compound from the information given?

3 Atoms of A contain 11 protons, 12 neutrons and 11 electrons.
Atoms of B contain 8 protons, 8 neutrons, and 8 electrons.
a Show how the electrons are arranged in
   (i) the atoms of A.
   (ii) the atoms of B.
b Which of these two elements is a metal?
c Cl^- is the symbol for an ion of chlorine. Write symbols for
   (i) an ion of A.
   (ii) an ion of B.
d Write the formula for the compound formed when A combines with B.
e Explain why the compound referred to in **d** has a high melting point.
f To which group of the periodic table does B belong?

(*Welsh Joint Education Committee CSE*)

4 Complete the table below. There are six omissions.

Table 13.5

Element	Atomic number	Arrangement of electrons in energy levels (shells)	Metal or non-metal or noble (inert) gas
A	11		metal
B	10		
C		2,8,7	
D	18		noble gas

(*West Midlands Examinations Board CSE*)

5 Complete the following table by putting in the appropriate numbers of protons, neutrons, electrons and mass numbers into the eight empty spaces.

Table 13.6

Particle	Number of electrons	neutrons	protons	Mass number
Magnesium ion Mg^{2+}		12	12	
Bromine atom Br	35	45		
Sulphide ion S^{2-}	18			32
Aluminium atom Al			13	27

(*Joint Matriculation Board/West Midlands Examination Board 16+*)

6 The following list contains six elements with their atomic numbers:
   hydrogen (1)   fluorine (9)   sodium (11)   magnesium (12)
   phosphorus (15)   chlorine (17)

Complete the following table. An example is given to help you. You should use the atomic numbers to work out the number of electrons in the outer energy level of the atoms.

Table 13.7

Elements in the compound	Formula of the compound	Type of bonding	Electrical conductivity when solid	Electrical conductivity when liquid
Magnesium and chlorine	MgCl$_2$	Ionic	Non-conductor	Good
Phosphorus and hydrogen				
Sodium and fluorine				

(*Joint Matriculation Board/West Midlands Examinations Board 16+*)

7 A list of elements and their atomic numbers is given below:

hydrogen	1	fluorine	9
helium	2	neon	10
carbon	6	sodium	11
nitrogen	7	magnesium	12
oxygen	8	chlorine	17

Answer the following questions by selecting the correct elements from the list.

Each element may be used once, more than once or not at all.

a Name two elements which have one electron in their outer shells.
b Name two elements which have full outer shells.
c Name two elements which form singly charged anions readily.
d Name two elements which form ions readily by *either* gaining *or* losing *two* electrons.
e Name two elements which react readily to form a covalent compound which dissolves in water to give an acidic solution.
f Two elements X and Y form compounds with hydrogen which have the formulae XH$_3$ and YH$_4$, respectively. Name X and Y.

(*Welsh Joint Education Committee CSE*)

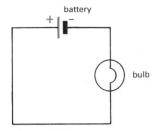

Figure 14.1

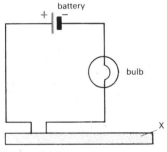

Figure 14.2

If a bulb and battery are connected together by two wires the circuit can be represented as in figure 14.1

The bulb lights because the **wires** (usually made of copper) **conduct electricity**. Electricity passes through the wire without chemically changing the wire. **Metals** have a **high electrical conductivity**, that is, electricity passes easily through the metal without changing it chemically. Silver, copper and aluminium are the three best conductors of electricity. Carbon is the only non-metallic element which is a good conductor of electricity.

If the circuit represented by figure 14.2 is connected, the bulb will only light up if the substance X conducts electricity. If X is aluminium (a metal) the bulb will light. If X is wood the bulb will not light.

Substances which conduct electricity are called **conductors**. Substances which do not conduct electricity are non-conductors or **insulators**. **Semiconductors**, widely used for making transistors, are crystals of metalloids like silicon or germanium with impurities added. These have a greater conductivity than insulators but not as great as conductors.

Household electric wires are covered with rubber or **P.V.C.** (polyvinyl chloride) to act as an **insulator**. High-voltage electric cables are insulated by the air that surrounds them. They are supported by metal pylons. The cables and the pylons are separated by a porcelain or toughened glass insulator.

Substances that conduct electricity

Although metals (and carbon) are the only substances to conduct electricity when solid, a greater range of substances conduct electricity when molten. Many substances conduct electricity when in solution using water as the solvent. Substances conducting electricity when molten or in solution but not when solid are called **electrolytes**.

The following substances are electrolytes: acids, alkalis, metal oxides, salts. However, when an electrolyte conducts electricity, the passing of electricity causes a splitting up of the electrolyte. The splitting up of an electrolyte by the passage of electricity is called **electrolysis**.

Insulators on an electricity pylon.

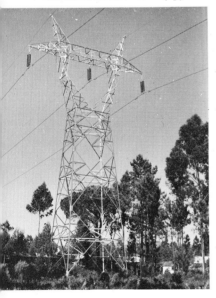

Electrolysis of molten lead bromide

The electrolysis of molten lead bromide is frequently used as an introduction to electrolysis. This is because lead bromide melts at a temperature which is lower than many other electrolytes. During the electrolysis of molten lead bromide, lead bromide is split up into lead and bromine. Solid lead bromide has a regular arrangement of lead (Pb^{2+}) and bromide (Br^-) ions.

The two **carbon rods** are called **electrodes**. The electrode connected to the positive terminal of the battery is positively charged and is called the **positive electrode** (or **anode**). The electrode attached to the negative terminal of the battery is negatively charged and is called the **negative electrode** (or **cathode**).

Making the ions move

Before an electric current can pass and electrolysis take place, the regular arrangement of ions in the solid must be broken down. This can be done by melting or dissolving in water. When this regular arrangement has been broken down the ions are more mobile.

Positively charged ions (or cations) move towards the cathode (negatively charged electrode). Negatively charged ions (or anions) move towards the anode (positively charged electrode). This process is called **migration of ions**. It occurs because of attraction between ions and the electrode with the opposite charge.

In the electrolysis of molten lead bromide, **lead ions** (Pb^{2+}) migrate towards the cathode (negatively charged) and **bromide ions** (Br^-) migrate towards the anode (positively charged).

At the electrodes

When the ions reach the electrodes they may be discharged. Discharging of ions involves the **transfer of electrons** between electrode and ion. This means that electrons move to or from the electrode. At the **anode** ($+$), electrons come from the negative ions to the anode because the anode is short of electrons. When the bromide ions lose electrons, neutral bromine results. At the **cathode** ($-$), electrons are transferred from the cathode to the lead ions because the cathode has too many electrons. When positively charged lead ions gain electrons, neutral lead metal results. During the electrolysis, there is a **flow of electrons** through the wires, bulb and battery from anode to cathode. It is this flow of electrons that we call an **electric current**.

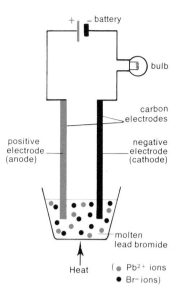

Figure 14.3 Electrolysis of molten lead bromide

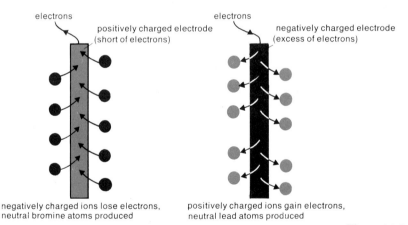

Figure 14.4

In summary

The anode ($+$) attracts negatively charged ions

Bromide ions→ Bromine + electrons (flow to the cathode)
(negative)   (gas at the
                   temperature of the
                   experiment)

The cathode ($-$) attracts positively charged ions

Lead ions + electrons   →lead metal
(positive)   (from the anode)   (neutral)

Electrolysis of solutions of electrolytes

Molten electrolytes produce products that are easily predicted. For example, electrolysis of molten **sodium chloride** produces sodium and chlorine. Solutions of electrolytes in water sometimes produce less obvious products on electrolysis. Some examples are shown in Table 14.1.

Table 14.1 Products of electrolysis.

Electrolysis of aqueous solution of	Produced at a carbon anode $(+)$	Produced at a carbon cathode $(-)$
Conc. hydrochloric acid HCl	Chlorine	Hydrogen
Copper(II) chloride $CuCl_2$	Chlorine	Copper
Sodium chloride NaCl	Chlorine	Hydrogen
Sulphuric acid H_2SO_4	Oxygen	Hydrogen
Copper(II) sulphate $CuSO_4$	Oxygen	Copper
Potassium iodide KI	Iodine	Hydrogen

The electrolysis of concentrated hydrochloric acid and copper(II) chloride leads to predictable products, but the products in the other cases are, at first sight, unexpected.

The products can be explained if it is known that water splits up into hydrated hydrogen ions $H^+(aq)$ and hydroxide ions $OH^-(aq)$. A hydrated hydrogen ion can also be considered as an $H_3O^+(aq)$ ion (that is, a hydrogen ion stabilised by one water molecule). This can be called an **oxonium**, or **hydronium**, ion.

$$H_2O(l) \rightarrow H^+(aq) + OH^-(aq)$$

or

$$2H_2O(l) \rightarrow H_3O^+(aq) + OH^-(aq)$$

In the electrolysis of sodium chloride solution, both sodium ions (Na^+) and hydrogen ions from the water migrate to the cathode. In practice, one ion is discharged in preference to the other. In this case, the hydrogen ions are discharged as they receive electrons from the cathode. The gas produced at the cathode is hydrogen.

$$2H^+(aq) + 2e^- \rightarrow H_2(g)$$

Both the chloride ions from the sodium chloride and the hydroxide ions from the water migrate to the anode. At the anode, the chloride ions are discharged (unless the solution is very dilute). The gas produced at the anode is chlorine.

$$2Cl^-(aq) \rightarrow Cl_2(g) + 2e^-$$

The apparatus in figure 14.5 can be used to collect the gases frequently produced during electrolysis of solutions.

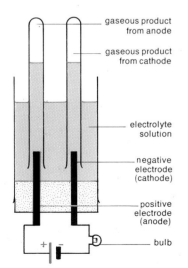

gaseous product from anode

gaseous product from cathode

electrolyte solution

negative electrode (cathode)

positive electrode (anode)

bulb

Figure 14.5 Collection of gases during electrolysis of solutions

Which ion is discharged in any particular case?

The higher an ion is placed in Table 14.2 the more readily it is discharged.

An example of the use of Table 14.2 is as follows. If **hydroxide** and **sulphate** ions migrate to an **anode, hydroxide ions** are discharged in preference to sulphate ions.

However this situation can be changed by varying the conditions of the electrolysis.

Table 14.2 Positive and negative ions arranged in order of discharge.

Positive ions	Negative ions
Silver Ag^+	Hydroxide OH^-
Copper Cu^{2+}	Iodide I^-
Hydrogen H^+	Bromide Br^-
Lead Pb^{2+}	Chloride Cl^-
Iron(II) Fe^{2+}	Nitrate NO_3^-
Zinc Zn^{2+}	Sulphate SO_4^{2-}
Magnesium Mg^{2+}	
Sodium Na^+	
Calcium Ca^{2+}	
Potassium K^+	

N.B. The order of metals in the reactivity series (Chapter 9) should be compared with the order of positive ions in the list

a Concentration

The order of discharge of ions applies if the two ions competing for discharge are present in approximately equal concentrations. If the concentrations of the two ions are very different, the order of discharge of ions can give the wrong results. Electrolysis of **dilute sodium chloride** solution produces **oxygen** at the **anode** from the discharge of hydroxide ions. This is as expected from the order of discharge because the hydroxide and chloride ion concentrations are similar. Electrolysis of **concentrated sodium chloride** solution produces **chlorine** at the **anode** from the discharge of chloride ions. In this case, the concentration of chloride ions is much greater than the concentration of hydroxide ions and the order of discharge is overruled.

b Electrode

Both **carbon** and **platinum electrodes** are commonly used because they do not interfere with the discharging of ions.

In the electrolysis of **sodium chloride** solution, **hydrogen gas** is produced at the **cathode** from the discharge of hydrogen ions if a carbon or platinum electrode is used. If a **mercury cathode** is used, **sodium ions** are discharged in preference to hydrogen ions. This is used in the electrolysis of sodium chloride (brine) in the Kellner-Solvay process which is used to produce sodium hydroxide.

Factors affecting the rate at which electrolysis occurs

In some experiments, the bulb is replaced by an ammeter which measures the current flowing through the wires, that is, the flow of electrons from anode to cathode. Figure 14.6 shows a circuit diagram with an ammeter included so that the rate of electrolysis can be measured.

It is incorrect to assume that the ways of speeding up chemical reactions (Chapter 18) have any effect on the rate at which electrolysis occurs. An electrolysis experiment like the one in figure 14.6 can be speeded up by

    i) increasing the voltage of the battery,
    ii) moving the electrodes closer together,
    iii) pushing the electrodes deeper into the solution, so that a larger area of electrode is in contact with the solution and
    iv) using a more concentrated electrolyte solution.

An increased rate of electrolysis will be recognised by faster escape of gases from the anode and/or cathode and by an increase in the reading on the ammeter.

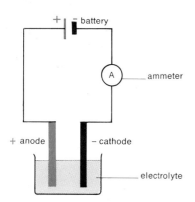

Figure 14.6 An ammeter is used to measure the electrical conductivity of a solution

A.C. or D.C.?

Electrolysis experiments are always carried out with a D.C. (or direct current) supply, for example, a dry cell battery. If an A.C. (or alternating current) supply is used electrolysis does not occur. This is because the electrodes do not remain positively or negatively charged but keep changing (or alternating) making electrolysis impossible.

If an A.C. supply was used in an experiment like the one in figure 14.6, a reading would still be obtained on the ammeter although electrolysis was not taking place. The ammeter is measuring the electrical conductivity of the solution. The electrical conductivity depends upon the concentration of ions in the solution.

Uses of electrolysis

1 Extraction of metals

Metals high in the reactivity series (Chapter 9) form stable compounds. In order to obtain these metals from their ores electrolysis is required. Potassium, sodium, calcium, magnesium and aluminium are obtained by electrolysis. The electrolysis of molten sodium chloride is an example.

Sodium chloride has a high melting point (801°C, 1074 K). By adding **calcium chloride**, the melting point of the mixture is reduced to about 600°C (873 K). This reduces the amount of fuel required to melt the electrolyte. During electrolysis, sodium and calcium ions migrate to the cathode, but the sodium ions are discharged in preference to the calcium ions.

$$Na^+ + electron \rightarrow Na$$

At the anode, chloride ions are discharged to form chlorine gas.

$$2Cl^- \rightarrow Cl_2 + 2\ electrons$$

The wire gauze prevents the sodium and chlorine coming into contact because at 600°C (873 K) they would immediately recombine to form sodium chloride. It also prevents metallic sodium conducting electricity

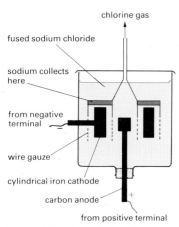

Figure 14.7 Electrolysis of molten sodium chloride

directly between the anode and cathode. This would cause 'short circuiting'.

All extractions of metals by electrolysis are expensive because of the high cost of electricity and the large amount of electricity required. The electricity required to produce one tonne of sodium metal by electrolysis would be sufficient for all households in a city like Exeter to use a small electric fire for one hour. Factories extracting metals by electrolysis are frequently sited near hydroelectric power stations.

2 Purification of metals

Metals including copper, nickel and lead can be purified by electrolysis. It is important, for instance, to use copper that is as pure as possible for **electric wires** because impurities reduce the electrical conductivity of the copper. Figure 14.8 shows a cell for the purification of copper.

During electrolysis, pure **copper** is deposited on the **cathode** from the discharge of copper ions (Cu^{2+}) in the solution.

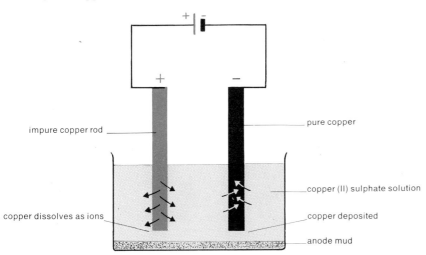

impure copper rod

pure copper

copper (II) sulphate solution

copper deposited

copper dissolves as ions

anode mud

Figure 14.8 Purification of copper

Purification of copper: pure copper cathodes being removed from the electrolysis cell.

At the anode, neither hydroxide nor sulphate ions are discharged but copper atoms on the surface of the copper anode lose electrons to the anode and the resulting copper ions go into solution to replace the ones discharged at the cathode. Impurities in the copper anode collect at the bottom of the solution in the form of an 'anode mud'. From this, precious metals like silver and gold can be obtained. During the electrolysis the anode decreases in mass and the cathode increases in mass.

3 Electroplating

Metal objects can be coated with another metal by electrolysis. This is called electroplating. A metal may be electroplated to prevent corrosion or to improve the appearance. A metal object can be electroplated by the apparatus in figure 14.9.

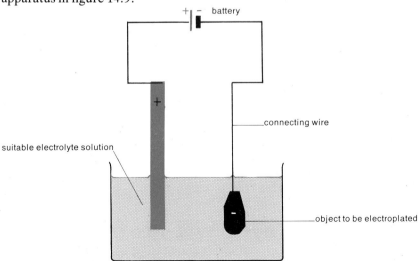

Figure 14.9 Electroplating of a metal object

Copper from the solution is deposited on the cathode. Careful control of conditions is necessary in order to obtain a firm deposit.

Other examples of electroplating include: car bumpers which are **chromium plated**, cutlery that is **silver plated**, heat-reflecting shields on space rockets that are **gold plated**.

A chromium-plated object is first plated with nickel and then plated with chromium. The nickel plating provides the essential protection against corrosion and the chromium plating gives a nice hard, shiny surface. The thickness of the chromium coating is about 0.0000003 m.

4 Anodising aluminium

The surface of a piece of aluminium is covered with a coating of aluminium oxide. Aluminium oxide is not readily soluble in water or acids and this explains the slow rate of reaction of aluminium in some experiments. Many aluminium objects are finished by thickening the oxide coating by electrolysis and dyeing the oxide layer. The apparatus in figure 14.10 is suitable and should be left for fifteen minutes. Oxygen produced at the anode thickens the oxide coating.

The object is then dipped into a suitable dye solution to dye the oxide coating. The result is a decorative coating which is not easily removed. A popular brand of chocolate is wrapped in a purple-coloured aluminium foil. Coloured milk bottle tops are produced in a similar way.

5 Electrotyping

Electrolysis can be used to produce copies of printing plates by a process of electrotyping. The original **metal plate** is coated with wax and a **wax mould** is produced. The surface of the mould is coated with graphite (carbon). This mould is then used as a cathode with a copper anode and copper(II) sulphate solution as electrolyte. During electrolysis, copper is deposited on the graphite-coated mould and a copper plate is built up. The wax and the graphite are removed and the copper plate remaining is an exact copy of the original plate.

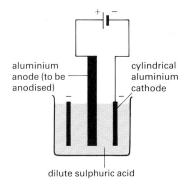

Figure 14.10 Anodising aluminium

Electroplating in progress: the items to be plated go in the perspex barrel which is lowered between the anodes.

something to think about . . .

1 Copy and complete the following crossword.

Figure 14.11

Across
1. A scientist who made a great contribution to the study of electrolysis. (7)
3. A metal used to electroplate jewellery. (4)
5. Coat a metal with another metal using electricity. (12)
9. Deposited on a cathode during electrolysis. (5)
10. Positively charged electrode. (5)
11. Negatively charged ion. (5)
12. This coating is thickened during anodising. (5)
13. Unit of electrical resistance. (3)
14. This may occur if the electroplating is carried out too fast. (14)
15. A molten electrolyte may be called a ____ . (4)

Down
1. Melting is used to ____ ions. (4)
2. This must not come in contact with a molten metal produced by electrolysis. (3)
3. A semi-solid colloidial solution. (3)
4. 'The bulb has ____'. This shows the solid tested is a conductor. (3)
6. Negatively charged electrode. (7)
7. Process used to colour aluminium. (7)
8. A substance whose atoms are all the same type. (7)
10. Produced when a positive ion gains electrons. (4)
11. Symbol for a metal extracted by electrolysis. (2)

2 Electrolysis of molten sodium hydride (NaH) produces hydrogen at the anode($+$) and sodium at the cathode($-$). What is unusual about this statement? How can you explain this?

3 Lead, sodium chloride, sulphur, copper, plastic, carbon, wood, magnesium, copper(II) chloride, calcium oxide, sodium hydroxide. From the above list select:
 a Three substances which do not conduct electricity under any conditions.
 b Four substances which conduct electricity when solid.
 c One non-metal which conducts electricity.
 d Four substances that are electrolytes.
 e Two substances that produce oxygen at the anode (positive electrode) during electrolysis of the molten substance.
 f One substance producing a metal at the cathode (negative electrode) during electrolysis of aqueous solutions (that is, water is the solvent).

4 Draw a diagram to show how you would prepare and collect some hydrogen and oxygen by electrolysis of dilute sulphuric acid. Then

a label the battery, electrolyte, anode($+$) and cathode($-$), the oxygen produced and the hydrogen produced;
b write down the ions that migrate to
  (i) the cathode($-$).
  (ii) the anode($+$).
c explain how the ions are discharged at
  (i) the cathode($-$).
  (ii) the anode($+$).

5 The diagram shows an apparatus which can be used to investigate the effect of electricity on various substances.

What is observed at the light bulb and at each electrode if the boiling tube contains distilled water at first and then some crystals of sodium chloride are added?

b If the solution in the boiling tube is copper(II) sulphate solution, name
  (i) the product at electrode (A).
  (ii) the product at electrode (B).
Why does the copper(II) sulphate solution lose its blue colour?

c If the electrolyte in the tube is dilute sulphuric acid, write an equation for the process occurring at electrode (B). Explain the process in terms of oxidation or reduction.

(*Joint Matriculation Board/West Midlands Examinations Board 16+*)

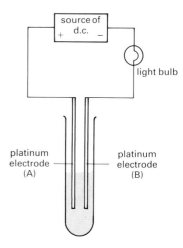

Figure 14.12

15. Carbon compounds

Carbon forms a very large number of compounds. This is because a carbon atom forms **stable bonds** with other atoms. Figure 15.1 is a simple two-dimensional representation of a carbon compound—in this case an amino acid.

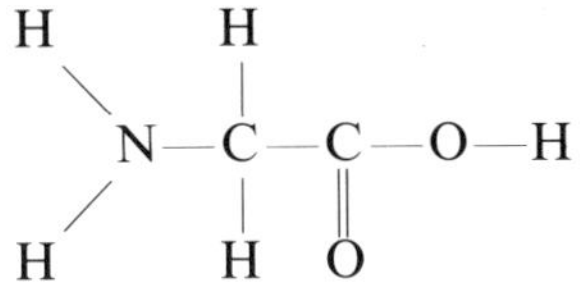

$$\begin{array}{ccccccc} H & & H & & & & \\ \diagdown & & | & & & & \\ & N & - & C & - & C & - O - H \\ \diagup & & | & & \| & \\ H & & H & & O & \end{array}$$

Figure 15.1

You will notice how
Each **carbon** atom forms **four bonds** with other atoms,
nitrogen forms **three bonds** with other atoms,
oxygen forms **two bonds** with other atoms, and
hydrogen forms a **single bond** with another atom.
    A diagram like this gives more information about the **arrangement** of atoms than does the molecular formula $C_2H_5NO_2$.

Hydrocarbons

There are many compounds that consist of just hydrogen and carbon and these are called **hydrocarbons**. The hydrocarbons are divided into families so that they can be studied easily. Three of these hydrocarbon families are the **alkanes** (or **paraffins**), **alkenes** (or **olefins**), and **alkynes** (or **acetylenes**).

Combustion of hydrocarbons
All **hydrocarbons** burn in air or oxygen. If they burn in a plentiful supply of air or oxygen, they form **carbon dioxide** and **water**. In a poor supply of air or oxygen, carbon monoxide and water are produced. In a **car engine** incomplete burning of the hydrocarbon (petrol) produces carbon monoxide. Running the engine of a car in a closed garage can lead to carbon monoxide poisoning.

Alkanes
Table 15.1 lists the simplest members of the alkane family. The important things to note are:

1 All alkanes are **saturated compounds**, that is, they contain only **single bonds**.
2 The names of all alkanes end in **-ane**.
3 All alkanes have a formula which fits the general formula C_nH_{2n+2}. For example, methane CH_4 is the formula obtained when n = 1.
4 The **melting** and **boiling points** of the alkanes increase as the mass of one mole increases.
5 Alkanes with four or more carbon atoms can exist in more than one arrangement of atoms. These different arrangements are called **isomers**. Two isomers of butane can exist (figure 15.2).

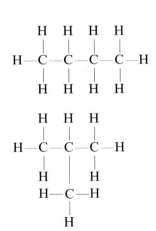

Figure 15.2

Table 15.1 Simplest members of the alkane family.

Alkane	Formula	Structure	Melting point °C	Boiling point °C	Mass of 1 mole g	State at room temperature and pressure
Methane	CH_4	H | H—C—H | H	−182 (91 K)	−161 (112 K)	16	Gas
Ethane	C_2H_6	H H | | H—C—C—H | | H H	−183 (90 K)	−89 (184 K)	30	Gas
Propane	C_3H_8	H H H | | | H—C—C—C—H | | | H H H	−188 (85 K)	−42 (231 K)	44	Gas
Butane	C_4H_{10}	H H H H | | | | H—C—C—C—C—H | | | | H H H H	−138 (135 K)	0 (273 K)	58	Gas
Pentane	C_5H_{12}	H H H H H | | | | | H—C—C—C—C—C—H | | | | | H H H H H	−130 (143 K)	36 (309 K)	72	Liquid
Hexane	C_6H_{14}	H H H H H H | | | | | | H—C—C—C—C—C—C—H | | | | | | H H H H H H	−95 (178 K)	68 (341 K)	86	Liquid

The next members of the alkane family are heptane (C_7H_{16}), octane (C_8H_{18}), nonane (C_9H_{20}) and decane ($C_{10}H_{22}$).

Uses of the alkanes

Natural gas is largely **methane** (CH_4). Large deposits of methane have been found under the North Sea and in Algeria. It has advantages over other types of gas. It is not poisonous, burns without soot and gives out a large amount of heat when it burns.

Ethane and **propane** are stored in cylinders for welding and cutting metals. **Butane** is used for heating and lighting. It is also used a fuel in cigarette lighters.

Petrol is a mixture of the isomers of **heptane** and **octane**. The octane number of a sample of petrol depends on the concentrations of the different alkanes. Substances like lead tetraethyl ($(C_2H_5)_4Pb$) added in small quantities to a sample of petrol increases its octane number. However, the long-term danger caused by lead compounds escaping into the atmosphere will lead to the removal of these additives.

Higher alkanes are present in paraffin, diesel oils, paraffin waxes and so on.

Source of alkanes

Crude oil is composed of a mixture of alkanes. The crude oil can be split into fractions by **fractional distillation** because the different alkanes have different boiling points.

In the laboratory the apparatus in figure 15.3 can be used to separate crude oil into fractions. Table 15.2 shows the properties of the different fractions of a sample of crude oil.

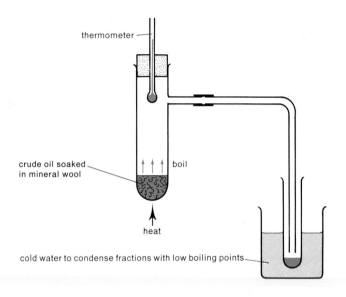

Figure 15.3 Separation of crude oil into fractions

Table 15.2: Properties of the different fractions in crude oil.

Fraction	Range of boiling point	Colour	Inflammability	Viscosity i.e. ease of flow
1st	Room temperature → 70°C	Yellow colour increases	Inflammability decreases	Viscosity increases
2nd	70°C–120°C			
3rd	120°C–170°C			
4th	170°C–220°C	↓	↓	↓

In an oil refinery fractional distillation is carried out on a large scale. The different fractions have different ranges of boiling point and, therefore, different uses (figure 15.4).

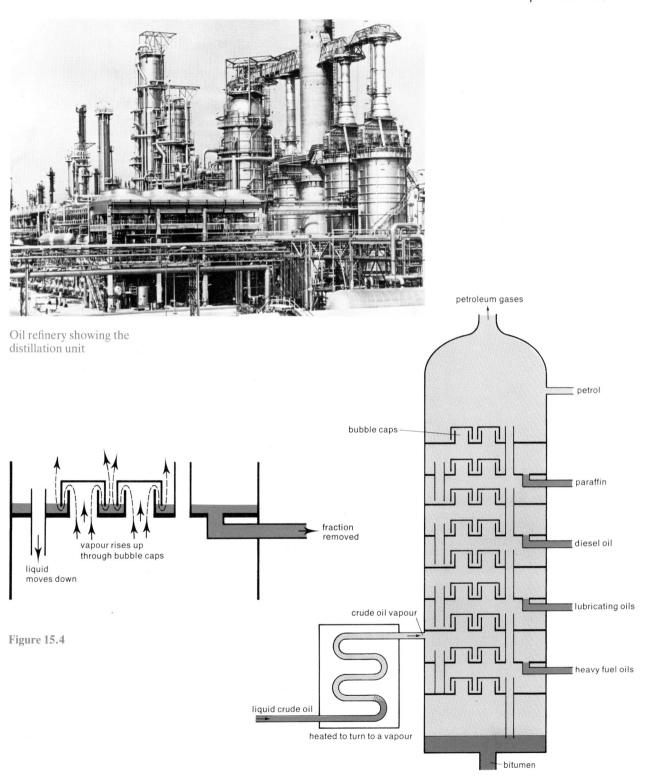

Oil refinery showing the
distillation unit

Figure 15.4

liquid
moves down

vapour rises up
through bubble caps

fraction
removed

petroleum gases

petrol

bubble caps

paraffin

diesel oil

crude oil vapour

lubricating oils

heavy fuel oils

liquid crude oil

heated to turn to a vapour

bitumen

Cracking

Crude oil contains many long-chain alkanes. Cracking is a process developed by the oil companies to produce larger quantities of the shorter-chain hydrocarbons such as butane and octane as these products can be sold more easily. Cracking is the breaking of long chain hydrocarbons and it can be carried out simply by heating (**thermal cracking**) or by using a catalyst (**catalytic cracking**).

Cracking of alkanes at high temperatures produces a residue of carbon black which has a range of uses including the blackening of rubber for car tyres.

The cracking of a long chain alkane must lead to at least one unsaturated product (a product containing a double bond). This is shown by the cracking of **hexane** in figure 15.5.

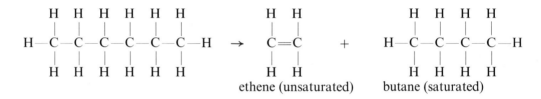

Figure 15.5

Thermal cracking of liquid paraffin

Liquid paraffin vapour is cracked when it is passed over strongly heated broken 'china' (figure 15.6). The broken 'china' does not act as a catalyst but it keeps the heat inside the tube. The single product is a gas, **ethene** C_2H_4 (an alkene) which is collected over water. Liquid paraffin is sometimes found floating on the water in the trough. It comes from the liquid paraffin vapour, which has not been cracked, but which condenses as it cools.

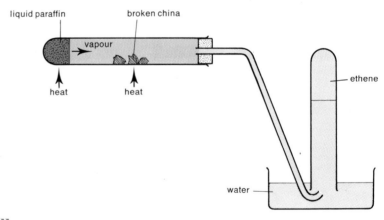

Figure 15.6 Thermal cracking of liquid paraffin

Alkenes

Table 15.3 lists the simplest members of the alkene family. The things to note are:

1 All alkenes contain a **double bond** between two carbon atoms. They are all unsaturated.

2 They all fit the general formula C_nH_{2n}. The simplest member is C_2H_4 because at least two carbon atoms are necessary.

Table 15.3: Simplest members of the alkene family.

Alkene	Formula	Structure	Melting point °C	Boiling point °C	Mass of 1 mole g	State at room temperature and pressure
Ethene	C_2H_4	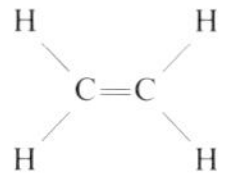	−169 (104 K)	−104 (169 K)	28	Gas
Propene	C_3H_6	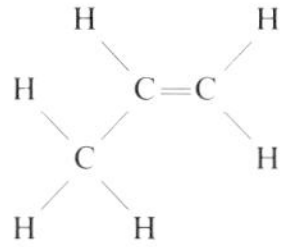	−185 (88 K)	−48 (225 K)	42	Gas
Butene	C_4H_8	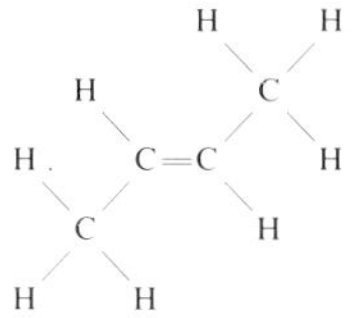	−139 (134 K)	−4 (269 K)	56	Gas
Pentene	C_5H_{10}	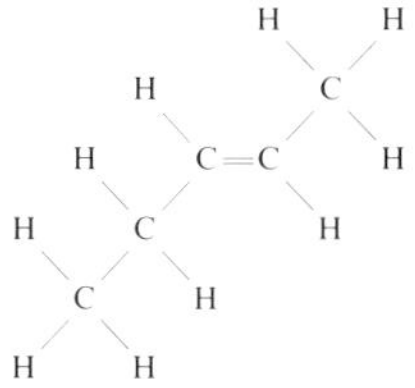	−138 (135 K)	30 (303 K)	70	Liquid

The next members of the alkene family are hexene (C_6H_{12}), heptene (C_7H_{14}), octene (C_8H_{16}), nonene (C_9H_{18}) and decene ($C_{10}H_{20}$).

3 The names of all alkenes end in **-ene** and the name comes from the alkane with the same number of carbon atoms. Ethene is named after ethane which is the alkane with the same number of carbon atoms.
4 The **melting points** and **boiling points** of alkenes increase as the mass of one mole increases.
5 Alkenes with four or more carbon atoms can exist in different **isomers**.

Addition reactions of alkenes

Ethene (and other alkenes) remove the red colour of **bromine** (dissolved in a suitable solvent). This is because bromine reacts with ethene to produce dibromoethane (a colourless oil).

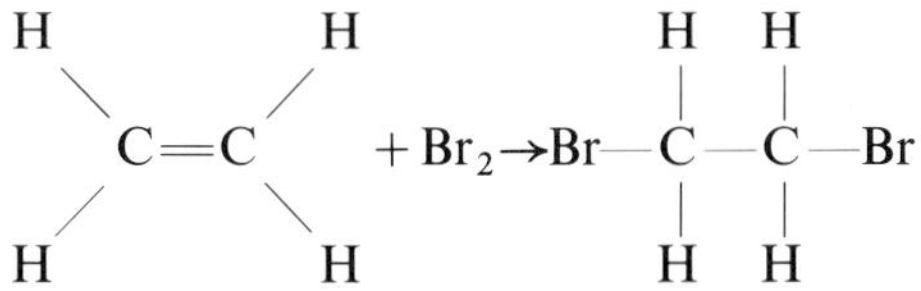

dibromoethane

Removing the colour from bromine dissolved in hexane is used as a test for compounds with double or triple bonds.

Alkynes

All alkynes contain a **triple bond** between two carbon atoms and fit the general formula C_nH_{2n-2}. The simplest member of the alkyne family is ethyne C_2H_2. Another name for ethyne is **acetylene**. Ethyne is a colourless gas which gives out a large amount of heat on burning in air or oxygen. Oxyacetylene equipment is used for cutting and welding metals. The structure of ethyne is $H-C\equiv C-H$.

Alcohols

Alcohols are compounds of carbon, hydrogen and oxygen. If a hydrogen atom in an alkane is replaced by an —OH (**hydroxyl group**), the result is an alcohol. Table 15.4 lists the simplest alcohols. The things to note are:
1 All alcohols have a general formula $C_nH_{2n+1}OH$.
2 Alcohols are named by taking the first part of the name of the alkane with the same number of carbon atoms and the ending **-ol** from alcohol.
3 Simple alcohols resemble water in many ways. They react with alkali metals (such as sodium) to produce hydrogen. They differ from water, however, because they burn readily. They are liquids that do not conduct electricity.

Table 15.4 The simplest alcohols.

Alcohol	Formula	Structure	Melting point °C	Boiling point °C	State at room temperature and pressure
Methanol	CH_3OH	H | H—C—OH | H	−94 (179 K)	64 (337 K)	Liquid
Ethanol	C_2H_5OH	H H | | H—C—C—OH | | H H	−117 (156 K)	78 (351 K)	Liquid
Propanol	C_3H_7OH	H H H | | | H—C—C—C—OH | | | H H H	−127 (146 K)	97 (370 K)	Liquid

Fermentation

Ethanol is the most common alcohol and is often just called alcohol. It can be prepared by the action of enzymes in yeast on sugar. The sugar is broken down into ethanol and carbon dioxide.

$$sugar \rightarrow ethanol + carbon\ dioxide$$

This process takes place at 20–30°C. At lower temperatures the enzymes do not operate and, at higher temperatures, the enzymes are killed.

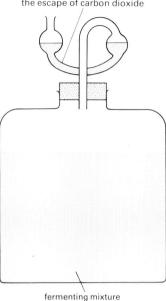

Fermentation during the brewing of beer by the traditional method. The froth is produced by the escaping carbon dioxide. In modern brewing the fermentation is carried out in an enclosed container.

The fermentation is carried out in a fermentation jar (figure 15.7). This enables carbon dioxide to escape without air entering the jar. The reaction of ethanol with oxygen in the presence of certain bacteria causes souring. The resulting solution contains ethanoic acid (acetic acid). Vinegar is a dilute solution of ethanoic acid.

Fermentation produces only a dilute solution of ethanol—up to about 20% ethanol. Fermentation stops at this stage because the enzymes are poisoned.

Beers contains about 3–4% ethanol. They are prepared by the fermentation of malt from barley. Wine can be made by fermentation of a wide range of fruits and berries. Wines contain up to about 15% ethanol. Sherry and port are called fortified wines and are prepared by adding extra ethanol to wine. Spirits such as whisky and gin contain about 35% ethanol and are prepared by fractional distillation of dilute solutions of ethanol.

Figure 15.7

Dehydration of ethanol

When ethanol vapour is passed over heated aluminium oxide, water is removed from the ethanol and the gas ethene is produced.

ethanol → water + ethene

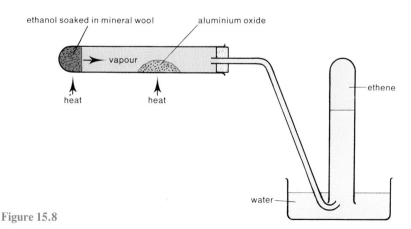

Figure 15.8

Polymerisation

Polymerisation is the opposite process to cracking. It is the joining of small molecules called **monomers** together to form long chain molecules called **polymers**. Polymerisation can be either addition polymerisation or condensation polymerisation.

Table 15.5: Common addition polymers and the monomers they come from.

Monomer	State of monomer at room temperature and pressure	Polymer
Ethene	Gas	Poly(ethene)
Vinyl chloride (chloroethene)	Liquid	Poly(vinyl chloride) (PVC)
Styrene (phenylethene)	Liquid	Poly(styrene)
Methyl methacrylate (methyl 2-methylpropenoate)	Liquid	Perspex

Addition polymerisation

Many monomers contain a double bond between two carbon atoms. During polymerisation the monomers link together, without losing atoms, but losing double bonds. Table 15.5 shows the common addition polymers and their monomers.

Uses of addition polymers

Rubber is an example of a natural addition polymer. It is made from latex obtained by tapping rubber trees. The final polymer is hardened by heating the polymer with sulphur. This process, called vulcanisation, hardens the rubber by forming cross links between chains. On exposure to air over long periods, rubber perishes, that is, it becomes hard and brittle. Synthetic rubbers such as neoprene have now been produced. These are more suitable for motor tyres etc.

Poly(ethene) was the first synthetic addition polymer to be produced in 1933. It was produced by heating ethene at very high pressures with a trace of oxygen as catalyst. The resulting polymer consists of about 50 000 ethene units joined together. This form of poly(ethene) is now called **low-density polythene**. It melts below 100°C but it is suitable for food wrappings and polythene sheeting to protect growing plants etc.

An alternative form of poly(ethene) is now produced called **high-density polythene**. It is produced at lower temperatures and pressures by using special catalysts called Ziegler catalysts. The polymer is more crystalline than low-density poly(ethene). The polymer chains are more regularly arranged and there is less space between the chains (hence the higher density). This polymer is rigid and melts at about 150°C. It is used for milk crates, washing-up bowls, dustbins and plastic bleach bottles.

It is very easy to polymerise **styrene** to make poly(styrene) and, as a result, poly(styrene) is cheap to produce. It is produced in a normal form and in an expanded form. The normal form is used for flowerpots, plastic model kits and yoghurt containers. It is easily moulded but melts below 100°C and can become brittle when exposed to sunlight. Expanded poly(styrene) is used as a packaging material and for ceiling tiles. It contains bubbles of air added during the manufacture. This makes it a better heat insulator, and it is less dense.

Poly(vinyl chloride) (or **PVC**) is widely used for making fashion clothes, electrical wire insulation and guttering. The monomer, vinyl chloride, is extremely unpleasant and there are strict regulations about the manufacture of PVC.

Perspex is used for boxes, safety screens etc. Both perspex and **poly(carbonate)** can be used as substitute for glass.

PTFE is used for coating saucepans and sawblades. It has a high melting point and a low coefficient of friction so that objects, such as fried eggs, slide over its surface very easily. It is also used for bridge bearings.

Condensation polymerisation

When two molecules react together to form a larger molecule and lose a small molecule like water or hydrogen chloride, this is called a condensation reaction.

Starch is a natural polymer formed from the monomer **glucose** by a series of condensation reactions. It is found in all green plants having been produced by photosynthesis. It has a molecular formula $(C_6H_{10}O_5)_n$.

Starch forms a dark blue-black colour when iodine solution is added and

Plastic materials in use: polythene for plants; PVC driving wheel; polythene sheeting underlay on the motorway.

Nylon being extruded through fine holes in a spinneret

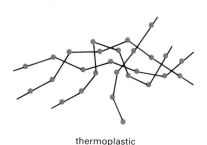

thermoplastic

cross-link

cross-link

cross-link

cross-link

thermosetting

Figure 15.10

this is used as a test for starch. Starch can be split up or hydrolysed in two ways.

1 Boiling with dilute hydrochloric acid breaks up the starch molecules to produce glucose.

2 When starch is mixed with enzymes in saliva and maintained at approximately 30°C, the starch is split up into maltose molecules. Maltose consists of two glucose molecules joined together.

Both glucose and maltose are reducing sugars—that is they reduce Fehling's solution or Benedict's solution to produce a precipitate of copper(I) oxide. Starch is not a reducing sugar.

Proteins are long-chain polymers which form a large part of the living tissue of the body. They are composed of carbon, hydrogen, oxygen and nitrogen with other elements like sulphur and phosphorus possibly present. They are condensation polymers and the monomers are **amino acid** molecules (like the one shown in figure 15.1).

The amino acids are joined together by **peptide links**. Each peptide link formed causes one molecule of water to be lost.

Nylon is a man-made condensation polymer copying the arrangement in proteins. There are different types of nylon. The form of nylon called nylon 6.6 (because both starting materials contain six carbon atoms) is made from hexane-1,6-diamine (hexamethylenediamine) and hexanedioyl dichloride (adipyl chloride). Both of the substances have molecules with **two reactive groups** one at each end of the molecule. When one of the reactive —NH_2 groups on the hexane-1,6-diamine molecule reacts with one of the reactive —COCl groups on the hexanedioyl dichloride, a condensation reaction takes place and a molecule of hydrogen chloride is lost. When a series of these reactions takes place, a condensation polymer results (figure 15.9). Unless the starting materials have two reactive groups no polymer is possible.

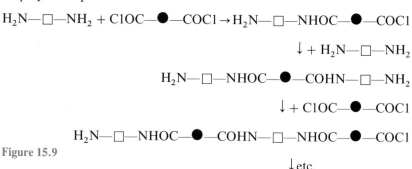

Figure 15.9

↓ etc.

Thermosetting and thermoplastic polymers

Polymers may be classified as addition or condensation polymers but may also be classified as thermosetting or thermoplastic according to the way they behave on heating.

Thermoplastics (e.g. poly(ethene) and other addition polymers), soften and melt when heated, but on cooling they turn solid again. They can therefore be moulded or extruded.

Thermosetting polymers decompose on heating and cannot be melted. Once they have been formed they cannot be reshaped by moulding. Bakelite is used for electrical switches and plugs.

The difference in structure between thermosetting and thermoplastic polymers is shown in figure 15.10.

Esters

Esters are compounds formed by the condensation reaction between **an acid** and **an alcohol**:

Acid + alcohol $\rightleftharpoons$ ester + water

This can be compared with:

Acid + alkali $\rightarrow$ salt + water (Chapter 17)

Esters are often sweet-smelling liquids. They are frequently found in flowers and fruits where they give scent and flavour. Table 15.6 shows the natural sources of some esters.

A simple ester can be made by warming ethanol and ethanoic acid (acetic acid) with a few drops of concentrated sulphuric acid as a catalyst. The ester produced is called ethyl ethanoate (ethyl acetate).

Ethanol + ethanoic acid $\rightleftharpoons$ ethyl ethanoate + water

Table 15.6 Where some esters are found.

Ester	Made from Acid	Made from Alcohol	Odour of
Pentyl acetate (amyl acetate)	Ethanoic acid (acetic acid)	Pentanol	Pear
Octyl acetate	Ethanoic acid	Octanol	Orange
Pentyl pentanoate	Pentanoic acid	Pentanol	Apple

Many of the very important naturally occurring **fats** and **oils** consist of esters. Figure 15.11 shows the world's supply of natural oils and fats. These oils are not to be confused with petroleum oil which is a mixture of alkanes, not esters.

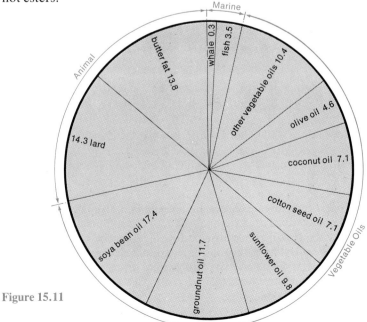

Figure 15.11

When esters are boiled with water they are partially split up into the constituent acid and alcohol. This splitting up with water is called **hydrolysis**. The hydrolysis is more complete if a solution of sodium or potassium hydroxide is used.

All of these oils or fats on hydrolysis with potassium hydroxide solution form the triol (alcohol with three —OH groups) called propane-1,2,3-triol (glycerine or glycerol) and the potassium salt of the appropriate acid. This potassium salt can be used as a soap and this hydrolysis reaction is sometimes called **saponification**. For example, propane-1,2,3-triyl trioctadecanoate (glyceryl tristearate) on saponification forms propane-1,2,3-triol and the potassium salt of octadecanoic acid (stearic acid).

Reaction of an alcohol containing two —OH groups and an acid containing two —COOH groups produces a long chain condensation polymer. This takes place by a series of steps, each step being a condensation reaction. This polymer can be produced in fibres and is called polyester.

HO—●—OH + HOOC—□—COOH → HO—●—OOC—□—COOH

↓ + HO—●—OH

HO—●—OOC—□—COO—●—OH

↓ + HOOC—□—COOH

HO—●—OOC—□—COO—●—OOC—□—COOH

Figure 15.12   etc.

Detergents

A detergent is a cleaning agent. Soap is the commonest detergent and has been used for thousands of years. It is still produced by the traditional process of boiling natural fats with strong alkali (sodium hydroxide or potassium hydroxide) in order to saponify the ester.

glyceryl tristearate + potassium hydroxide → glycerol + potassium stearate
(a soap)

After boiling, sodium chloride is added to the solution. Potassium stearate is much less soluble in salt solution and precipitates out. It can be removed by filtering.

Soap does not lather well in hard water, but produces scum (Chapter 6).

potassium stearate + calcium ions → calcium stearate + potassium ions
(scum)

Synthetic soapless detergents are used in washing powders and washing-up liquids. They lather well in hard and soft water. Soapless detergents are usually made by the action of fuming sulphuric acid (a very concentrated form of sulphuric acid) on an alkyl benzene (from crude oil). Early synthetic soapless detergents caused a problem of foaming in rivers. Modern soapless detergents are broken down by bacteria in the river. They are said to be **biodegradable**.

Structure of soap and soapless detergents

Both soap and soapless detergent molecules consist of a long hydrocarbon chain which repels water molecules, and a charged group of atoms forming a 'head' which readily attracts water molecules (figure 15.13). The difference between the molecules is the atoms making up the head.

Figure 15.14 shows you how a soap or soapless detergent cleans: the tails of the detergent molecules stick into the grease. Because the heads of the detergent molecules are attracted towards the water molecules, the grease is lifted from the material.

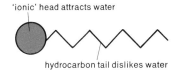

Figure 15.13

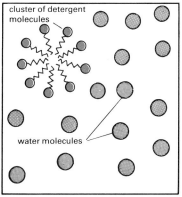

Detergent solution

Cluster of detergent molecules in solution.

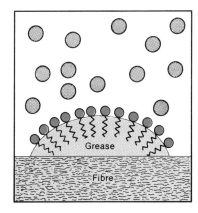

Tails of detergent molecules stick into the grease. Attraction between heads of detergent molecules and water molecules. Grease is lifted from the material.

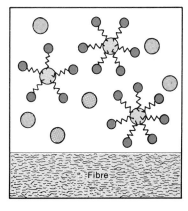

Grease is suspended in the solution. Repelling forces between droplets of grease prevents them coming together.

Figure 15.14

Figure 15.15 shows the approximate composition of a washing powder. **Sodium sulphate** and **sodium silicate** prevent the washing powder absorbing water from the atmosphere. The dirt-suspending agent prevents dirt settling on the washing again. **Sodium perborate** acts as a bleach to remove stains. The fluorescent agents help to overcome the yellowing of clothes with age.

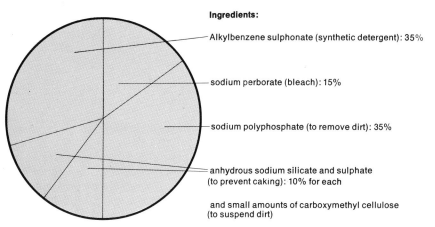

Figure 15.15 The constituents of a washing powder

Margarine

Margarine is produced by the reaction of **natural fats** and **oils** with **hydrogen gas** under pressure using a nickel catalyst at 300°C (573 K). This process is called the hardening of oils.

The natural oils and fats contain double bonds between two carbon atoms. The hydrogen adds on to the fat or oil reducing the double bonds to single bonds.

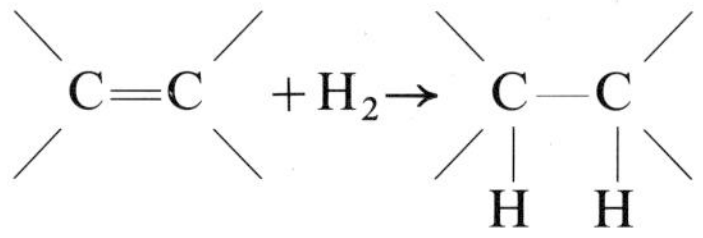

$$\begin{array}{c}\diagdown \\ \diagup\end{array} C{=}C \begin{array}{c}\diagup \\ \diagdown\end{array} + H_2 \rightarrow \begin{array}{c}\diagdown \\ \diagup\end{array} \underset{\underset{H}{|}}{C}{-}\underset{\underset{H}{|}}{C} \begin{array}{c}\diagup \\ \diagdown\end{array}$$

More expensive margarines contain only vegetable oils which, because of their low cholesterol content, are favoured by some people. Research has linked the cholesterol level in animal fats with heart disease. Cheaper margarines may contain quantities of hardened fish oil. Vitamins A and D are added to the margarine before packing. The spreading properties of margarine depend on the arrangement of the molecules in the margarine.

something to think about . . .

1 Figure 15.16 shows the structures of six carbon compounds labelled A–F.

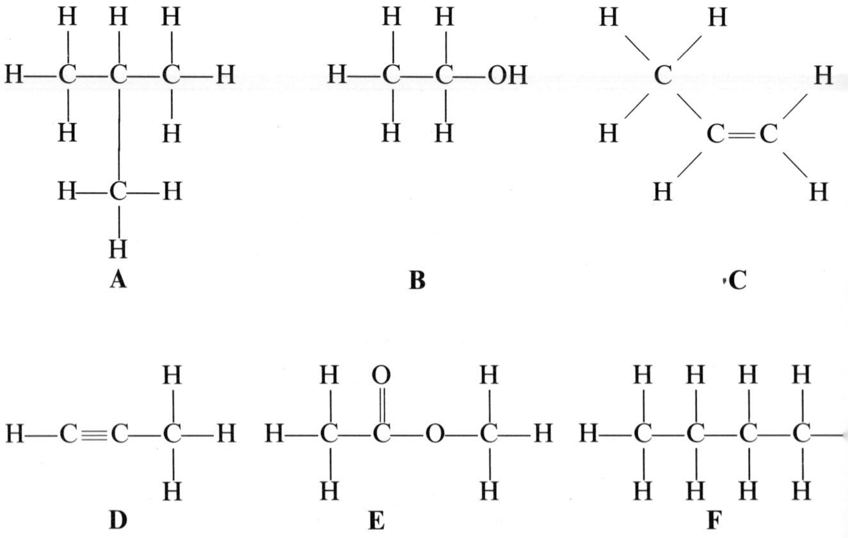

Figure 15.16

Write down which of these compounds

a are hydrocarbons
b have the same molecular formula
c are liquids
d are unsaturated hydrocarbons
e are alkanes
f is an alkene
g is an alkyne

h is an alcohol
i is an ester
j produces hydrogen with sodium
k is produced by fermentation
l is hydrolysed by potassium hydroxide solution?

2 Ethane and ethene are hydrocarbons containing two carbon atoms per molecule. Ethane is a saturated compound and ethene is unsaturated. Both compounds burn readily in air forming the same products. Ethene is more reactive, forming addition products with hydrogen and with bromine. The product with bromine is 1,2—dibromoethane. Ethane can be polymerised to form poly(ethene).

a Write the molecular formulae for
   (i) ethane,
   (ii) ethene.
b Explain what is meant by the term hydrocarbon.
c Draw the structural formula of:
   (i) ethane,
   (ii) ethene.
d What are the products of the complete combustion of ethane and ethene?
e Explain what is meant by the terms saturated and unsaturated with respect to the structures of ethane and ethene.
f Name the product formed when ethene reacts with hydrogen. State one industrial application of the reaction between unsaturated compounds and hydrogen.
g Write a symbol equation for the reaction between ethene and bromine.
h Draw the structural formula of 1,2—dibromoethane.
i Explain what is meant by the term polymerisation, using the conversion of ethene to poly(ethene) to illustrate your answer.
   (*Joint Matriculation Board/West Midlands Examination Board 16+*)

3 'Crimplene' and 'Terylene' are trade names for polyester (a condensation polymer). Suggest the monomer(s) necessary for the production of polyester.

The coloured substances that colour plants and vegetables are called **plant pigments**. They can be extracted from plants by crushing the plant material and adding a solvent like ethanol or propanone (acetone). The plant pigments dissolve in the solvent to form a **coloured solution**.

Indicators

Solutions of plant pigments can act as **indicators**. Indicators are substances which change colour when acids and alkalis are added. Examples of good plant indicators are solutions from red cabbage, red roses, beetroot and elderberries. Most plant extracts are suitable except those that are yellow or green in colour.

In the laboratory the plant extract most commonly used to detect acids and alkalis is **litmus**. Litmus is extracted from a lichen which grows in very cold areas of the world. Litmus solution (or litmus paper) changes colour as follows:

in **acid** solution —red
in alkali solution—blue

In neutral solutions the litmus solution turns **purple**.

However, litmus gives no indication of the strength of an acid or alkali. The **strength** of an acid or alkali solution can be determined using **universal indicator**. Universal indicator is a mixture of simple indicators designed to change colour a number of times depending on the strength of the acid or alkali solution. The strength of the acid or alkali solution is measured on the **pH scale**. Figure 16.1 shows the part of the pH scale commonly used in the laboratory. Table 16.1 shows the pH values of some common substances.

Figure 16.1 Part of the pH scale

pH	1	2	3	4	5	6	7	8	9	10	11	12	13	14
Colour of Universal Indicator	←	Red	→	Pink	Orange	Yellow	Green	Green-blue	Blue	Blue-violet	←		Violet	→
Conclusion from colour change	Acid — Stronger as the pH decreases — Increasing hydrogen ion (H^+) concentration (pH 1–6)						neutral (pH 7)	Alkali — Stronger as pH increases — Increasing hydroxide ion (OH^-) concentration (pH 8–14)						

Table 16.1: pH values of some common substances.

Substance	pH	Substance	pH
Water	7	Apples	3
Salt solution	7	Butter	6
Sugar solution	7	Sodium hydrogencarbonate	8.5
Ethanol	7	Ammonia solution	10
Paraffin	7	Washing soda	11.5
Lemon juice	2.5	Toothpaste	9
Vinegar	3		

Many household substances are acid or alkali

The pH of a solution can also be found using a **pH meter**. This is particularly useful for measuring the pH of coloured substances or if a large number of pH readings have to be made.

Acids

An acid is a compound containing **replaceable hydrogen**. Replaceable hydrogen is hydrogen which can be replaced by a metal during salt formation. When dissolved in water the solution produces an excess of hydrated hydrogen ions $H^+(aq)$.

The three common acids used in the laboratory are:

$$\text{sulphuric acid} \quad H_2SO_4$$
$$\text{nitric acid} \quad HNO_3$$
$$\text{hydrochloric acid} \quad HCl$$

These acids are called **mineral acids** because they can all be made from substances that have come from the ground.

There are also many **organic acids** composed of carbon, hydrogen and oxygen. Many of these organic acids are solids. Examples are citric acid, tartaric acid and oxalic acid.

In addition to using indicators, other tests can be used for recognising acids.

1 **Taste:** Many acids are poisonous. Those acids that are not poisonous have a sour taste. Acetic acid (vinegar) is an example.

2 Add **magnesium**: An acid produces hydrogen when magnesium ribbon or powder is added. **Hydrogen** is a colourless gas which burns with a squeaky pop.

3 Add **sodium carbonate** crystals. An acid produces **carbon dioxide** when sodium carbonate crystals are added. Carbon dioxide is a colourless gas which turns limewater milky.

An acid only shows these acidic properties when water is present. This can be shown by comparing the properties of the following two solutions (Table 16.2):

Solution A: a solution of dry hydrogen chloride in dry methylbenzene (toluene). No water is present.

Solution B: a solution of hydrogen chloride in water, called hydrochloric acid.

Table 16.2: Testing for acidity. Solution A contains no water; solution B contains water.

Test	Solution A (Dry hydrogen chloride in dry methylbenzene)	Solution B (Hydrogen chloride in water)
Dry Universal indicator	Green. pH 7, neutral.	Red. pH 1, strongly acidic.
Electrical conductivity	Does not conduct electricity.	Good conductor of electricity.
Addition of magnesium	No bubbles of hydrogen produced.	Bubbles of hydrogen produced.
Addition of sodium carbonate crystals	No bubbles of carbon dioxide produced.	Bubbles of carbon dioxide produced.

Water is needed to ionise the hydrogen chloride, which is present as molecules.

$$HCl \xrightarrow{\text{water}} H^+(aq) + Cl^-(aq)$$

Similar results can be obtained with pure or glacial ethanoic acid (acetic acid), which contains no water and dilute ethanoic acid.

Bases and alkalis

A base is an **oxide** or **hydroxide** of a **metal**. It reacts with an acid to form a salt and water only:

base + acid → salt + water

An **alkali** is a base which is soluble in water. A solution of an alkali contains an excess of hydroxide (OH^-) ions.
There are four common alkalis:

potassium hydroxide   KOH
sodium hydroxide   NaOH
calcium hydroxide $Ca(OH)_2$
ammonium hydroxide NH_4OH
(or ammonia solution NH_3aq)

Note: Ammonium hydroxide differs from the other alkalis because it contains no metal ions. It smells strongly of ammonia gas and if it is evaporated to dryness, no residue remains. Most other metal hydroxides are insoluble in water.

Figure 16.2 summarises the relationships between acids, bases and alkalis.

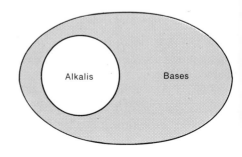

Figure 16.2

Neutralisation

A neutralisation reaction is any reaction between an **acid** and an **alkali** to form a **salt** and **water**. If sulphuric acid is spilt on the laboratory bench, a weak alkali should be added to neutralise the acid before the spill is cleared up.

The reaction between sodium hydroxide and hydrochloric acid is a neutralisation reaction producing sodium chloride and water only. The essential step in a neutralisation is the reaction of the hydrated hydrogen ion with the hydroxide ion from an alkali:

$$H^+(aq) + OH^-(aq) \rightarrow H_2O(l)$$

Applications of neutralisation

1 **Soil testing**: A soil with a pH value between 6.5 and 7.0 is suitable for growing most plants. If the pH falls below 6.0, the soil becomes too acidic for growing some plants. If the pH rises to 8.0 it will again be poor for plant growth because extreme alkalinity causes shortages of vital minerals. The chemical sequestrene helps acid-loving plants to grow in alkaline soils. Sequestrene contains special iron compounds which plants cannot normally get from alkaline soils.

Table 16.3 shows plants, trees and shrubs suited to acid and alkaline soils.

One interesting effect of soil acidity concerns the shrub **hydrangea**. In alkaline or neutral soils only white or pink flowers can be obtained. In acid soils blue flowers can be obtained. Treatment of the alkaline or neutral soil with 'blueing compound' consisting of **aluminium sulphate** makes the soil acidic and produces blue flowers.

The pH of the soil is found by mixing the soil with distilled water and adding pure, insoluble barium sulphate powder. The barium sulphate helps the solution to clear. Universal indicator is added to the clear solution and the colour of the resulting solution is compared with a universal indicator colour chart.

Excess acidity of soils is the most important cause of crop failure. It has been estimated that if this was always corrected properly there would be a one-fifth increase in food production. Excess acidity (or soil sourness as it is called) is caused by the washing of alkali out of the soil by rainwater. The excess acidity can be neutralised by adding alkali.

Calcium oxide (or **quicklime**) and calcium hydroxide (or slaked lime) are frequently used to make the soil less acidic. They are formed from calcium carbonate.

Calcium carbonate $CaCO_3$ $\xrightarrow[\text{carbon dioxide produced}]{\text{heat strongly}}$ Calcium oxide CaO

Addition of a calculated quantity of water $\downarrow$

Calcium hydroxide $Ca(OH)_2$

Table 16.3: Plants suited to acid soils and alkaline soils.

Acid soil	Alkaline soil
Rhododendron	Cherry
Azalea	Juniper
Lavender	Laburnum
Wallflowers	Lilac
Stocks	Birch
Heather	Broom
Hydrangea	Holly

above rhododendron, which grows on acid soil

above clematis, which grows on acid soil

Calcium oxide and calcium hydroxide are quick-acting. In order to correct excess soil acidity, these alkalis should be used in autumn or winter. In addition to neutralising the excess soil acidity, the addition of these substances to the soil improves the quality of heavy, clay soils and supplies the **calcium** required for plant growth.

Calcium carbonate can be used as an alternative. It has the advantage of being less soluble and therefore it continues to work in the soil for much longer. **Dolomite** (containing magnesium and calcium carbonates) has the advantage of supplying **magnesium** which is an important element for plant growth.

2 The digestive system: Every adult has several hundred cubic centimetres of dilute **hydrochloric acid** in the gastric juices in the stomach. This is used, together with enzymes, in the digestion of food. Digestion involves the breaking down of complex substances into simpler substances that can be used by the body. **Proteins** are broken down into amino acids, **fats** into propane-1,2,3-triol (glycerine or glycerol), and **organic acids** and **sugars** and **starches** into simple sugars like glucose.

The presence of hydrochloric acid in the stomach causes no problem to the healthy person. **Ulcers** of the stomach or duodenum (part of the digestive system) are caused by the digestion of the walls of the stomach or duodenum by the **gastric juices**. The ulcers are not due to an excess of hydrochloric acid but rather to a defect in the wall. About one person in ten suffers from this defect during their life.

Indigestion is caused by an excess of hydrochloric acid in the gastric juices. It can be corrected by swallowing a mild alkali to neutralise some of the hydrochloric acid. **Bicarbonate of soda** (sodium hydrogencarbonate) is frequently used for this. Other mixtures include magnesium hydroxide and/or aluminium hydroxide.

3 Health salts: A popular brand of health salts has the following ingredients: citric acid (anhydrous), sodium hydrogencarbonate, magnesium sulphate, sucrose (sugar).

On adding water, citric acid dissolves to form an acidic solution. This reacts with sodium hydrogencarbonate to produce carbon dioxide which bubbles off producing a fizzy or effervescent drink.

Excess sodium hydrogencarbonate acts as an **antacid**, that is, it neutralises excess hydrochloric acid in the gastric juices. Magnesium sulphate acts as a laxative and the sugar removes the bitter taste from the drink.

4 Insect bites and stings: Insect bites or stings involve the injection of a small amount of chemical into the skin. This causes irritation. Nettle stings and ant bites inject methanoic acid (formic acid) into the skin. Bee stings also involve the injection of an acid. The sting or bite should be treated with calamine lotion or bicarbonate of soda (sodium hydrogencarbonate) to remove the irritation. **Calamine lotion** is a suspension containing **zinc carbonate**. Both sodium hydrogencarbonate and zinc carbonate neutralise the injected acid and remove the irritation.

Wasp stings, however, are different. They are best treated by applying vinegar (acetic or ethanoic acid) because this sting involves the injection of an alkali.

something to think about . . .

The table below compares solutions of dry hydrogen chloride in water and also in dry toluene (a hydrocarbon solvent).

Table 16.4

	Dry hydrogen chloride dissolved in dry toluene	Dry hydrogen chloride dissolved in water
pH	7	1
Electrical conductivity	Non-conductor	Conductor
Reaction with magnesium ribbon	No reaction	Colourless gas rapidly evolved
Reaction with sodium carbonate crystals	No reaction	Colourless gas rapidly evolved

a Name the two colourless gases evolved with a solution of dry hydrogen chloride in water
   (i) with magnesium ribbon.
   (ii) with sodium carbonate crystals.
b What is the chemical name for a solution of dry hydrogen chloride in water?
c The toluene, before being used in this experiment, is kept in contact with anhydrous calcium chloride for 24 hours. Why?
d What structure does dry hydrogen chloride have
   (i)   as a gas.
   (ii) dissolved in dry toluene.
   (iii) dissolved in water.

Hydrogen chloride can be made by dropping concentrated sulphuric acid onto solid sodium chloride. The hydrogen chloride is then dried by passing it through concentrated sulphuric acid before being dissolved in dry toluene.
   The diagram (figure 16.3) shows apparatus set up to produce a solution of dry hydrogen chloride in dry toluene.
e Name the pieces of apparatus labelled X, Y, Z.
f List four mistakes in the design of the apparatus for this experiment.

(Southern Regional Examinations Board)

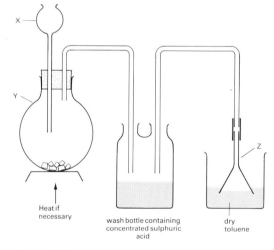

Figure 16.3

A **salt** is the compound formed by replacing hydrogen in an acid by a metal or ammonium ion. For example

$$H_2SO_4 \quad \xrightarrow[\text{replace by sodium ions}]{\text{remove hydrogen and}} \quad Na_2SO_4$$

sulphuric acid — an acid → sodium sulphate — a salt

Salts are **solids** with **high melting points** and **boiling points.** They undergo **electrolysis** when molten or in solution.

Acid salts

An acid salt is one in which only part of the hydrogen in the acid has been replaced by metal ions. When the acid salt is dissolved in water it frequently has properties similar to the acid.

If only one of the two hydrogens in sulphuric acid is replaced by sodium, an acid salt remains. This is $NaHSO_4$ sodium hydrogensulphate (sodium bisulphate). **Sodium hydrogensulphate** is a white crystalline solid. A solution of sodium hydrogensulphate behaves in a similar way to sulphuric acid. It is included in chemistry sets because it is easier to pack than sulphuric acid but it has similar properties. Solid lavatory cleaners contain sodium hydrogensulphate.

Sodium hydrogencarbonate ($NaHCO_3$)—sometimes called bicarbonate of soda—is an acid salt.

Solubility of salts

The following rules summarise the solubility of common salts.

1 All **nitrates** are soluble in water.
2 All potassium, sodium and ammonium salts are soluble in water.
3 All **carbonates** are insoluble except sodium, potassium and ammonium carbonates.
4 All **sulphates** are soluble in water except barium and lead sulphates. (Calcium sulphate is only slightly soluble in water.)
5 All **chlorides** are soluble in water except silver and lead chlorides.

Preparation of salts

The method used to prepare a salt depends on whether the salt is soluble or insoluble in water.

Preparation of soluble salts

One of the following reactions can be used to prepare a soluble salt.

metal + acid → salt + hydrogen gas
metal oxide + acid → salt + water
metal hydroxide + acid → salt + water
metal carbonate + acid → salt + water + carbon dioxide gas

In each case if the correct amounts of the two reacting substances are used, only a solution of the soluble salt in water remains.

Table 17.1 shows which acid should be used to prepare sulphates, nitrates, and chlorides.

Table 17.1 The acids used to prepare certain salts.

To produce a	Acid to use
Sulphate	Sulphuric acid
Nitrate	Nitric acid
Chloride	Hydrochloric acid

Examples of salt preparation:

   copper oxide + sulphuric acid → copper sulphate + water

   calcium carbonate + hydrochloric acid → calcium chloride + water + carbon dioxide

   magnesium + sulphuric acid → magnesium sulphate + hydrogen

The choice of **starting materials** depends on various factors.

1 The **cost** and **availability** of the different starting materials. Calcium chloride is best prepared from calcium carbonate because calcium carbonate is most readily available.

2 The **rate of reaction** of the two substances. Sodium chloride is not prepared from sodium and hydrochloric acid because the reaction would be too violent.

Copper sulphate and chloride are not prepared directly from copper because copper does not react with dilute sulphuric and hydrochloric acids.

Preparation of soluble salts

The method used to prepare a soluble salt (**copper sulphate** in this case) is summarised in figure 17.1. The acid is warmed at first to speed up the reaction of the **copper oxide** with the **sulphuric acid**. When all the sulphuric acid has been used up, no more copper oxide will react and any more copper oxide added will remain unreacted in the solution. It is not true to say that the copper oxide remains unchanged in the solution because the solution is saturated. The hot solution also ensures that the soluble salt remains in solution.

The salt is obtained from the solution by **evaporation**. It is important not to evaporate the solution to dryness. Evaporation to dryness may decompose the salt. The solution can be tested, during evaporation, to find the stage at which the solution will crystallise on cooling to room temperature. If a glass rod is dipped into the solution at intervals, a time will come when crystals form on the end of the glass rod on cooling in the air. At this stage the solution can be left to cool and crystallise.

Sometimes when preparing soluble sodium, potassium or ammonium salts, an alternative procedure is followed. This is shown in figure 17.2.

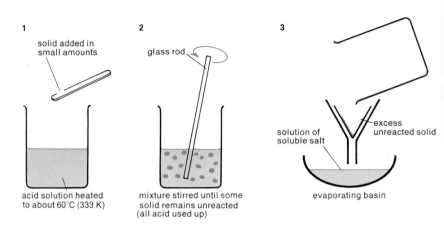

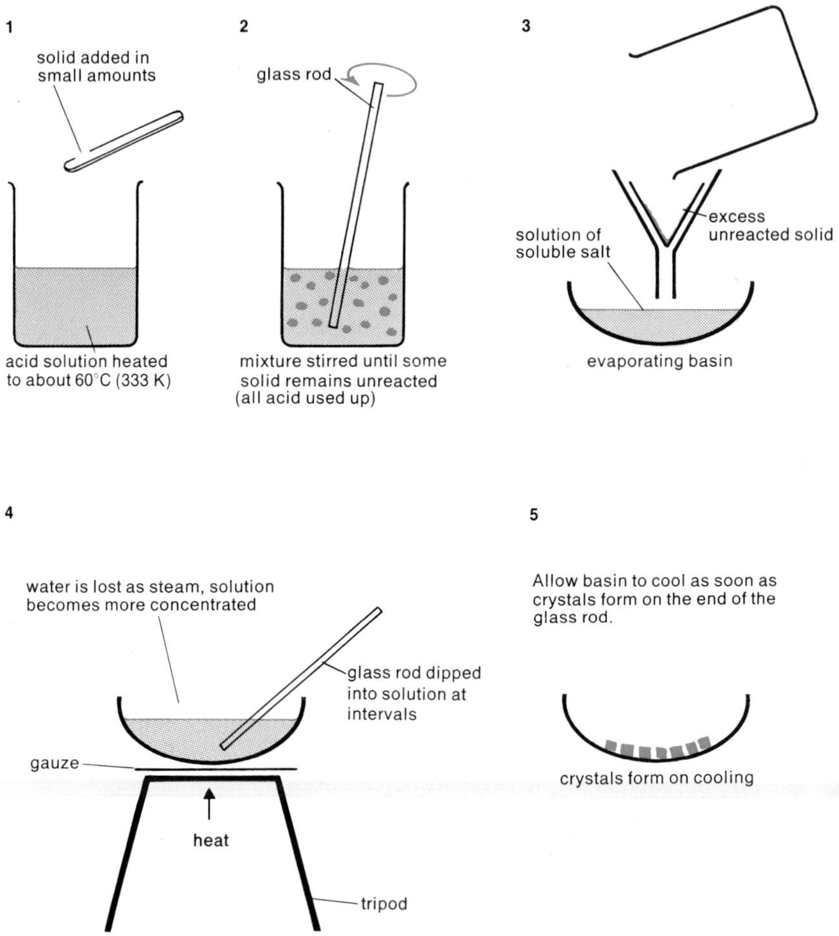

1
solid added in
small amounts

acid solution heated
to about 60°C (333 K)

2
glass rod

mixture stirred until some
solid remains unreacted
(all acid used up)

3

solution of
soluble salt

excess
unreacted solid

evaporating basin

4

water is lost as steam, solution
becomes more concentrated

glass rod dipped
into solution at
intervals

gauze

heat

tripod

5

Allow basin to cool as soon as
crystals form on the end of the
glass rod.

crystals form on cooling

Figure 17.1 Preparation of
copper sulphate

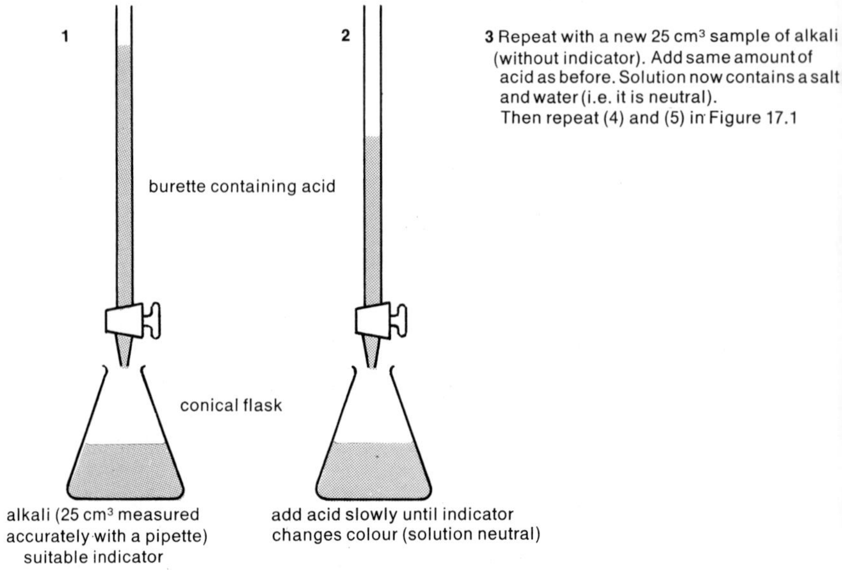

1

burette containing acid

conical flask

alkali (25 cm³ measured
accurately with a pipette)
suitable indicator

2

add acid slowly until indicator
changes colour (solution neutral)

3 Repeat with a new 25 cm³ sample of alkali
(without indicator). Add same amount of
acid as before. Solution now contains a salt
and water (i.e. it is neutral).
Then repeat (4) and (5) in Figure 17.1

Figure 17.2 Preparation of alkali
metal salts

Table 17.2 Useful soluble salts.

Chemical name	Formula	Common name
Sodium chloride	NaCl	Common salt
Sodium carbonate	$Na_2CO_3.10H_2O$	Washing soda
Sodium sulphate	$Na_2SO_4.10H_2O$	Glauber's salt
Magnesium sulphate	$MgSO_4.7H_2O$	Epsom salt

Preparation of insoluble salts

Insoluble salts can be prepared by a process of **precipitation**. In order to form an insoluble salt, two suitable solutions are prepared. For example, if insoluble **lead sulphate** is to be prepared, solutions of lead nitrate (containing lead ions) and sulphuric acid (containing sulphate ions) would be suitable. When the two solutions are mixed, lead sulphate is precipitated:

$$Pb^{2+}(aq) \ + \ SO_4^{2-}(aq) \ \rightarrow \ PbSO_4(s)$$

lead ions in   sulphate ions   lead sulphate
solution   in solution   precipitated

The solution still contains oxonium (hydronium) ions and nitrate ions.

The lead sulphate, being a solid suspended in the solution, can be filtered off from the solution. The lead sulphate is then washed with distilled water to remove any soluble impurities and dried.

Barium sulphate can be prepared by mixing solutions of barium hydroxide (containing barium ions) and sulphuric acid (containing sulphate ions):

barium hydroxide + sulphuric acid → barium sulphate + water
                                     (precipitated)   (not ionised)

If the process is carried out slowly by adding portions of dilute sulphuric acid from a burette to 100 cm³ barium hydroxide solution, the point at which all the barium hydroxide has been used up and further additions of sulphuric acid will remain unused, can be found using an indicator or by electrical conductivity measurements (figure 17.3). The graph obtained from electrical conductivity measurements is shown in figure 17.4.

The **electrical conductivity** depends on the concentration of ions in solution. Electrolysis does not take place because an alternating current (A.C.) is used. Barium hydroxide solution and sulphuric acid conduct electricity. During the addition of the first 10 cm³ of dilute sulphuric acid (AB on the graph), the electrical conductivity decreases due to the removal of ions from the solution.

$$Ba^{2+}(aq) + SO_4^{2-}(aq) \rightarrow BaSO_4(s) \text{ ions removed from solution}$$
$$H^+(aq) + OH^-(aq) \rightarrow H_2O(l) \text{ ions removed by reaction}$$

After addition of 10 cm³ of sulphuric acid (i.e. at point B) the solution has zero electrical conductivity because all the ions have been removed from the solution. This is the **neutral point**. All the barium hydroxide (the alkali) have been used up but there is no unused sulphuric acid.

When more than 10 cm³ of sulphuric acid is added, the amount of barium sulphate does not increase at all because the barium ions have

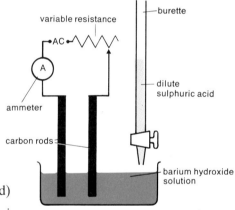

Figure 17.3 Preparation of barium sulphate

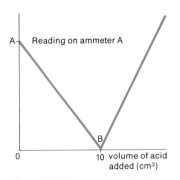

Figure 17.4 When all the barium hydroxide has been neutralised the ammeter reading falls to zero

been used up. The excess sulphuric acid causes the electrical conductivity to rise.

Uses of insoluble salts

1 A most important use of insoluble salts is as **pigments** in **paint manufacture**. A typical gloss paint is made by grinding thoroughly together a hardening oil, pigment, driers, extenders, and solvent.

The paint dries partly by evaporation of the solvent. The important process, however, is the reaction of the oil with oxygen of the air (oxidation) to form a hard film. Only certain oils harden in this way. Examples of hardening oils are linseed oil, dehydrated castor oil and tung (or wood) oil. Driers are compounds like cobalt or lead naphthanates. These catalyse the oxidation of the oils, that is, they speed up the drying process.

The **pigment** is the insoluble substance (often a salt) which gives the paint its colour and covering power. The pigment is not dissolved in the oil but suspended. Some examples of common pigments are shown in Table 17.3.

Table 17.3: **Some common pigments.**

Pigment	Colour
Lead sulphate	White
Copper carbonate	Mountain green
Lead carbonate	White
Zinc chromate	Yellow
Titanium dioxide	White

Paint manufacture: loading pigment for a batch of emulsion.

Extenders are substances like china clay and chalk which are added to reduce the amount of pigment required. This reduces the cost of the paint produced. Solvents such as white spirit (a hydrocarbon solvent) are added to produce the correct consistency.

A paint should not be confused with a **varnish**. A varnish consists of a substance dissolved in a solvent. For instance, a simple varnish can be prepared by dissolving naturally occurring shellac in ethanol. When applied, the varnish dries by evaporation of the ethanol leaving a thin coating of shellac.

2 In the **control of water pollution** precipitation of insoluble salts is used to remove toxic substances from the water. **Cyanides** dissolved in the water are removed by precipitation of complex cyanides when iron(II) sulphate is added. The precipitate is removed by filtration.

something to think about . . .

1 Ammonium chloride, copper sulphate, sodium chloride, sodium hydroxide, barium chloride, silver chloride, magnesium chloride, barium sulphate.

From the list of compounds above select
a A compound that is not a salt.
b Two salts that are insoluble in water.
c A coloured salt.
d The salt which is the major constituent of table salt.
e The compound which would form a white precipitate when dilute sulphuric acid is added to a solution of it in water.

2 Complete the following word equations. (The number in brackets is the number of products in each case.)
a zinc + dilute sulphuric acid   (2)
b zinc + dilute hydrochloric acid   (2)
c copper oxide + dilute hydrochloric acid   (2)
d copper oxide + dilute nitric acid   (2)
e potassium hydroxide + dilute hydrochloric acid   (2)
f potassium hydroxide + dilute sulphuric acid   (2)
g potassium hydroxide + dilute nitric acid   (2)
h magnesium carbonate + dilute hydrochloric acid   (3)
i magnesium carbonate + dilute sulphuric acid   (3)
j magnesium carbonate + dilute nitric acid   (3)

3 This question is about the preparation of copper(II) sulphate crystals. Read the passage carefully and then answer the questions.
    'Black copper(II) oxide powder was added to a colourless liquid (A) until no more would dissolve. The resulting coloured solution (B), after removing any excess copper(II) oxide, was concentrated to solution (C). After leaving this solution for a few days, crystals of copper(II) sulphate began to separate out. These were separated from the solution by filtration, the filtrate being called D.'
a What is the name of liquid A?
b What is the formula of copper(II) oxide?
c What will be the colour of solution B?
d Draw a labelled diagram to show how you would separate the excess copper(II) oxide from solution B.
e Draw a labelled diagram to show the apparatus you would use to concentrate solution B.
f Which of the solutions A, B, C and D are saturated solutions of copper(II) sulphate?
g If liquid A was heated would it react with more copper(II) oxide? Give a reason for your answer.
h To which solution A, B, C or D is given the name 'mother-liquor'?
i Consider the three changes which take place: A to B; B to C; C to D.
    (i) Which of these changes can be considered **physical** changes?
    (ii) Which of these three changes can be considered to be **chemical** changes?
j What is the percentage of water in blue copper(II) sulphate crystals $CuSO_4, 5H_2O$? (Relative atomic masses $Cu = 64$; $S = 32$; $O = 16$; $H = 1$)
(*East Anglian Examinations Board CSE*)

18. Rate of chemical reaction

Some chemical reactions like the explosion of hydrogen and oxygen occur very rapidly. Other chemical reactions like the rusting of iron or the souring of milk are slower. It is possible to speed up or slow down any chemical reaction by changing the conditions under which it occurs. For instance, the souring of milk can be slowed down by cooling the milk.

We cannot measure the rate of reaction directly in a simple experiment. We can, however, time how long it takes for a reaction to be completed or to reach a certain stage of completeness. If a 5 cm length of magnesium ribbon is put into 25 cm^3 of dilute hydrochloric acid, we can time how long it takes for the magnesium to react.

A reaction which is completed in a fraction of a second is a very fast reaction (i.e. has a **high rate of reaction**). If a solution of hydrochloric acid is added to a solution of silver nitrate, a white precipitate of silver chloride forms instantaneously. As the time taken for a reaction increases, the rate of reaction decreases (that is, the rate of reaction is inversely proportional to the time).

If we consider the reaction between **magnesium ribbon** and **dilute hydrochloric acid**, we can follow the course of the reaction by measuring the **volume of hydrogen** gas produced at various times during the reaction. The apparatus in figure 18.1a or b can be used for this purpose.

The divided flask allows the magnesium ribbon and hydrochloric acid to be placed in the same flask without them coming into contact and reacting. The reaction is started by shaking the flask so that the magnesium ribbon and hydrochloric acid come into contact. The apparatus in figure 18.2 can be used as an alternative to the divided flask.

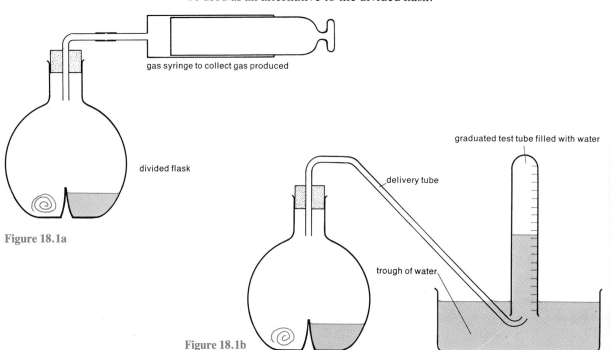

gas syringe to collect gas produced

divided flask

Figure 18.1a

graduated test tube filled with water

delivery tube

trough of water

Figure 18.1b

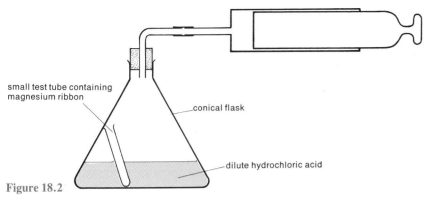

small test tube containing
magnesium ribbon

conical flask

dilute hydrochloric acid

Figure 18.2

It is easy to see that the reaction is faster at the beginning and slows
down as the reaction proceeds. The results of a typical experiment are
shown in Table 18.1. These results are plotted in a graph in figure 18.3.

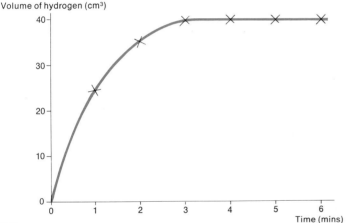

Figure 18.3

**Table 18.1 Results of the reaction
between magnesium ribbon and
hydrochloric acid.**

Time (minutes)	Volume of hydrogen gas collected (cm^3)
0	0
1	24
2	35
3	40
4	40
5	40
6	40

You will notice that the volume of hydrogen produced in the first
minute (24 cm^3) was greater than the volume produced in the second
minute (11 cm^3). In the third minute less hydrogen (5 cm^3) was produced
and after three minutes no more hydrogen was produced, in other words,
the reaction had stopped. A measure of the rate of reaction at any time
can be obtained from the steepness of the graph at that time. The steeper
the graph at that point the faster the reaction.

After three minutes the reaction had stopped and the graph is flat, that
is, it is parallel to the axis. The reaction has stopped because either all the
magnesium ribbon had been used up or all the acid had been used up. It is
easy to tell which is the case because if magnesium ribbon remained
unreacted at the end of the experiment, the magnesium was in excess.

If the experiment was repeated using an equal mass of magnesium
turnings with all other conditions the same as before, a graph like the one
in figure 18.4 overleaf would be obtained.

The rate at the beginning of the reaction was greater than before (the

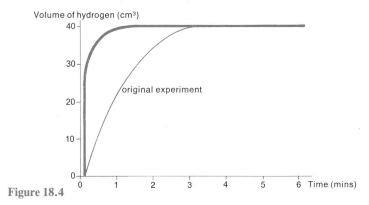

Figure 18.4

graph is steeper in the early stages). The reaction was completed in one minute and the volume of hydrogen produced when the reaction had stopped was the same as in the original experiment (40 cm^3).

Catalysis

Over one hundred years ago the German chemist Döbereiner put a cold platinum wire into a mixture of hydrogen and oxygen. Combination took place at room temperature to produce water vapour. No reaction took place if a copper or iron wire was used in place of platinum. The platinum wire was acting as a **catalyst**.

A catalyst is a substance which alters the rate of a chemical reaction. Catalysts usually speed up chemical reactions but some catalysts called negative catalysts or inhibitors slow down chemical reactions. A catalyst only affects the rate of a reaction that is proceeding, however slowly. It does not produce an otherwise impossible reaction.

At the end of the experiment the mass of catalyst remaining is unchanged. It may, however, be in a different form.

Catalysts are important in many industrial processes including:
    making ammonia from nitrogen and hydrogen (Chapter 19);
    conversion of ammonia into **nitric acid** (Chapter 11);
    hardening of natural oils to make **margarine** (Chapter 15);
    production of **sulphuric acid** (Chapter 19).

Catalysts are usually **heavy** (or transition) **metals** or **compounds of heavy** (or transition) **metals**.

Catalysts in industrial processes are frequently in the form of pellets or a wire mesh. The addition of **promoters** make the catalyst more effective.

Enzymes are biological catalysts. They are important in many reactions including the digestion of food and the fermentation of sugars. They differ from other catalysts because they operate only under certain conditions. They act only within a range of temperature and often within a certain pH range. **Biological washing powders** contain enzymes that 'digest' proteins in stains. The enzymes are only able to digest proteins below 60°C (333 K). In a cool wash or in soaking, the enzymes can remove stains but in a very hot wash the enzymes are not active.

Factors affecting the rate of reaction

Table 18.2 summarises the changes in rate of reaction that occur when changes in conditions are made.

Selection of industrial catalysts.

Table 18.2: Factors affecting rate of reaction.

Factor	Reactions affected	Change made in conditions	Effect on the rate of reaction
Temperature	All	Increase 10°C (10 K) Decrease 10°C (10 K)	Approx. double Approx. half
Concentration	All	Increase in concentration of one of the reactants	Increase in the rate of reaction
Light	Wide variety of reactions including reactions of mixtures of gases including chlorine or bromine	Reaction in sunlight or ultraviolet light	Effect varies. Often dramatic in case of gases
Particle size	Reactions involving solids and liquids, solids and gases or mixtures of solids	Powdering the solid—greatly increasing surface area	Great increase

Suitable reactions for rate of reaction study

1 Calcium carbonate and dilute hydrochloric acid

The course of the reaction can be followed by measuring the volume of **carbon dioxide** produced (figure 18.1). Because carbon dioxide is more soluble in water than hydrogen, figure 18.1a is better than figure 18.1b. The course of the reaction can also be followed by weighing the reaction flask and contents at intervals (figure 18.5).

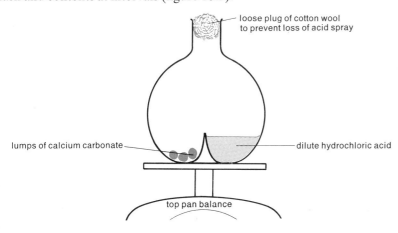

loose plug of cotton wool
to prevent loss of acid spray

lumps of calcium carbonate

dilute hydrochloric acid

top pan balance

Figure 18.5 Rate of reaction when calcium carbonate reacts with dilute hydrochloric acid

The loss of mass corresponds to the mass of the carbon dioxide escaping. The graph produced has the same shape as the graph in figure 18.3.

2 Sodium thiosulphate solution and dilute hydrochloric acid

The reaction of **sodium thiosulphate solution** and **dilute hydrochloric acid** slowly produces a creamish-white precipitate of **amorphous sulphur**. If a pencil line is viewed through the beaker containing the reacting solutions the time is measured until the pencil line is just obscured.

3 Decomposition of hydrogen peroxide

A solution of **hydrogen peroxide** very slowly decomposes into **water** and **oxygen**. The course of the reaction can be followed using the apparatus in figure 18.1

The decomposition is **catalysed** by a range of substances. These include metal oxides such as copper(II) oxide, manganese(IV) oxide and lead oxides. The decomposition is catalysed by enzymes in blood or potatoes.

4 Silver chloride precipitation

The precipitate of **silver chloride** produced by the reaction between **silver nitrate** solution and dilute **hydrochloric acid** is white in colour. On standing in sunlight it turns greyish-blue due to the partial decomposition of silver chloride by sunlight.

Applications of rate of reaction

1 Surface area

Although lumps of coal do not react with the oxygen in the air without heating, mixtures of coal dust and air can be explosive in coal mines. About thirty years ago fifty-one men were killed in such an explosion at Sneyd Colliery, Stoke-on-Trent. Often explosions of coal dust are started by the burning of fire-damp (a mixture of gases of which methane CH_4 is the major constituent). Careful control of ventilation and dust underground is essential if explosions are to be avoided.

Similarly, flour dust can explode when mixed with air in a flour mill.

2 Temperature

Epoxy adhesives were originally developed in World War II to replace metal rivets in aircraft construction. An epoxy adhesive consists of two substances called the resin and the hardener which have to be mixed thoroughly. After mixing polymerisation takes place but the final cross-linking that links the molecules together and gives the adhesive its strength is a slow process. This cross-linking or curing, as it is called, can be speeded up by heating.

Food goes bad because of oxidation processes that occur slowly. This spoiling of food can be slowed down by cooling. Food stored in a deep freeze at −18°C (255 K) does not spoil rapidly. Meat stored in a deep freeze for months is still in good condition when it is thawed. The oxidation processes are not stopped completely but slowed down.

3 Use of inhibitors

Inhibitors are added to rubber during manufacture to slow down the oxidation of the rubber. Phosphoric acid is added to hydrogen peroxide to slow down its decomposition into water and oxygen.

Examples of catalysts used in industry to carry out chemical processes economically are in Chapter 19.

4 Light

Some chemicals such as hydrogen peroxide are stored in dark bottles to keep out light and slow down decomposition. The reaction between hydrogen and chlorine occurs only very slowly in the dark. In sunlight the mixture reacts explosively to produce hydrogen chloride.

Gammexane, an insecticide, is produced by the reaction of benzene and chlorine. The reaction is speeded up by illuminating the mixture with ultraviolet lights.

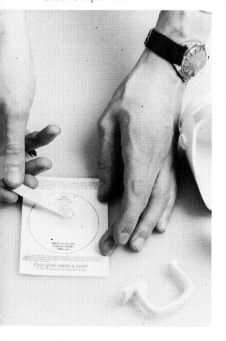
Household epoxy adhesive being used to repair broken china.

something to think about . . .

1 During an experiment to brew beer the percentage of ethanol formed was measured at the end of each day using a beer hydrometer. Throughout the experiment the temperature was kept at 20°C. The results are given in Table 18.3.

a In the experiment, enzymes in yeast convert sucrose (sugar) into ethanol and carbon dioxide. What name is given to this chemical process?

b Plot a graph of the percentage of ethanol formed against the number of days the reaction has been in progress. (At the start of the experiment the solution contained no ethanol.)

c On what day was the rate of production of ethanol greatest?

d On what day did the reaction stop?

e Assuming conditions remain unchanged, what would be the effect on the **initial rate** of reaction of
   (i) increasing the constant temperature to 25°C.
   (ii) decreasing the concentration of the sucrose solution used?

f Assuming conditions remain unchanged, what would would be the effect on the **final percentage of ethanol** of
   (i) increasing the constant temperature to 25°C.
   (ii) decreasing the concentration of sucrose solution used?

g The rate of reaction can also be investigated by measuring the volume of carbon dioxide released. Assuming you are given $50 \, cm^3$ of the original brewing mixture, draw and label a diagram of suitable apparatus set up for carrying out this experiment. State briefly what measurements you would take.

(Southern Regional Examinations Board CSE)

Table 18.3

End of day	Percentage of ethanol
1	3.0
2	3.8
3	4.2
4	4.4
5	4.5
6	4.5
7	4.5

2 a A small flask was connected to a gas syringe by means of a stopper and delivery tube. $40 \, cm^3$ of water and $1.0 \, g$ of manganese(IV) oxide (manganese dioxide), a catalyst, were placed in the flask. $5 \, cm^3$ of hydrogen peroxide solution was added, the flask stoppered and readings of the volume of gas in the syringe at room temperature and pressure were recorded at timed intervals. The results are shown in Table 18.4.
   The equation for the reaction is:

$$2H_2O_2 \rightarrow 2H_2O + O_2.$$

(i) Plot a graph of gas volume against time. Label the curve A.

(ii) Why is the curve steepest at first?

(iii) Why does the curve eventually become parallel to the time axis?

(iv) Calculate the total number of moles of oxygen given off in the reaction. (1 mole of any gas occupies 24 litres at normal room temperature and pressure.)

(v) Without emptying the flask, another $20 \, cm^3$ of water and $5 \, cm^3$ of hydrogen peroxide solution were added, and the experiment was repeated exactly as before. On the same axes, sketch a graph to show how the volume of gas would vary with time. Label the curve B. (You may assume the reaction is complete within the axes given.)

(vi) Draw another curve for the results of another experiment in which all the conditions are the same as for curve B, except that only $2.5 \, cm^3$ of hydrogen peroxide solution were used. Label the curve C.

Table 18.4

Time (seconds)	Volume (cm³)
0	0
10	20
20	33
30	44
40	52
50	58
60	59
70	60
80	60

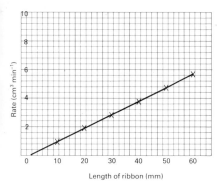

Figure 18.6

b Strips of magnesium ribbon of the same width but of different lengths were cut. Each strip was added to excess 2 M hydrochloric acid at 20°C and the mixture was shaken. The rate at which hydrogen was given off was measured. The graph in figure 18.6 was plotted.

    (i) What conclusion about the rate of reaction can you draw from the graph? What is the reason for this?

    (ii) On the same axes, draw a graph to show the results you would expect to obtain from an identical experiment at 50°C. Label the graph X.

    (iii) On the same axes, draw a graph to show the results you would expect to obtain with all the conditions as in **b** (ii) except that the experiments were carried out using a wider magnesium ribbon. Label the graph Y.

c The table shows the results of nine experiments to find the rates of the reaction between magnesium and hydrochloric acid.

In each experiment the acid was placed in a flask and its temperature taken. A weighed amount of magnesium was added. The mixture was stirred and the time taken for the magnesium to disappear was noted. The highest temperature of the mixture was also noted. The results are shown in Table 18.5

Table 18.5

Experiment	Molarity of acid	Volume of acid (cm³)	Temperature (°C) before	Temperature (°C) after	Mass of magnesium (g)	Form of magnesium	Times (seconds)
A	0.5	40	21	31	0.1	ribbon	500
B	0.6	40	21	32	0.1	powder	50
C	0.7	40	21	32	0.1	ribbon	250
D	0.8	40	21	33	0.1	ribbon	160
E	0.9	40	21	39	0.2	ribbon	230
F	1.0	40	21	33	0.1	ribbon	100
G	1.0	40	35	44	0.1	ribbon	50
H	1.1	40	21	33	0.1	ribbon	75
J	1.5	40	21	31	0.1	ribbon	30

    (i) A graph can be drawn to show how the rate of the reaction varies with the molarity of the acid.
The results of three of the experiments could not be used when drawing such a graph. Give the letters of these three experiments and say why the results could not be used for the graph.

    (ii) Write an ionic equation for the reaction of magnesium with hydrochloric acid.

    (iii) Choose the fastest reaction from A, F, H or J and suggest a reason why it would be the fastest of the four.

    (iv) How does the rate of the reaction in B compare with that in A and C?
Suggest a reason for the difference.

(Joint Matriculation Board/West Midlands Examinations Board 16+)

19. Reversible reactions

In other chapters there are examples of reversible reactions. A reversible reaction is a reaction which can go in either direction (either forward or backward) depending on the reaction conditions. In an equation for a reaction which goes in only one direction (i.e. it cannot be reversed) a single arrow → is written. In an equation for a reversible reaction a double arrow ⇌ is written.

Examples of reversible reactions

1 Blue copper(II) sulphate-5-water crystals on heating lose steam and leave white anhydrous copper(II) sulphate. On adding water to cold anhydrous copper(II) sulphate, heat is evolved and blue copper(II) sulphate is reformed:

copper(II) sulphate + heat ⇌ anhydrous copper(II) sulphate + water

2 Calcium carbonate on heating decomposes to form calcium oxide and carbon dioxide. Calcium oxide reacts with carbon dioxide to reform calcium carbonate:

calcium carbonate ⇌ calcium oxide + carbon dioxide

3 Mercury, on heating in air, produces a red powder, mercury(II) oxide. On heating mercury(II) oxide alone, it decomposes to form mercury and oxygen:

mercury + oxygen ⇌ mercury(II) oxide

Reversible reaction of iron and steam

If **steam** is passed over red-hot **iron**, then hydrogen and an iron oxide (Fe_3O_4—iron(II)diiron(III) oxide or ferrosoferric oxide) are formed. Figure 19.1 shows the apparatus necessary to carry out this reaction.

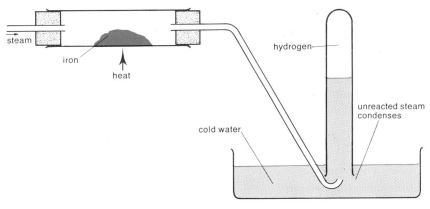

Figure 19.1 Reversible reaction of steam and iron

As soon as the hydrogen is produced it is swept over by the steam and can be collected over water. The iron oxide remains in the hard glass tube.

If **hydrogen** is passed over heated **iron oxide** (Fe_3O_4), the iron oxide is reduced to **iron** and **steam** is produced. The steam condenses to form water. Unused hydrogen is burnt at the jet to prevent it escaping into the

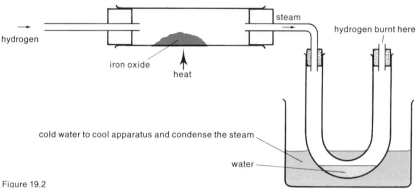

Figure 19.2

Figure 19.2

room. In figure 19.2, the apparatus necessary to produce samples of iron and water in this reaction is shown. As soon as the steam is produced, it is swept away by the stream of hydrogen.

In both cases the reaction goes in only one direction because the reaction in the opposite direction is stopped as the products are separated as soon as they are formed.

If the **iron** and **steam** are heated at 300°C (573 K) in a **closed metal globe** the results are different. Figure 19.3 represents the situation inside the globe at the start and at one day intervals for the first three days.

Key: ● Fe   ● H   ○ O

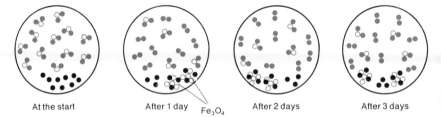

At the start   After 1 day Fe_3O_4 After 2 days   After 3 days

Figure 19.3

At first the iron reacts with steam to produce hydrogen and the iron oxide. As the amounts of hydrogen and iron oxide increase, the reverse reaction becomes possible and speeds up. After one day there is no further change in the quantities of iron, iron oxide, steam and hydrogen inside the globe providing no change is made to the conditions.

The reaction has not, however, stopped but is in a system of **equilibrium** (plural equilibria). When a system is in equilibrium the forward and reverse reactions are still continuing but both at the same rate so no change in any concentration of reacting substance or product takes place.

When a system is in equilibrium the sign ⇌ is used in the equation.

$$\text{iron} + \text{steam} \rightleftharpoons \text{iron oxide} + \text{hydrogen}$$
$$3Fe(s) + 4H_2O(g) \rightleftharpoons Fe_3O_4(s) + 4H_2(g)$$

Factors affecting an equilibrium

An equilibrium mixture of iron, iron oxide, hydrogen and steam with unchanging concentrations can be disturbed by altering a condition. If the equilibrium moves to produce more iron oxide and hydrogen (that is, the forward reaction for a time becomes faster than the reverse reaction) the equilibrium is said to have moved to the right. The equilibrium is said to have moved to the left if the equilibrium changes to produce more iron and steam.

Consider a reaction where A, B, C and D represent reacting substances and products:

$$A + B \rightleftharpoons C + D + \text{heat}$$

The **forward reaction** is **exothermic**, that is, heat is evolved as the reaction proceeds. Table 19.1 shows the changes that affect an equilibrium.

Table 19.1 Changes that affect equilibrium of the reaction
$A + B \rightleftharpoons C + D + \text{heat}$.

Factor	Type of equilibrium affected	Effect on equilibrium
Increase in concentration of A and/or B	Any	Moves to the right
Decrease in concentration of A and/or B	Any	Moves to the left
Increase in concentration of C and/or D	Any	Moves to the left
Decrease in concentration of C and/or D	Any	Moves to the right
Increase in pressure	Reactions involving gases	May move to left, right or remain unchanged (see Note 1)
Catalyst added	Certain reactions only	No change
Increase in temperature	Exothermic forward reaction	Moves to the left
	Endothermic forward reaction	Moves to the right
Decrease in temperature	Exothermic forward reaction	Moves to the right
	Endothermic forward reaction	Moves to the left (see Note 2)

Things to note are:
1 The resulting change in the equilibrium position when **pressure is increased** depends on the **number of gas molecules** on the left-hand side and on the right-hand side of the equation. If there are more gas molecules on the left-hand side increasing the pressure moves the equilibrium to the right. For example

$$2SO_2(g) + O_2(g) \rightleftharpoons 2SO_3(g)$$

If there are more molecules on the right-hand side increasing the pressure moves the equilibrium to the left.
   If there are equal numbers of gas molecules on both sides of the

equation increasing the pressure has no effect on the equilibrium. For example:

$$H_2(g) + I_2(g) \rightleftharpoons 2HI(g)$$

2 Increasing the temperature helps to establish the equilibrium more quickly. This is because it speeds up both the forward and the reverse reactions. Rapid cooling of a system in equilibrium at a high temperature may 'freeze' an equilibrium, that is, it may slow down both the forward and reverse reactions so that amounts of reacting substances and products remain unchanged for a considerable time.

Industrial processes where equilibrium is important

1 The Haber process for producing ammonia from nitrogen and hydrogen

This is an important process for 'fixing' nitrogen from the air in compounds (Chapter 10).

$$\text{Nitrogen} + \text{hydrogen} \rightleftharpoons \text{ammonia} + \text{heat}$$
$$N_2(g) \quad + 3H_2(g) \quad \rightleftharpoons 2NH_3(g) \ + \text{heat}$$

This equation tells us that the combination of nitrogen and hydrogen is exothermic, that is, heat is evolved.

Nitrogen gas (from fractional distillation of liquid air) and hydrogen (from water or natural gas) are purified and mixed in a ratio of three parts of hydrogen to one part of nitrogen. Impurities like carbon oxides, water vapour and sulphur compounds have to be removed or they will poison the catalyst at a later stage.

The mixture of gases is then compressed to about 200 atmospheres. **High pressures** favour a move to the right to produce more ammonia because there are fewer gas molecules on the right hand side.

The mixture of compressed gases is passed over a **heated catalyst** at a temperature of between 350°C (623 K) and 550°C (823 K). Any attempt to **increase** the **temperature** produces less ammonia because ammonia decomposes at high temperatures. At lower temperatures, although a greater proportion of nitrogen and hydrogen would combine, the reaction would be very slow unless a catalyst is used. The **catalyst**, which was the big advance that Fritz Haber made, is finely divided **iron** with substances like **aluminium oxide** and **potassium hydroxide** that act as **promoters**. Under these conditions between ten and twenty per cent of the gases combine. The unreacted gases are recycled until they react.

When the mixture of gases containing ammonia is cooled the ammonia liquefies and can be removed. Alternatively, the ammonia can be removed by dissolving in water because it is much more soluble than nitrogen or hydrogen. Figure 19.4 shows a simplified ammonia manufacturing plant.

About 15 million tonnes of ammonia are produced this way each year.

2 The Contact process for the manufacture of sulphuric acid

The manufacture of sulphuric acid by the Contact process takes place in three stages.

Stage 1: Sulphur dioxide is produced by the burning of sulphur in air, from crude oil or natural gas or from naturally occurring sulphur compounds like anhydrite ($CaSO_4$ calcium sulphate).

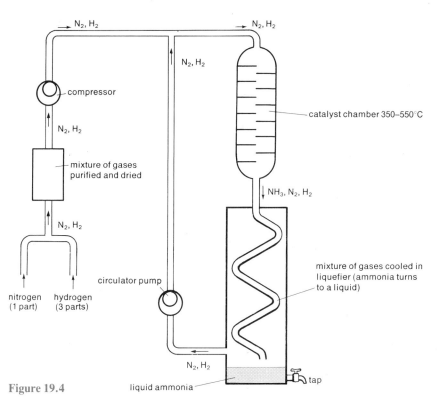

Figure 19.4

The sulphur dioxide is purified to remove substances like arsenic that would poison the catalyst in the next stage.

Stage 2: This stage involves the reversible reaction:

sulphur dioxide + oxygen (present in air) $\rightleftarrows$ sulphur trioxide + heat
$2SO_2(g)$ $+ O_2(g)$ $\rightleftarrows 2SO_3(g)$

The treatment of the mixture of sulphur dioxide and air at this stage will determine the amount of sulphuric acid eventually produced.

A low temperature is suggested because the forward reaction is exothermic. But a low temperature, which would produce a good conversion to sulphur trioxide, would cause the reaction to be very slow. A balance has to be struck. The temperature used is 450°C (723 K) and a catalyst of vanadium(V) oxide (vanadium pentoxide), in the form of pellets, is used. An effective catalyst would be **platinum**. This is less easily poisoned but is no longer used because it is too expensive.

Increasing the pressure would also produce a larger proportion of sulphur trioxide in the resulting equilibrium mixture but, in practice, the extra sulphur trioxide does not justify the extra costs of increasing the pressure.

Stage 3: The **sulphur trioxide** is removed from the mixture of gases and converted to sulphuric acid. The sulphur trioxide is not directly dissolved in water because the reaction is too violent on a large scale.

Instead, it is dissolved in fairly concentrated sulphuric acid which can be diluted later with water to give sulphuric acid of the required concentration. The overall equation for this stage is:

$$SO_3(g) + H_2O(l) \rightarrow H_2SO_4(aq)$$

Figure 19.5 shows a simplified plan of a **sulphuric acid plant**.
About 90 million tonnes of sulphuric acid are produced in the world each year.

Figure 19.5

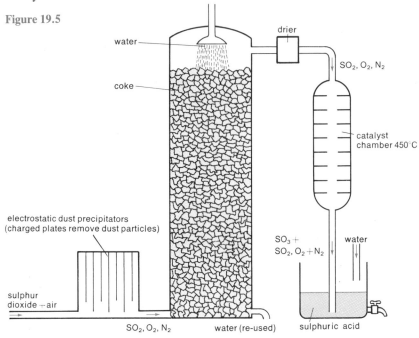

General view of a sulphuric acid plant.

something to think about . . .

1 This question refers to the Haber process (page 134).

a In order to start the process the catalyst is heated electrically or by using jets of burning hydrogen gas. After the process has started no further heating is required to maintain the catalyst temperature. Explain why this is not necessary.

b It has been found that more nitrogen and hydrogen combine in the catalyst chamber if the pressure is increased further (say up to 1000 atmospheres). What are the disadvantages of carrying out this process at a higher pressure?

c More ammonia can be produced in the equilibrium mixture leaving the catalyst chamber if the proportions of nitrogen and hydrogen are changed from 1:3 to 2:3 (that is, more nitrogen is used). Why is this not done?

d The catalyst is put into the catalyst chamber in the form of irregular granules of iron(II) diiron(III) oxide (Fe_3O_4) containing some aluminium oxide and potassium hydroxide. What change occurs to the catalyst when the mixture of nitrogen and hydrogen is passed over the catalyst before it starts to operate?

e Powdered iron would provide a much larger surface area for the catalyst. Why are powdered catalysts rarely used?

f Supposing each time the nitrogen and hydrogen mixture passes over the catalyst 10 per cent of the mixture is converted to ammonia, is it true to say that the conversion would be complete after 10 cycles? Explain your answer.

2 When an organic acid is boiled for some time with an alcohol, an ester and water are formed. An equilibrium is set up which can be represented by:

$$acid(l) + alcohol(l) \rightleftharpoons ester(l) + water(l)$$

State, giving an explanation in each case, whether at equilibrium:
  (i) the rate of reaction between the acid and the alcohol is equal to the rate of reaction between the ester and water.
  (ii) the concentrations of all the reactants and products must be equal.
  (iii) more ester would be produced if a catalyst were used.
  (iv) the concentrations of the substances are independent of the pressure at which the reaction is carried out.

3 Consider the following equilibrium:

$$Zn(s) + H_2O(g) \rightleftharpoons ZnO(s) + H_2(g)$$

Some zinc and steam were heated in a sealed container for a long time. (Assume the container can withstand any pressure changes.)
  (i) Name the substances present in the container after prolonged heating.
  (ii) What would be the effect of forcing more steam into the container during the heating?
  (iii) Under what conditions would zinc be completely converted into zinc oxide in this reaction?

20. Radioactive decay

Many atoms, particularly atoms containing large numbers of protons, neutrons and electrons, can split up with the loss of α, β or γ rays. This splitting up or decay is not affected by changes of condition that alter the rate of chemical reactions (Chapter 18). For example, the rate of decay of a **radioactive decay** is not changed by a change of temperature.

In schools, radioactive experiments are often designed using uranium, thorium and potassium compounds. When carrying out radioactivity experiments care must be taken not to spill radioactive chemicals. It is very important to dispose of radioactive chemicals carefully.

Types of radioactive decay

Table 20.1

Radiation	Nature	Charge	Penetrating power
α	Stream of helium nuclei (2 protons + 2 neutrons)	Positive	Low; up to 0.00001 m of metal.
β	Stream of electrons	Negative	Medium; pass through up to 0.01 m of metal.
γ	Very high energy X-rays		Very high; pass through 0.1 m of metal.

Changes within the atoms

When **uranium-238** decays it loses α **particles**; that means that it decays by α decay. The product of decay (the atom that is left) of uranium-238, therefore, contains two fewer protons and two fewer neutrons than the uranium-238:

$$^{238}_{92}U \rightarrow ^{4}_{2}He + ^{234}_{90}Th$$

The product **thorium-234** contains two fewer protons and is, therefore, two places to the left of uranium in the periodic table.

Thorium-234 itself undergoes radioactive decay. It decays by losing β **particles**. In order to lose β particles, a neutron in the nucleus is changed into a proton and an electron. The electron is then lost. The new atom produced contains the same number of particles in the nucleus as the original atom (that means that it has the same **mass number**). However it contains one more proton than the original atom and is therefore one place to the right of thorium in the periodic table. Because uranium-238 decays much more slowly than thorium-234 the thorium-234 does not have a chance to build up in deposits in the earth.

When γ **rays** are lost by a radioactive substance **electromagnetic radiation**, which is similar to light but of much shorter wavelength, is lost. The γ rays are lost when there is a rearrangement of protons and neutrons in the nucleus. The resulting atom is not changed by the loss of γ rays. γ radiation accompanies most α and β decays.

Making radioactivity measurements

In order to make readings of radioactive decay a **scaler** is needed. This records the number of atoms undergoing radioactive decay in the sample. The scaler is connected by a lead to a G–M tube (Geiger–Muller) which holds the sample. The design of the G–M tube varies to suit the sample being used. Figure 20.1 shows a G–M tube suitable for using with a radioactive liquid or solution.

A G–M operates at a high voltage (around 400 volts). Only high energy β particles and γ rays pass through into the centre portion of the G–M tube. β particles, however, can **ionise the halogen gas** in the G–M tube and this ionisation (one for each β particle) is recorded on the scaler. The G–M tube and scaler, therefore, only measure β decay.

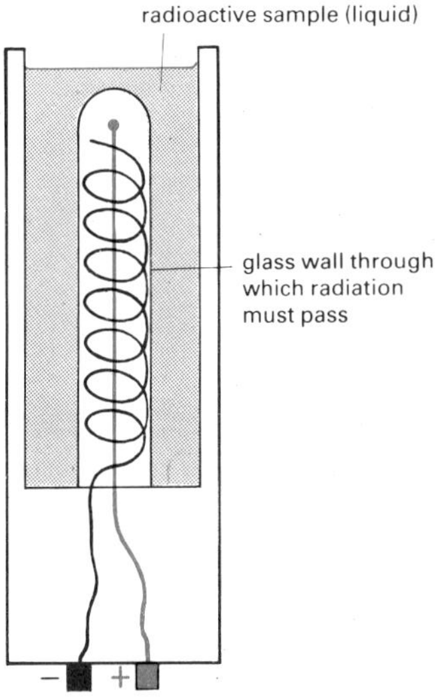

Background radiation

Even when there is no radioactive substance near the scaler and G–M tube, radioactivity will still be recorded on the scaler. This is because of small quantities of radioactive materials in the air, in building materials, and even on the luminous face of the experimenter's watch.

During radioactivity experiments the G–M tube can be surrounded by a casing of lead in order to try to keep out stray radioactivity. Alternatively, the average background count can be found by experiment and deducted from all experimental results. The background count can be found either by taking readings with no sample in the tube for one minute and repeating a number of times and working out an average count per minute or taking a reading for, say, thirty minutes and dividing this reading by thirty to find an average count per minute.

Sample radioactivity measurements

The graph in figure 20.2 shows the results of an experiment to measure the radioactive decay of a radioactive sample. Before readings are taken the radioactive substance has been treated in some way (for example, by solvent extraction) to remove any unwanted radioactive substances that would interfere.

In order to get readings, measurements were taken for one minute periods each fifteen minutes. The readings were then corrected by subtracting the experimental background count.

radioactive sample (liquid)

glass wall through which radiation must pass

terminals connecting GM tube to scaler

Figure 20.1 Geiger-Muller tube

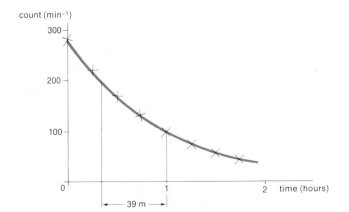

Figure 20.2 Measurement of radioactive decay

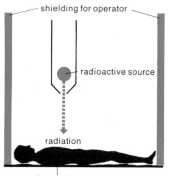

Figure 20.3

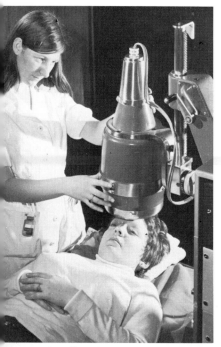

A radioactive isotope is used in the treatment of a cancerous tumour.

Figure 20.4 Radioactivity measurements can be used to control the thickness of materials

Half-life

It is not possible to predict when a particular radioactive atom is going to decay. It is possible, however, to find the time required for half the atoms in the sample to decay. This is called the **half-life** of the radioactive substance.

Applications of radioactivity

There are many examples of radioactivity in use today. They can be divided into medical, industrial and 'detective' uses.

1 Medical uses

a The **γ rays** from radioactive substances like **cobalt-60** can destroy both healthy and cancerous tissue. If a patient is exposed to the correct dose of γ radiation it is possible to destroy a cancerous growth without killing the patient. It is possible either to put the patient under a radioactive source (figure 20.3); or a small radioactive source (sometimes radon) can be placed below the skin close to the tumour.

b Instruments and equipment used by doctors can be sterilised to remove the germs by putting them in boiling water. All the germs are not killed by this method and it is not suitable for delicate instruments. It is common for instruments and equipment to be made germ-free or sterile by submitting them to γ radiation.

c Radioactive substances can be used to carry out diagnosis tests on patients. For instance, radioactive **iodine-131** can be used to test whether the thyroid gland in the neck is working correctly. The thyroid gland takes in iodine from the food. If the thyroid gland is working properly the radioactive iodine-131 is detected in the thyroid gland.

2 Industrial uses

a The **thickness of paper, plastic** or **metal sheets** can be controlled by a mechanism using a radioactive substance (figure 20.4).

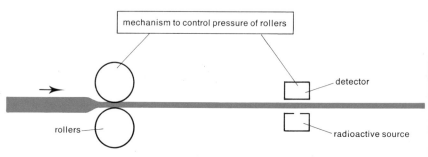

The radioactive source producing β or γ radiation gives a steady reading on the detector providing the thickness of the sheet remains constant. If the sheet becomes too thick the detector reading goes down because a greater proportion of the radiation is absorbed by the sheet. The detector is connected to the mechanism that controls the pressure of the rollers. The pressure of the rollers increases to make the sheet thinner.

This has been used in producing aluminium sheet of constant thickness. This is necessary in producing new beer cans with the top that is opened by pulling a ring. These were not possible until constant thickness aluminium sheet was available.

b Radioactive substances are used to check the contents of containers like **fire extinguishers** or **food packets** (figure 20.5). The radioactive source and detector are moved up slowly and the top limit of the contents is shown by a sudden increase in the reading on the detector.

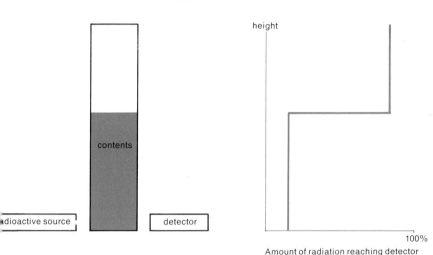

Figure 20.5 The radioactive source checks the amount in the container

c Faults in castings can be discovered by radiography using γ radiation. The γ radiation passes through metals better than X-rays. It can be used to test **turbine blades** in aero engines for faults inside the casting. Any other method used to check the quality of a casting would destroy the casting in the process. Similar methods can be used to test the quality of welding, for instance in steel reactor vessels for nuclear power stations.

d Ethene and similar substances (Chapter 15) can be polymerised more easily using radiation from a radioactive source. The resulting polymers have more links between molecules (cross-linking) than in ordinary polymers. This makes them melt at higher temperatures.

3 Detective uses
Radioactivity can be used to solve a wide range of problems that would be difficult to solve by other methods.

a **Napoleon Bonaparte I** died on the island of St Helena in 1821. The doctor attending him at his death gave cancer of the stomach as the cause of death. Close friends of Napoleon suspected that he had been poisoned.

About 1960 it was decided to confirm the reason for Napoleon's death. A few tufts of his hair taken shortly after his death by a friend were still available. These tufts were sealed in an aluminium container and put into a nuclear reactor to be subjected to neutrons. Naturally occurring arsenic (arsenic-75) is not radioactive but when it absorbs neutrons it forms arsenic-76 (with an extra neutron) which is radioactive. The amount of arsenic in the hair can be found by radioactive measurements.

The sample of Napoleon's hair was found to contain thirteen times as much arsenic as ordinary hair. Because the arsenic-75 is not radioactive, the amount of arsenic in the hair now must be the same as when Napoleon died. This suggests that Napoleon had been slowly poisoned by arsenic. Although the arsenic can be detected and the quantity measured by radioactivity measurements, the quantities are so small that they cannot be detected in any other way.

A similar method can be used to monitor the **mercury** absorbed by dental nurses. Dental nurses are more likely to suffer mercury poisoning because of the tooth filling amalgams (containing mercury) that they mix. Samples of toe nail, for example, are exposed to neutrons in a nuclear reactor. Mercury contains several isotopes. Mercury-202 (which makes up about 30 per cent of the mercury) absorbs a neutron to form mercury-203 which decays by β decay. The level of mercury in the nail can be found by radioactivity measurements.

b A **leak** in **an underground water main** is difficult to find without digging away all of the earth from the main. A small quantity of **radioactive sodium** in the form of soluble sodium carbonate is fed into the main. A counter is then taken along the line of the main on the surface until a large reading is obtained. This must be where the water is escaping.

c The **age of an object**, like a wooden axe handle, can be found by **radiocarbon dating**. A living tree or plant takes in radioactive **carbon-14** in the form of carbon dioxide along with non-radioactive carbon-12 and 13. This taking in of carbon-14 stops when the tree is felled. The carbon-14 then decays. The half-life of carbon-14 is 5760 years. The age of the wooden axe handle can be found by measuring the carbon-14 content of the handle using radioactivity measurements. This method can be used to date objects up to 40 000 years old.

Dating using carbon-14.

Nuclear fission

In 1939 Otto Hahn, a German scientist, showed that uranium-235 atoms ($^{235}_{92}U$) could absorb slow moving neutrons and break into two almost equal parts. This is called **fission**. It is accompanied by the giving out of a large amount of **energy**.

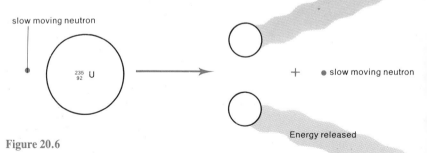

slow moving neutron

$^{235}_{92}U$

+   ● slow moving neutron

Energy released

Figure 20.6

Extra neutrons are lost and these, in turn, can cause the fission of other uranium-235 atoms. Thus a chain reaction is possible.

An **atomic bomb** is an uncontrolled fission of uranium atoms. If the mass of uranium-235 is greater than a certain critical mass, neutrons produced by the fission of uranium-235 atoms are able to continue the process. The temperature at the centre of an atomic explosion is about one million degrees Celsius.

It is necessary to separate the uranium-235 from the uranium-238 which is present in natural uranium ores in far larger amounts. This separation is done by producing uranium hexafluoride (UF_6) and separating the uranium hexafluoride containing uranium-235 by diffusion of gases.

In an **atomic power station** the same process is carried out as in an atomic bomb but it is carefully controlled to release energy over a period of time. A moderator such as graphite is used to slow the neutrons sufficiently so that they can be absorbed by other uranium atoms. The speed of the decay can be slowed by using control rods made of metals such as cadmium or hafnium. When these rods are lowered into the reactor, they absorb neutrons and so slow down the process.

The energy released by fission is carried away from the reactor by the **coolant**. This can be a gas such as helium or carbon dioxide. If the reactor is operating at a higher temperature, liquid sodium or potassium can be used. The coolant removes heat from the reactor and this heat is used to boil water and the steam produced generates electricity.

The heat, generated in the core of the reactor, is carried away by a **coolant** under high pressure. In the American Pressure Water Reactor (PWR), now under serious consideration for use in Britain, the coolant is water. In the British Magnox and the Advanced Gas-cooled Reactor (AGR) the coolant is carbon dioxide gas. Steam produced turns a turbine which drives an electricity generator.

A single atomic power station will produce sufficient electricity for a million small electric fires.

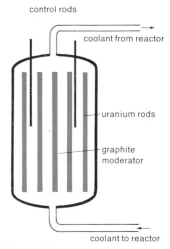

Figure 20.7 An atomic power station

Atomic fusion

The ultimate source of energy for the earth is the sun. The energy produced in the sun may be produced by the joining of hydrogen atoms to form helium atoms. This is accompanied by the evolution of a large amount of energy. This **joining of atoms** is called **fusion**. It has been estimated that there is sufficient hydrogen in the sun for several thousand million years.

A **hydrogen bomb** copies this fusion of hydrogen atoms to form helium. A temperature of at least one million degrees Celsius is required to start the process but much larger amounts of energy are liberated by fusion than by fission.

If the hydrogen bomb is controlled to release its energy slowly it could be a most valuable way of generating electricity.

Making new elements

It is possible to produce elements that do not occur naturally by bombarding large atoms with suitable particles. Charged particles like α particles or protons can be easily accelerated.

When uranium-238 is bombarded by α particles a new element, plutonium, is produced:

$$^{238}_{92}U + {}^{4}_{2}He \rightarrow {}^{242}_{94}Pu$$

It is therefore possible to change one element into another. For hundreds of years alchemists tried unsuccessfully to make their fortunes by turning a common metal into a valuable metal like gold. Man now, at last, has the ability to change one element into another.

something to think about . . .

1 A radioactive isotope A decays by β decay to produce another radioactive isotope B which decays very slowly by α decay. The initial decay rate of A, after correcting for background radiation, is 384 decays per minute and the half-life of A is 45 minutes.

a Draw a graph of the decay of A over the first 4.5 hours.
b If the original sample of A had a mass of 64 g, what mass of A remains after 4.5 hours?
c Explain how the graph would be different if B decayed by β decay and had a short half-life.

2 There are five radioactive isotopes of sodium (half-lives in brackets).

Sodium-20 (0.3s)
Sodium-21 (23s)
Sodium-22 (2.6 years)
Sodium-24 (54 000s)
Sodium-25 (62s)

a Which one of these isotopes would be most suitable for detecting a leak in a water pipe? Explain.
b Explain, with word equations, how you could safely change a radioactive sample of sodium metal into a solution of sodium carbonate.

3 Bismuth-212 is a radioactive isotope with a half-life of 1 hour. In an experiment using a sample of Bismuth-212, the count recorded in the first minute was 524. The average background reading taken immediately before the experiment was started was 12 per minute.
a Explain briefly how the average background count could be found.
b Correct the reading for the first minute for background count.
c Plot this reading on a graph.
d On the graph, plot points corresponding to the corrected count after 1 hour, 2 hours, 3 hours, 4 hours and 5 hours. Complete this graph by drawing a curve through these points.

Bismuth-212 ($^{212}_{83}Bi$) decays by β decay to produce X which in turn decays to produce Y by α decay.

Atomic number	81	82	83	84	85
Element	thallium	lead	bismuth	polonium	actinium

e Using the information above, identify:
(i) mass number of X   (ii) mass number of Y
atomic number of X   atomic number of Y
name of element X   name of element Y
f Why is it possible to make readings of the rate of decay of Bismuth-2 without the decay of X interfering? (The half-life of X is about 10^{-7} seconds.)   (*Southern Regional Examinations Board CSE*)

21. Energy

Substances can possess two kinds of energy:

1 Kinetic or movement energy
The particles of solids, liquids and gases at room temperature have kinetic energy because they are constantly moving. As temperature rises the particles move faster and, therefore, have more kinetic energy.

2 Potential or bonding energy
When elements combine together to form compounds, bonds are formed and energy is released. In Chapter 3, the formation of water from hydrogen and oxygen, aluminium iodide from aluminium and iodine, and iron(II) sulphide from iron and sulphur are accompanied by a release of energy. If these bonds are to be broken, energy has to be supplied.

It is not possible to measure the actual energy content of any substance. It is only possible to measure changes in energy content.

In most chemical reactions, the energy change varies little at different temperatures. This suggests that changes in potential or bonding energy are more important (and larger) than changes in kinetic energy.

Exothermic reactions
An exothermic reaction is one where energy is lost to the surroundings during the reaction. During the reaction more new bonds are formed than old ones broken and the unwanted energy is lost often in the form of heat. If the reaction is carried out in solution, the temperature of the solution rises:

ΔH Heat (or energy) change = Energy of products − Energy of reactants

In an exothermic reaction, ΔH is always **negative** because the products contain less energy than the reactants (figure 21.1).

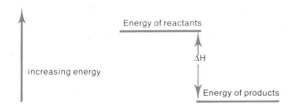

Figure 21.1

The products are more stable (they contain less energy). The change from **diamond** to **graphite** is exothermic but it does not take place instantly.

In figure 21.2 it can be seen that before the energy can be lost, heat or energy in some other form has to be supplied. This energy is called **activation energy**. In the formation of **iron(II) sulphide**, the mixture of iron and sulphur has to be heated to start the reaction. Once the reaction has started, the heat produced by the reacting substances maintains the temperature of the mixture until the reaction is complete.

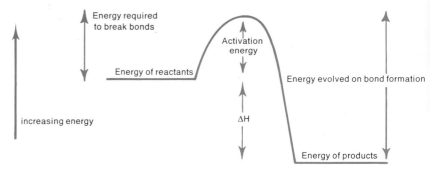

Figure 21.2

In the case of the change from diamond to graphite, the activation energy is large and the reaction does not take place at room temperature. If the activation energy is reduced the reaction will be speeded up. Addition of a **catalyst** lowers the activation energy of a slow reaction and, therefore, speeds it up.

Endothermic reactions

An endothermic reaction is one where energy is gained from the surroundings during the reaction. During the reaction more bonds are broken than are formed. If the reaction is carried out in solution, the temperature of the solution falls. There are few endothermic reactions compared to the large number of exothermic reactions.

ΔH heat (or energy) change = energy of products − energy of reactants.

In an endothermic reaction, ΔH is always positive because the products contain more energy than the reactants (figure 21.3).

Figure 21.3

Again, before the reaction can take place activation energy has to be supplied (figure 21.4).

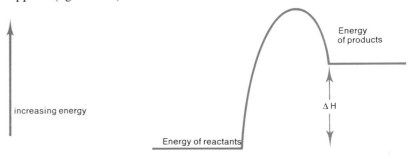

Figure 21.4

Heat of reaction

This is the heat gained or lost when the quantities of chemicals expressed in an equation react together. For example:

$$2Mg(s) + O_2(g) \rightarrow 2MgO(s)$$

The energy evolved when 48 g of magnesium is completely burnt in oxygen is 1200 kJ. ΔH is negative because the reaction is exothermic.

If the heat of reaction (1200 kJ) could be converted into mechanical energy without energy losses, it would be sufficient to lift a weight of 1 tonne nearly 120 metres into the air or to lift a 1 kg mass well above the height of Mount Everest.

Heat of formation

The heat of formation of a compound is the heat produced or absorbed when 1 mole of molecules of a compound is formed from its constituent elements. Some heats of formation are shown in Table 21.1.

Table 21.1 Heats of formation of some compounds.

Compound	Heat of formation kJ mole^{-1}
Hydrogen fluoride HF (g)	-268
Hydrogen chloride HCl(g)	-92
Hydrogen bromide HBr(g)	-36
Hydrogen iodide HI(g)	$+26$
Carbon monoxide CO(g)	-111
Carbon dioxide CO_2(g)	-394

Heat of neutralisation

The heat of neutralisation is the heat evolved when 1 mole of hydrogen ions from an acid is neutralised by an alkali.

The heats of neutralisation of many acids and alkalis is -58 kJ mole^{-1}. This is because, providing the acid and alkali are fully ionised, the reaction in each case is the same:

$$H^+(aq) + OH^-(aq) \rightarrow H_2O(l)$$

Heat of combustion

The heat of combustion is the heat evolved when 1 mole of a substance is completely burnt in oxygen.

Table 21.2 shows the heats of combustion of some common substances.

Table 21.2 Heats of combustion of some carbon compounds.

Compound	Heat of combustion kJ mole^{-1}
Methane CH_4(g)	-883
Ethane C_2H_6(g)	-1545
Propane C_3H_8(g)	-2200
Butane C_4H_{10}(g)	-2860
Pentane C_5H_{12}(g)	-3510

Table 21.3 Energy value of certain foods.

Food	Energy value kJ kg^{-1}
Bread, brown	9 930
Rice	15 040
Cheddar cheese	17 260
Butter	31 220
Minced beef	8 880
Cabbage, boiled	340
Chips	9 890
Pork sausage	22 080
Peas, canned	4 020
Potatoes, boiled	3 310

The food we eat is the fuel we need. It is burnt inside us to produce energy. The fuel value of food is measured in joules or calories (1 calorie = 4.2 joule).

The 30 tonnes of food we eat during our lifetime contains a mixture of carbohydrate, fat and protein. The energy value of the food depends on its composition. The energy values of some common foods are given in Table 21.3.

An active adult uses up to 9 kJ of energy each day. If more food is eaten than is required for supplying energy, fat is deposited.

Cells and batteries

The energy produced by a chemical reaction can be used in three ways.
As heat: Burning of fossil fuels like coal can be used to produce heat.
To do work.
To produce electricity: A cell or battery is a controlled chemical reaction. The energy produced by the reacting chemicals is in the form of electricity. When one of the reacting substances in the battery is used up, no more electricity is produced.

Daniell cell

The overall chemical reaction in the cell is:

$$Zn(s) + Cu^{2+}(aq) \rightarrow Cu(s) + Zn^{2+}(aq)$$

or

zinc + copper sulphate solution → copper + zinc sulphate solution.

The heat of the reaction is -52kJ. This is produced as electricity. The voltage of a Daniell cell is 1.1 volts.

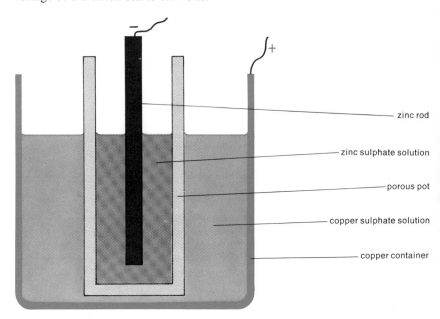

zinc rod

zinc sulphate solution

porous pot

copper sulphate solution

copper container

Figure 21.5 Daniell cell

Dry cell

A dry cell is the convenient form of the Leclanché cell used widely in cycle lamps, torches and portable radios. A single dry cell produces a voltage of 1.5 volts.

The overall reaction is

$$Zn(s) + 2MnO_2(s) + NH_4^+(aq) \rightarrow Zn^{2+}(aq) + Mn_2O_3(s) + \\ NH_3(g) + OH^-(aq)$$

Other types of battery

Lead–acid batteries are rechargeable batteries used widely in cars. They are very heavy and this is a disadvantage when they are used in battery powered cars and milk floats. Also, they cannot travel far without being recharged. They do, however, have the advantage of being pollution free.

Much research has been carried out to devise alternatives to the lead – acid battery. Many of these batteries contain solid electrolytes. These are solid ceramic materials which allow ions to migrate through them. The rate of movement of ions through a solid electrolyte is slow but can be speeded up by heating.

The most promising battery is the sodium–sulphur cell shown in figure 21.7. The electrolyte is a complex ceramic material composed of sodium, aluminium and oxygen compounds. At 300°C, sodium ions pass through the electrolyte. The reactions taking place at the electrodes are:

$$\text{Positive electrode} \quad S + 2e^- \rightarrow S^{2-}$$
$$\text{Negative electrode} \quad 2Na \rightarrow 2Na^+ + 2e^-$$

This battery produces a voltage of 2.3 volts and has a performance close to that of the petrol engine. It is much lighter than lead–acid batteries. If further research can lead to a reduction of the working temperature, there is every prospect that these batteries could provide a pollution-free alternative to the petrol engine.

Fuel cells

In an ordinary cell or battery, electrical energy is produced from chemicals. Chemicals can be changed very efficiently into electrical energy in a fuel cell. Also, electrical energy can be produced continuously providing fuel is supplied.

A simple fuel cell devised by Bacon in 1938 used hydrogen and oxygen as fuels. The cell consisted of a box containing two porous nickel electrodes. Hydrogen and oxygen were pumped into the cell separately under pressure. Within the cell, hydrogen and oxygen combined to form water and the energy produced is in the form of electricity (figure 21.8).

At the negative electrode, electrons from the electrode are used to produce hydroxide ions:

$$4e^- + 2H_2O(g) + O_2(g) \rightarrow 4OH^-(aq)$$

These negatively charged **hydroxide ions** move to the positively charged electrode. At the positively charged electrode, they react with hydrogen held on the surface of the electrode.

$$2OH^-(aq) + H_2(g) \rightarrow 2H_2O(g) + 2e^-$$

The electrons then flow through the wire from the positive to the negative.

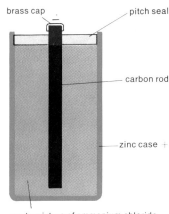

pasty mixture of ammonium chloride and manganese (IV) oxide

Figure 21.6 Dry cell

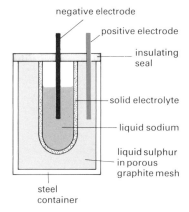

Figure 21.7

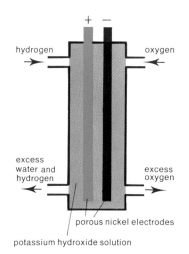

Figure 21.8 Fuel cell

The main disadvantages of this type of fuel cell are the high temperatures and pressures that are required for it to operate. Also, this fuel cell is heavy and bulky.

Developments in fuel cells have overcome these problems. Other fuels such as propane (C_3H_8), methanol (CH_3OH) and hydrazine (NH_2NH_2) have been used in place of hydrogen and other electrode systems including metal-coated plastics have been developed. Working temperatures have been reduced to 100°C (373 K).

Fuel cells have been used in space flights, for example, Gemini and Apollo flights.

something to think about . . .

1 Divide the following reactions into (i) exothermic reactions (ii) endothermic reactions.

$$Ag^+(aq) + Cl^-(aq) \rightarrow AgCl(s) \qquad \Delta H = -58.6 \text{ kJ}$$
$$Ca^{2+}(aq) + CO_3^{2-}(aq) \rightarrow CaCO_3(s) \qquad \Delta H = +13 \text{ kJ}$$
$$H_3O^+(aq) + OH^-(aq) \rightarrow 2H_2O(l) \qquad \Delta H = -54 \text{ kJ}$$
$$4Al(s) + 3O_2(g) \rightarrow 2Al_2O_3(s) \qquad \Delta H = -3360 \text{ kJ}$$
$$C(s) + O_2(g) \rightarrow CO_2(g) \qquad \Delta H = -394 \text{ kJ}.$$

Draw energy diagrams similar to figure 21.1 for each of the above reactions.

2 Using the information in Table 21.2 estimate the heat of combustion of hexane C_6H_{14}.

3 Using the information in Table 21.3, calculate the energy content of the following two meals.

Meal A   minced beef 50 g   **Meal B**   grilled sausage 50 g
            potatoes, boiled 100 g   chips 100 g
            cabbage, boiled 50 g   peas, canned 50 g
    Which of these two meals has the lower energy content?

4 The combination of hydrogen and iodine to form hydrogen iodide is endothermic even though new bonds between hydrogen and iodine are formed. Explain.

22. Carbon and sulphur

In this chapter two important non-metallic elements are discussed. Both carbon and sulphur can exhibit **allotropy**, that is, they can exist in two or more forms in the same state. The different forms are called **allotropes**. Allotropy is sometimes called polymorphism and the different forms (or allotropes) may be called polymorphs.

Carbon

Carbon forms two crystalline allotropes—diamond and graphite. Graphite is the more stable allotrope at room temperature. Both diamond and graphite are made up from regular arrangements of carbon atoms, but the arrangements in the two allotropes are different. The carbon atoms are more closely packed in diamond than in graphite. A comparison of the two allotropes is shown in Table 22.1.

Table 22.1 Comparison of the properties of diamond and graphite.

	Diamond	Graphite
Appearance	Transparent crystals, can be colourless or coloured.	Black shiny solid, slippery to the touch.
Hardness	Very hard indeed.	Very soft.
Density $(g\ cm^{-3})$	3.5	2.2
Volume of 12g of carbon (cm^3)	3.4	5.4
Electrical conductivity	Non-conductor	Conductor of electricity, electrons can move through the structure.
Burning in oxygen	Burns with difficulty when heated to a high temperature. Carbon dioxide produced and no residue.	Burns readily to produce carbon dioxide. No residue.
	Equal masses of diamond and graphite on complete combustion produce equal masses (and volumes) of carbon dioxide.	

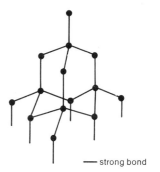

— strong bond

Figure 22.1 Diamond structure

In the **diamond** structure, each **carbon atom** is strongly attached to **four** other carbon atoms. One large crystal is built up with the distance between any two carbon atoms the same (0.154 nm between centres).

The diamond structure is very difficult to break up because the forces between the carbon atoms are very strong. This gives diamond its great **strength** and **high melting point**.

Graphite has a **layer structure**. In each layer the carbon atoms are regularly arranged and tightly held together. The distance between the centres of carbon atoms in each layer is the same (0.142 nm). However, the

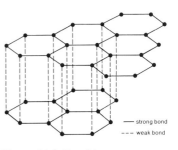

— strong bond
--- weak bond

Figure 22.2 Graphite structure

separate layers are widely spaced (0.335 nm) and are not tightly held together. The layers are able to slide over one another.

Making diamonds

Diamonds have been found naturally in the earth for many thousands of years. Having realised that graphite, like diamond, was a form of carbon, chemists tried for many years to convert graphite to diamond. The presence of small fragments of diamond associated with nickel and iron in meteorites suggested methods that could be used.

In the late nineteenth century many chemists, including Moissan, claimed to have produced diamonds from graphite. The method used was to dissolve graphite in molten iron and to cool the iron quickly using cold oil or water. As the iron solidified the carbon was subjected to great pressure at a high temperature. When the iron was removed by reaction with acid, grey diamonds remained.

However, other chemists had great difficulty in repeating these experiments. In 1962, the General Electric Company in America succeeded in making diamonds although again they were only suitable for industrial use.

In order to produce synthetic diamonds carbon containing quantities of metals including nickel is subjected to a pressure of 50 000 atmospheres at a constant temperature around 1700°C (1973 K) in a large press. Diamonds suitable for industrial use are produced.

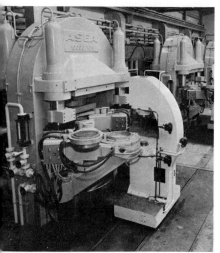

A press used to produce synthetic diamonds

Highly magnified synthetic diamonds. They are used for tips of drills and for the cutting teeth of saws.

Other forms of carbon

An interesting new material is called **carbon fibre**. It is produced by the partial decomposition of a textile fibre like rayon. It is done at a temperature of about 1000°C (1273 K) in an atmosphere of a noble gas. This is done in this way so that the fibre structure of the textile fibre remains. The resulting fibre is crystalline with a graphite-like structure. It has a wide range of uses because it is very strong but very light. It also has a high melting point. In order to use its mechanical strength to the full, it is used with a polymer, metal or ceramic material to form a composite. It has been used in **turbines** and **compressor blades** in aeroplane engines. It has also been used for heat shields in spacecraft and in sports equipment like golf clubs.

Other forms of carbon such as coal, charcoal and soot are non-crystalline

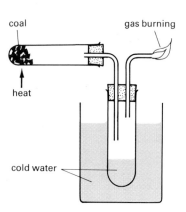

coal   gas burning

heat

cold water

Figure 22.3 Apparatus for destructive distillation of coal

Coal

Coal is the remains of plants and trees which once grew on the earth. The dead plants and trees were turned to coal by the effects of high temperatures and pressures over millions of years. Coal is a fossil fuel. The coal deposits in the earth can never be replaced, but, despite being widely mined for several centuries, ample stocks remain. Coal can be mined in two ways.

1 Open cast mining. This is used for deposits close to the surface. The soil is removed until the deposits are exposed. The coal is removed by excavator and, finally, the soil is replaced.

2 Deep mining. This is used when the seams are deep underground. A shaft is sunk down to the seam. Tunnels are then cut horizontally into the seams by automatic cutting machinery.

Destructive distillation of coal

When coal is heated in excess air it burns to produce carbon dioxide as the main product. When coal is heated out of contact with air the coal splits up to form four products. The apparatus in figure 22.3 can be used to carry out the process in the laboratory. The four products are:

1 Coal gas which contains largely hydrogen and carbon monoxide. This mixture of gases was used for household gas supplies before the discovery of natural gas.

2 Coke (or smokeless fuel) which remains in the test tube. Coke is a good solid industrial fuel.

3 Coal tar which is a dark brown tarry residue. It contains a wide range of valuable chemicals. It can be treated to produce creosote, dyes, drugs etc.

4 Ammonia solution which can be used to produce fertilisers, e.g. ammonium sulphate.

Charcoal

Charcoal is formed by heating wood, bones or other carbon-rich compounds, out of contact with air. The apparatus in figure 22.4 can be used to prepare charcoal in the laboratory from wood chippings.

Charcoal has a very large surface area and a wide range of uses. Gas masks contain charcoal which filters out poisonous gases. Charcoal can be boiled with a solution of crude sugar to decolourise the sugar. On crystallisation white sugar is produced. The charcoal used for these purposes is called activated charcoal. Charcoal is also used by artists, and as a fuel for barbecues.

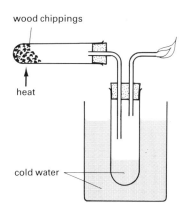

Figure 22.4 Apparatus for the preparation of charcoal

Sulphur

Most of the world's uncombined sulphur is found in Texas and Louisiana in the United States. It is found in deposits deep underground in an area where conventional deep mining is impossible because of quicksand. The sulphur is obtained by the **Frasch process**. A hole is drilled down to the deposits with an oil drilling rig. A sulphur pump is inserted in the hole. The sulphur pump (shown in figure 22.5) consists of three pipes of different diameters. Superheated water at 170° (443 K), produced by heating water under pressure, is pumped down the outer tube. When the water reaches the deposits, the sulphur melts (melting point of sulphur 113°C, 386 K). Hot compressed air is pumped down the centre tube. A mixture of sulphur, air and water is forced up the remaining tube to the surface. It is then cooled and sticks of solid sulphur called 'roll sulphur' are produced which are 99.5% pure sulphur. Coal cannot be mined in this way because it cannot be melted.

Sulphur is also extracted from natural gas in certain parts of the world. In Lacq, in Southern France, the natural gas extracted contains about 15% hydrogen sulphide. The natural gas is treated with an alkaline solution under pressure. The hydrogen sulphide and carbon dioxide (present only in small amounts) are dissolved because they are acid gases. The solution is then acidified to release these gases. Partial combustion of the hydrogen sulphide with a limited supply of air in the presence of a catalyst produces sulphur.

$$\text{hydrogen sulphide} + \text{oxygen} \rightarrow \text{sulphur} + \text{water}$$

Allotropy of sulphur

There are two crystalline allotropes of sulphur. These are α-sulphur (called rhombic sulphur) and β-sulphur (called monoclinic sulphur). Table 22.2

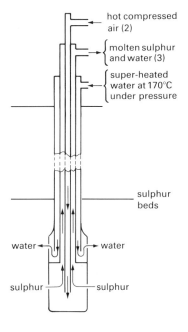

three concentric tubes

Figure 22.5 Frasch pump

Table 22.2 The properties of α-sulphur and β-sulphur.

	α-sulphur	β-sulphur
Appearance	Bright yellow crystals.	Orange-brown needle shaped crystals.
Density (g cm^{-3})	2.02	1.96
Volume of 32 g of sulphur (cm^3)	15.8	16.3
Solubility	Insoluble in water. Soluble in organic solvents like methylbenzene (toluene) and carbon disulphide.	
Effect of heat	Rapidly heated it melts at 113°C (386 K).	Melts at 119°C (392 K).
Range of stability	More stable below 96°C (369 K).	More stable above 96°C (369 K).
Burning in oxygen	Burns to produce sulphur dioxide. No residue. Equal masses of both allotropes produce equal masses of sulphur dioxide.	

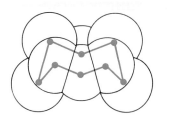

Figure 22.6 Sulphur molecules

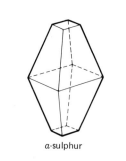

α-sulphur

β-sulphur

Figure 22.7

compares the properties of α- and β-sulphur.

Both allotropes of sulphur are made up from regular arrangements of sulphur molecules. The arrangement of molecules is different in the two allotropes. The sulphur molecules are **rings** of **eight sulphur atoms** (figure 22.6).

The **transition temperature** (96°C or 369 K) is the temperature at which both allotropes are stable. Below this temperature the α-sulphur is more stable and above this temperature the β-sulphur is more stable.

Table 22.3 shows the effect of heating powdered sulphur in a test tube. It shows how the changes in appearance can be explained in terms of changes in structure.

Note: When molten sulphur is cooled quickly by pouring into cold water, a non-crystalline solid is produced which is called **plastic sulphur**. Plastic sulphur resembles plastic materials because it consists of long chains of sulphur atoms tangled up. On standing at room temperature, plastic sulphur changes to α-sulphur.

Preparation of α-sulphur

A saturated solution of sulphur in methylbenzene (toluene) is prepared. The methylbenzene is warm but below 96°C (369 K). The solution is filtered to remove undissolved sulphur. The solution is allowed to stand until crystals of α-sulphur are formed.

Preparation of β-sulphur

Crystals of β-sulphur are produced when a saturated solution of sulphur in methylbenzene is allowed to crystallise above 96°C (369 K). Alternatively, β-sulphur crystals are produced when molten sulphur is allowed to cool and

Table 22.3 Effect of heat on powdered sulphur.

Temperature	State	Colour	Ease of pouring out of the test tube	Structure
Up to 113°C (386 K)	Solid	Yellow	—	A regular arrangement of S_8 rings.
113°C (386 K) –180°C (453 K)	Liquid	Amber	Easy to pour	Irregular arrangement of S_8 rings. Rings are free to move.
180°C (453 K) –220°C (493 K)	Liquid	Dark reddish brown.	Difficult to pour	Rings open and short chains join together to produce long chains. Long chains are tangled up.
220°C (493 K) –444°C (717 K)	Liquid	Black	Easy to pour	Long chains break up to form short chains.
At 444°C (717 K)	Turns to gas	Colourless	—	Pairs of sulphur atoms.

crystallise. Crystals of β-sulphur change to α-sulphur on standing at room temperature.

Uses of sulphur

Most of the sulphur produced is used for producing sulphuric acid. Other uses of sulphur include vulcanisation of rubber and the fumigation of greenhouses.

something to think about . . .

This question is about the chemistry of sulphur.
a Draw a neatly labelled diagram to show how sulphur is obtained from underground deposits by the Frasch process.
b A sulphur atom has six electrons in its outer shell, while the sodium atom and the hydrogen atom only have one electron in the outer shell. Draw a neat diagram to show how these electrons are arranged in
  (i) a molecule of hydrogen sulphide where the sulphur and hydrogen atoms are covalently bonded to each other.
  (ii) sodium sulphide where the sodium is ionically bonded to the sulphur.
c How could you show that sodium sulphide is an ionic substance?
d Hydrogen sulphide dissolves in water to form a slightly acidic solution. Write the name of the ion which must have been formed from the hydrogen sulphide to cause this acidity.
e Write down the formula of one other ion which is formed when hydrogen sulphide dissolves in water.
f Name one chemical which can be used to detect a sulphide ion and state what would happen to prove its presence.
                    (*East Anglian Examinations Board CSE*)

23. Study of group 4 elements

In any group of the periodic table it is possible to see gradual changes within the group. In this chapter we are going to study the changes within group 4. Table 23.1 shows the elements in group 4, their chemical symbols, atomic numbers, melting points, boiling points and atomic radii.

Table 23.1 The group 4 elements.

Element	Symbol	Atomic number	Melting point °C	Boiling point °C	Atomic radii nm
Carbon	C	6	3500 (3773 K)	3900 (4173 K)	0.077
Silicon	Si	14	1410 (1683 K)	2480 (2753 K)	0.117
Germanium	Ge	32	958 (1231 K)	2880 (3153 K)	0.122
Tin	Sn	50	232 (505 K)	2600 (2873 K)	0.141
Lead	Pb	82	327 (600 K)	1750 (2023 K)	0.154

Atoms of each of these elements have **four electrons** near the outside of the atom (because they are in group 4). These four electrons can be involved in bonding atoms together. **Carbon** is able to use these four electrons to form four covalent or sharing bonds. The tendency to form four covalent bonds decreases down the group. On the other hand, lead atoms form ions with a 2+ charge by losing two electrons. The tendency to form ions increases down the group.

Down any group in the periodic table there is an increase in the size of the atoms of the different elements. There is not the same simple relationship between atomic number and melting and boiling point (as was seen with group 0 èlements in Chapter 10 because the elements have different structures.

The elements

There is a gradual change down the group from non-metal to metal. **Carbon** is definitely a non-metal and can exist in two crystalline allotropes: diamond and graphite (Chapter 22). When carbon burns in excess oxygen it forms carbon dioxide which is an acidic oxide.

Silicon is again definitely non-metallic although it has a shiny grey metallic appearance. Crystalline silicon has a structure similar to diamond.

Germanium is not obviously metallic or non-metallic. It is a **metalloid**. Germanium has a non-metallic diamond structure and a melting point between the high values of carbon and silicon and the lower values of tin and lead. It resembles a metal in appearance.

Tin can exist in three solid allotropes:

α-tin $\rightleftarrows$ β-tin $\rightleftarrows$ γ-tin
(grey tin)   (white tin)   (brittle tin)

stable below stable between stable above
13°C (286 K) 13°C (286 K) and 161°C (434 K)
             161°C (434 K)

In the α form, tin has a non-metallic diamond structure. Tin has a metallic appearance and properties but still retains one or two properties of a non-metal.

Lead has a typical metallic structure (cubic close-packed ABCABC . . ., see Chapter 13). Its appearance and properties are more metallic than the other members of group 4.

Oxides of group 4 elements

The oxides formed by these elements are:

CO_2	CO	
carbon dioxide	carbon monoxide	
SiO_2		
silicon(IV) oxide		
GeO_2		
germanium(IV) oxide		
SnO_2	SnO	
tin(IV) oxide	tin(II) oxide	
PbO_2	PbO	Pb_3O_4
lead(IV) oxide	lead(II) oxide	dilead(II) oxide lead(IV) red lead

Carbon dioxide and carbon monoxide are both **gases**. They are composed of separate molecules. For example:

$$O=C=O$$

Silicon(IV) oxide, however, has a giant structure of atoms (figure 13.12) because silicon–oxygen double bonds are not possible.

All dioxides will dissolve to some extent in alkalis—either molten alkalis or alkali solutions. In this respect they are behaving as **acidic oxides**. Carbon dioxide dissolves in alkali to form carbonate ions. Carbon dioxide can be removed from a mixture of gases by passing the mixture through potassium or sodium hydroxide.

When silicon(IV) oxide, sodium carbonate and calcium carbonate are heated together, the resulting mass of sodium and calcium silicates with excess silicon(IV) oxide is called **glass**. Glass can be coloured by the presence of small quantities of coloured compounds (Table 23.2).

'Pyrex' glass, which is more resistant to changes of temperature, contains borates in addition to silicates.

Glass blowing: TOP making sulphuric acid carboy; BELOW making a condenser.

Table 23.2 Impurities added to glass to produce colour.

Colour of glass	Impurity
Blue	Cobalt(II) oxide, copper(II) oxide
Red	Copper(I) oxide
Violet	Manganese(IV) oxide
Green	Chromium(III) oxide

Preparation of carbon dioxide

Carbon dioxide can be prepared by the action of dilute hydrochloric acid on marble chips (calcium carbonate). Thus:

calcium carbonate + hydrochloric acid → calcium chloride + water
+ carbon dioxide

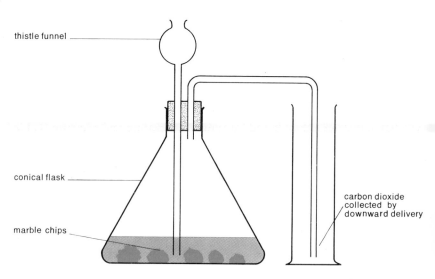

Figure 23.1 Preparation of carbon dioxide

Stability of the oxides

The stability of the oxides decreases down the group. **Carbon dioxide** and **silicon(IV) oxide** require a strong reducing agent such as magnesium to split them up and produce carbon and silicon.

If a mixture of silicon(IV) oxide (sand) and magnesium powder are strongly heated in a test tube, a reaction takes place:

silicon(IV) oxide + magnesium → silicon + magnesium oxide

The magnesium oxide can be removed from the silicon by adding warm, dilute hydrochloric acid. This dissolves the magnesium oxide forming soluble magnesium chloride and leaving silicon to be filtered off.

During the heating of the test tube some of the magnesium reacts with the glass to form magnesium silicide. The formation of **metal silicides** can be compared with the formation of metal carbides. When the warm, dilute acid is added to the resulting mixture, the magnesium silicide reacts with the acid solution forming silicon hydrides.

Both lead(IV) oxide and red lead lose oxygen on heating forming lead(II) oxide. Lead(II) oxide is not decomposed by heating but can be reduced to lead using carbon, carbon monoxide or hydrogen (see figure 6.7).

Hydrides of group 4 elements

Hydrides are compounds of elements with hydrogen. There are more hydrides formed by the elements in group 4 than by all other elements together. Hydrides of carbon (called **hydrocarbons**) were studied in Chapter 15. The wide range of hydrocarbons possible is due to the great strength of **C–C covalent bonds** which enables long chains and rings to exist. It is also possible to form double and triple bonds between carbon atoms.

Silicon and germanium form a limited number of hydrides called **silanes** and **germanes**. Double and triple bonds do not exist and long chains are not possible.

Tin and lead form only one hydride and these (SnH_4 and PbH_4) are difficult to obtain.

Chlorides of group 4 elements

The chlorides formed are:

CCl_4 tetrachloromethane (carbon tetrachloride)
$SiCl_4$ silicon tetrachloride
$GeCl_4$ germanium tetrachloride
$SnCl_4$ tin(IV) chloride $SnCl_2$ tin(II) chloride
$PbCl_4$ lead(IV) chloride $PbCl_2$ lead(II) chloride

The tetrachlorides are all liquids at room temperature and pressure. Table 23.3 shows the melting and boiling points of the tetrachlorides.

Table 23.3 Melting points and boiling points of tetrachlorides.

Tetrachlorides	Melting point °C	Boiling point °C
CCl_4	−23 (250 K)	77 (350 K)
$SiCl_4$	−70 (203 K)	60 (333 K)
$GeCl_4$	−50 (223 K)	86 (359 K)
$SnCl_4$	−33 (240 K)	114 (387 K)

The low melting and boiling points suggest that the tetrachlorides are composed of molecules. The melting and boiling point of tetrachloromethane (carbon tetrachloride) do not fit the same pattern as the other tetrachlorides.

Another difference between tetrachloromethane and the other tetrachlorides is the reaction with water. Tetrachloromethane does not react with water but the tetrachlorides of other elements react readily with water; that means that they are hydrolysed by water. For example:

silicon tetrachloride + water → silicon(IV) oxide + hydrogen chloride

The dichlorides of tin and lead are very different from the tetrachlorides.

They are both largely composed of ions. Tin(II) chloride is usually hydrated and, on heating, the tin(II) chloride is hydrolysed. Tin(II) chloride is also soluble in organic solvents. This suggests tin(II) chloride is not completely ionic.

Table 23.4 Melting points and boiling points of the dichlorides of tin and lead.

Dichlorides	Melting point °C	Boiling point °C	State
$SnCl_2$	38 (311 K)	Decomposes	Solid
$PbCl_2$	501 (774 K)	950 (1223 K)	Solid

Summary

It can be seen within group 4 that:

1 The elements become more metallic down the group.

2 All elements form four covalent bonds in some compounds although the stability of these compounds decreases down the group.

3 Elements lower in the group form positive ions with a 2+ charge.

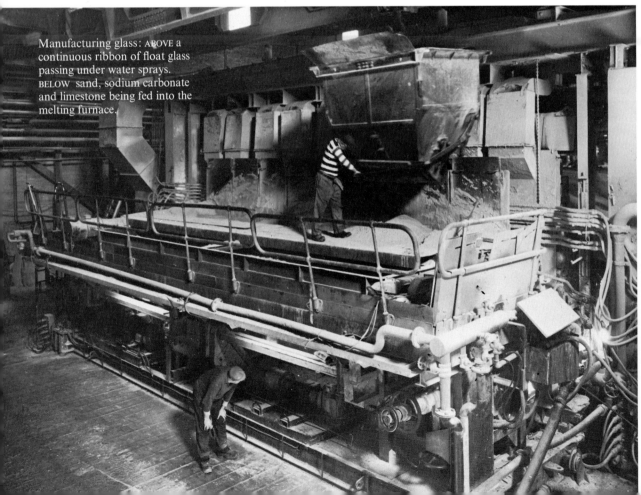

Manufacturing glass: ABOVE a continuous ribbon of float glass passing under water sprays. BELOW sand, sodium carbonate and limestone being fed into the melting furnace.

something to think about . . .

The passage below describes the chemistry of the element **boron**. Boron is the first element in group 3. We would not expect boron to be identical to any element in group 4. Read the passage and list all the similarities and all the differences between boron and the elements carbon and silicon of group 4.

The element boron occurs in the earth as boric(III) acid and borates. About 0.001 per cent of the earth's crust is boron.

The element was first prepared in 1808 by J. L. Gay Lussac. He prepared it by heating boron(III) oxide B_2O_3 with metallic potassium. It has also been prepared by the action of alkali on boron trichloride and the reduction of boron(III) oxide with magnesium.

Laubengayer and others (1943) produced a deposit of pure crystalline boron on a heated tantalum filament in an atmosphere of hydrogen and boron tribromide vapour.

Pure boron can exist in crystalline and powder forms. In the crystalline form it has a dull metallic lustre. It exists in a three-dimensional giant structure with strong bonds between boron atoms. As a result it has a high melting point (2030°C, 2303 K) and is chemically unreactive.

Powdered boron is more reactive than crystalline boron. At high temperatures it acts as a **reducing agent** and reduces many metal oxides often with the formation of metal borides as a side reaction. Boron powder reacts with steam at high temperatures to produce boric(III) acid. It also reacts with molten alkalis to produce borates.

Boron trichloride (boiling point 12°C, 285 K) is prepared by the action of chlorine gas on heated boron.

Boron hydrides (called boranes) are produced when hydrochloric acid is added to the residue remaining from the heating of boron(III) oxide and magnesium. The boron hydrides produced are colourless gases with a sickly odour and they usually burn spontaneously in air. A series of boranes were isolated by Stock in 1912. The best known of the boranes is diborane B_2H_6.

When boron(III) oxide is strongly heated a glassy solid is formed. This can be coloured by the presence of certain metal oxides. This is used as the basis of the borax bead test in chemical analysis.

Now answer the following questions:

a How could the tantalum filament be heated in the mixture of hydrogen and boron tribromide?

b Four hydrides isolated by Stock were
   diborane B_2H_6, pentaborane B_5H_9, hexaborane B_6H_{10}, decaborane $B_{10}H_{14}$.
These formulae all fit the same general formula. What is this general formula?

c Name the following compounds:
   B_2O_3, Mg_3B_2, BN, H_3BO_3.
d Write equations for the reactions between
   (i) boron and chlorine;
   (ii) boron(III) oxide and magnesium;
   (iii) boron and lead(II) oxide.

Appendix 1. Units

The International System of Units (called **SI Units**) is widely accepted now. In this book, SI units are used unless using non-SI units causes a simplification.

The SI system is based on seven base units. Some of these are shown in Table A.1.1.

Table A.1.1 Basic SI units.

Physical quantity	Name of unit	Symbol
Length	metre	m
Mass	kilogram	kg
Time	second	s
Electric current	ampere	A
Temperature	kelvin	K
Amount of substance	mole	mol

Table A.1.2 shows some units derived from SI base units.

Table A.1.2 Derived SI units.

Physical quantity	Name of derived SI unit	Symbol
Energy, heat	joule	J
Power	watt	W
Electric charge	coulomb	C
Electric potential difference	volt	V

Non-SI units

Atomic mass unit (symbol u): This unit is used for comparing the masses of atomic particles. The mass of a proton or neutron is approximately 1 u.

Litre: This is an alternative to 1 dm^3. It is equal to 1000 cm^3. A one thousandth part of a litre (volume 1 cm^3) is sometimes called a millilitre (ml).

Tonne: This is a common unit in everyday life. A tonne is one thousand kilograms.

Degree Celsius (°C) This is used throughout the book with kelvin temperatures in brackets.

$$\text{temperature in K} = \text{temperature in °C} + 273$$

Atmosphere: A pressure of 1 atmosphere is the normal room pressure. It is equal to 10^5 pascal (Pa).

Prefixes

Units can be varied by putting the appropriate prefix before the unit. Some of these are shown in Table A.1.3.

Table A.1.3 **Prefixes for SI units.**

Factor	Prefix	Symbol
1000 000 or 10^6	mega	M
1000 or 10^3	kilo	k
10	deca	da
$\frac{1}{10}$ or 10^{-1}	deci	d
$\frac{1}{100}$ or 10^{-2}	centi	c
$\frac{1}{1000}$ or 10^{-3}	milli	m
$\frac{1}{1000\,000}$ or 10^{-6}	micro	μ
$\frac{1}{1000\,000\,000}$ or 10^{-9}	nano	n

A complete list of suggested units and symbols is to be found in *Chemical Nomenclature, Symbols and Terminology*, 1979 (A.S.E.)

Appendix 2. Naming compounds

For many compounds there are a variety of possible names. In this book the recommendations of *Chemical Nomenclature, Symbols & Terminology*, 1979. (A.S.E.) have generally been followed.

However, the systematic names for certain negative ions containing oxygen and their parent acids are not widely used at this level at present. In fact using the systematic names could cause confusion. A list of some of these common ions and their parent acids together with their systematic names are shown in Table A.2.1.

Table A.2.1 Common ions and their parent acids. *The systematic names are preferred in these cases as they simplify the name.

Common name	Formula	Systematic name
Sulphuric acid	H_2SO_4	Sulphuric(VI) acid
Sulphurous acid	H_2SO_3	Sulphuric (IV) acid
Nitric acid	HNO_3	Nitric(V) acid
Nitrous acid	HNO_2	Nitric(III) acid
Phosphoric acid	H_3PO_4	Phosphoric(V) acid
Sulphate ion	$SO_4{}^{2-}$	Sulphate(VI) ion
Sulphite ion	$SO_3{}^{2-}$	Sulphate(IV) ion
Nitrate ion	$NO_3{}^-$	Nitrate(V) ion
Phosphate ion	$PO_4{}^{3-}$	Phosphate(V) ion
Chlorate ion	$ClO_3{}^-$	Chlorate(V) ion
Chromate ion	$CrO_4{}^{2-}$	Chromate(VI) ion
Hypochlorite ion	OCl^-	Chlorate(I) ion
Manganate ion	$MnO_4{}^{2-}$	Manganate(VI) ion
Permanganate ion	$MnO_4{}^-$	Manganate(VII) ion
Thiosulphate ion	$S_2O_3{}^{2-}$	Thiosulphate(VI) ion
Nitrite ion	$NO_2{}^-$	Nitrate(III) ion
Bicarbonate ion	$HCO_3{}^-$	Hydrogencarbonate ion*
Bisulphate ion	$HSO_4{}^-$	Hydrogensulphate ion*

The following five points are worth remembering

1 Compounds ending in **-ide** contain **two elements**. For example, sodium chloride is a compound of sodium and chlorine.

2 Compounds ending in **-ite** or **-ate** contain **oxygen**. For example, sodium sulphate and sodium sulphite are both compounds of sodium, sulphur and oxygen.

The compound ending in -ate contains more oxygen than the compound ending in -ite.

3 Compounds with a prefix **per-** contain extra oxygen. This extra oxygen is often easily lost. For example, Na_2O sodium **oxide**, Na_2O_2 sodium **peroxide**.

4 Compounds with a prefix **thio-** contain an extra sulphur atom replacing an oxygen atom. For example:

Na_2SO_4 $Na_2S_2O_3$
sodium **sulphate**   sodium **thiosulphate**

5 If a compound contains water of crystallisation this is shown in the formula. For example, blue copper(II) sulphate crystals are called copper(II) sulphate(VI)-5-water showing five molecules of water of crystallisation.

something to think about . . .

1 Write down the elements present in each of the following compounds:

a sodium nitrate   f potassium chromate
b magnesium nitride   g lead carbonate
c potassium chloride   h ammonium hydroxide (Chapter 11)
d calcium hydride   i calcium carbide
e sodium chlorate   j calcium phosphate.

2 When potassium chlorate is heated a residue of potassium chloride is formed. Name the substance lost when potassium chlorate is heated.

Appendix 3. Chemical equations

A chemical equation is a summary of a chemical reaction. Throughout this book word equations are used. For example,

copper oxide + sulphuric acid → copper(II) sulphate + water

These are useful to help you remember chemical reactions but it is more valuable to write equations using **symbols** that can be understood by any chemist throughout the world whatever language he uses. The shorthand symbol for each element will be found on pages 186–8. **Symbol equations** also enable you to check that you have remembered all the products; to work out quantities of reacting substances and products and, providing you do it sensibly, to predict possible reactions. An example of a symbol equation is:

$$CuO(s) + H_2SO_4(aq) \rightarrow CuSO_4(aq) + H_2O(l)$$

Writing the formulae for compounds

From electrolysis calculations it is possible to work out the charges on common ions. These include the ions in Table A.3.1.

Table A.3.1 Common ions and their charges.

Sodium	Na^+	Chloride	Cl^-
Potassium	K^+	Bromide	Br^-
Ammonium	NH_4^+	Iodide	I^-
Silver	Ag^+	Hydroxide	OH^-
Copper	Cu^{2+}	Nitrate	NO_3^-
Lead	Pb^{2+}	Hydrogencarbonate	HCO_3^-
Magnesium	Mg^{2+}	Sulphate	SO_4^{2-}
Calcium	Ca^{2+}	Carbonate	CO_3^{2-}
Zinc	Zn^{2+}	Oxide	O^{2-}
Barium	Ba^{2+}	Sulphide	S^{2-}
Iron(II)	Fe^{2+}	Phosphate	PO_4^{3-}
Iron(III)	Fe^{3+}	Aluminium	Al^{3+}

From these ions it is possible to work out the correct formula of a range of common compounds. For example, **copper(II) sulphate** is composed of Cu^{2+} and SO_4^{2-} ions. The ions are present in equal numbers so that the number of positive charges equals the number of negative charges. The formula of copper(II) sulphate is written as $CuSO_4$.

Sodium oxide contains Na^+ and O^{2-} ions. In order to have equal numbers of positive and negative charges, twice as many sodium ions as oxide ions are needed. The formula is, therefore, written as Na_2O.

The formulae of the common acids can be worked out using the hydrogen ion H^+.

hydrochloric acid	$H^+ Cl^-$	HCl
sulphuric acid	$H^+ SO_4^{2-}$	H_2SO_4
nitric acid	$H^+ NO_3^-$	HNO_3
carbonic acid	$H^+ CO_3^{2-}$	H_2CO_3

Table A.3.2 gives the formulae of some common substances made up from ions.

Table A.3.2 Some common substances, their ions and formulae.

Substance	Ions present	Formula
Potassium oxide	$K^+ O^{2-}$	K_2O
Potassium chloride	$K^+ Cl^-$	KCl
Potassium nitrate	$K^+ NO_3^-$	KNO_3
Potassium sulphate	$K^+ SO_4^{2-}$	K_2SO_4
Potassium carbonate	$K^+ CO_3^{2-}$	K_2CO_3
Potassium hydroxide	$K^+ OH^-$	KOH
Zinc oxide	$Zn^{2+} O^{2-}$	ZnO
Zinc chloride	$Zn^{2+} Cl^-$	$ZnCl_2$
Zinc nitrate	$Zn^{2+} NO_3^-$	$Zn(NO_3)_2$
Zinc sulphate	$Zn^{2+} SO_4^{2-}$	$ZnSO_4$
Zinc carbonate	$Zn^{2+} CO_3^{2-}$	$ZnCO_3$
Zinc hydroxide	$Zn^{2+} OH^-$	$Zn(OH)_2$
Aluminium hydroxide	$Al^{3+} OH^-$	$Al(OH)_3$
Aluminium oxide	$Al^{3+} O^{2-}$	Al_2O_3
Aluminium chloride	$Al^{3+} Cl^-$	$AlCl_3$

something to think about . . .

Write the formulae for each of the following compounds.

a sodium chloride	b calcium carbonate
c calcium bromide	d lead carbonate
e lead bromide	f aluminium carbonate
g magnesium nitrate	h calcium hydrogencarbonate
i ammonium sulphate	j calcium phosphate.

In addition, you should try to remember the formulae of the common substances in Table A.3.3.

These are not made up of ions. There are rules that enable chemists to work out these formulae and many others. There is little benefit learning these rules for the few formulae needed at this stage.

Table A.3.3 Formulae of some important substances that are not ionised.

H_2O water	SO_3 sulphur trioxide
CO_2 carbon dioxide	SO_2 sulphur dioxide
CO carbon monoxide	NH_3 ammonia
NO nitrogen monoxide	HCl hydrogen chloride
NO_2 nitrogen dioxide	CH_4 methane

In chemical equations letters after the formulae show the state of the substance:

    (s) solid
    (l) liquid
    (g) gas
    (aq) in solution in water

In some books (c) is used for a crystalline solid.

The steps in writing a chemical equation

1 Write the corresponding **word equation**. You will have to use your chemical knowledge to complete this. For example:

    calcium carbonate + hydrochloric acid → calcium chloride + water + carbon dioxide.

2 Fill in the correct **formulae** and states:

$$CaCO_3(s) + HCl(aq) \rightarrow CaCl_2(aq) + H_2O(l) + CO_2(g)$$

3 **Balance** the chemical equation.

In any chemical reaction no atoms are created or destroyed. There must be the same number of atoms before and after the reaction. This 'accounting' cannot be done by altering any formulae. Only the proportions of the reacting substances and products can be changed. Thus:

$$CaCO_3(s) + 2HCl(aq) \rightarrow CaCl_2(aq) + H_2O(l) + CO_2(g)$$

something to think about . . .

1 Using information in the book, complete the following word equations.

    a magnesium + oxygen → ———
    b magnesium oxide + sulphuric acid → ——— + ———
    c sodium hydroxide + nitric acid → ——— + ———
    d potassium carbonate + hydrochloric acid → ——— + ——— + ———
    e calcium hydroxide + carbon dioxide → ——— + ———

2 Some of these equations contain one or more mistakes. Write out all the equations correcting any mistakes.

    a $Al(s) + HCl(aq) \rightarrow AlCl_3(aq) + H(g)$
    b $Mg(s) + CO_2(aq) \rightarrow MgO_2(s) + C(s)$
    c $Al(s) + O(g) \rightarrow Al_2O_3(s)$
    d $CH_4(g) + Cl(g) \rightarrow CH_3Cl(l) + HCl(g)$
    e $NH_3(g) + CuO(s) \rightarrow N_2(g) + H_2O(l) + Cu(s)$

Common chemical equations

Here is a check list of some of the chemical equations you have met in this book:

Chapter

3
$Fe(s) + S(s) \rightarrow FeS(s)$
$2Al(s) + 3I_2(s) \rightarrow 2AlI_3(s)$
$2H_2(g) + O_2(g) \rightarrow 2H_2O(l)$

5
$2H_2O_2(aq) \rightarrow 2H_2O(l) + O_2(g)$
$2Cu(s) + O_2(g) \rightarrow 2CuO(s)$

6
$CaCO_3(s) + H_2O(l) + CO_2(g) \rightleftarrows Ca(HCO_3)_2(aq)$
$Mg(s) + H_2O(g) \rightarrow MgO(s) + H_2(g)$
$Zn(s) + 2HCl(aq) \rightarrow ZnCl_2(aq) + H_2(g)$
$Zn(s) + H_2SO_4(aq) \rightarrow ZnSO_4(aq) + H_2(g)$
$PbO(s) + H_2(g) \rightarrow Pb(s) + H_2O(g)$

8
$C(s) + O_2(g) \rightarrow CO_2(g)$
$CO_2(g) + C(s) \rightarrow 2CO(g)$
$Fe_2O_3(s) + 3CO(g) \rightarrow 2Fe(l) + 3CO_2(g)$

(and 19)
$CaCO_3(s) \rightleftarrows CaO(s) + CO_2(g)$
$CaO(s) + SiO_2(g) \rightarrow CaSiO_3(l)$

9
$Mg(s) + PbO(s) \rightarrow MgO(s) + Pb(s)$
$Fe_2O_3(s) + 2Al(s) \rightarrow 2Fe(s) + Al_2O_3(s)$
$Cr_2O_3(s) + 2Al(s) \rightarrow 2Cr(s) + Al_2O_3(s)$
$CuSO_4(aq) + Fe(s) \rightarrow Cu(s) + FeSO_4(aq)$

10
$2Li(s) + 2H_2O(l) \rightarrow 2LiOH(aq) + H_2(g)$
$2Na(s) + 2H_2O(l) \rightarrow 2NaOH(aq) + H_2(g)$
$2K(s) + 2H_2O(l) \rightarrow 2KOH(aq) + H_2(g)$
$2Li(s) + Cl_2(g) \rightarrow 2LiCl(s)$
$2Na(s) + Cl_2(g) \rightarrow 2NaCl(s)$
$H_2(g) + Cl_2(g) \rightarrow 2HCl(g)$
$H_2(g) + Br_2(g) \rightarrow 2HBr(g)$
$H_2(g) + I_2(g) \rightleftarrows 2HI(g)$
$Cl_2(g) + 2KBr(aq) \rightarrow Br_2(aq) + 2KCl(aq)$

10
$2HOCl(aq) \rightarrow 2HCl(aq) + O_2(g)$

11
$(NH_4)_2SO_4(s) + 2NaOH(aq) \rightarrow 2NH_3(g) + Na_2SO_4(aq) + 2H_2O(l)$
$2NH_4OH(aq) + H_2SO_4(aq) \rightarrow (NH_4)_2SO_4(aq) + 2H_2O(l)$
$4NH_3(g) + 5O_2(g) \rightarrow 4NO(g) + 6H_2O(g)$
$2NO(g) + O_2(g) \rightleftarrows 2NO_2(g)$

15
$C_2H_5OH(g) \rightarrow H_2O(g) + C_2H_4(g)$
$H_2O(l) + C_{12}H_{22}O_{11}(aq) \rightarrow 4C_2H_5OH(aq) + 4CO_2(g)$
$CH_3COOH(l) + C_2H_5OH(l) \rightleftarrows CH_3COOC_2H_5(l) + H_2O(l)$

17
$CuO(s) + H_2SO_4(aq) \rightarrow CuSO_4(aq) + H_2O(l)$

17,18,23
$CaCO_3(s) + 2HCl(aq) \rightarrow CaCl_2(aq) + CO_2(g) + H_2O(l)$

17
$Mg(s) + H_2SO_4(aq) \rightarrow MgSO_4(aq) + H_2(g)$

17
$Ba(OH)_2(aq) + H_2SO_4(aq) \rightarrow BaSO_4(s) + 2H_2O(l)$

18
$Na_2S_2O_3(aq) + 2HCl(aq) \rightarrow 2NaCl(aq) + SO_2(g) + S(s) + H_2O(l)$

19
$CuSO_4.5H_2O(s) \rightleftarrows CuSO_4(s) + 5H_2O(l)$
$3Fe(s) + 4H_2O(g) \rightleftarrows Fe_3O_4(s) + 4H_2(g)$
$2Hg(l) + O_2(g) \rightleftarrows 2HgO(s)$

22
$2H_2S(g) + O_2(g) \rightarrow 2S(s) + 2H_2O(l)$

23
$SiO_2(s) + 2Mg(s) \rightarrow 2MgO(s) + Si(s)$
$SiCl_4(l) + 2H_2O(l) \rightarrow SiO_2(s) + 4HCl(aq)$

Appendix 4. Chemical calculations

Approximate relative atomic masses

H = 1	He = 4	C = 12
N = 14	O = 16	Na = 23
Mg = 24	Al = 27	P = 31
S = 32	Cl = 35.5	K = 39
Ca = 40	Fe = 56	Ni = 59
Cu = 64	Br = 80	Ag = 108
Sn = 118	Hg = 200	Pb = 207

1 mole of molecules of any gas has a volume of 24 dm³ (24 000 cm³) at room temperature and pressure.

The understanding of the **quantities** of **chemicals** used and produced in chemical reactions, together with the quantity of **energy** required or produced, can be extremely important, particularly in industrial chemistry. It enables a manufacturer to work out his costs and, therefore, the price that has to be paid for his product.

Relative atomic mass

The particles that make up all substances are very small indeed. Whether they are atoms, molecules or ions, they are too small to be weighed individually. An individual atom would weigh about 10^{-23} g but the most sensitive balance in the world can only weigh objects with masses greater than 10^{-7} g.

A hydrogen atom is the lightest of all atoms. The atoms of all other elements are heavier than a hydrogen atom. The **relative atomic mass** of an element is the number of times the mass of one atom of the element is heavier than one atom of hydrogen.

$$\text{Relative atomic mass} = \frac{\text{mass of one atom of the element}}{\text{mass of one atom of hydrogen}}$$

For example, one atom of magnesium is 24 times heavier than an atom of hydrogen. The relative atomic mass of magnesium is 24.

The relative atomic masses of some common elements are printed at the top of the page throughout this section.

The mole

The relative atomic mass of helium is 4. (**note** this is a ratio or number and has no units.) This means:

1 atom of helium weighs 4 times as much as 1 atom of hydrogen

2 atoms of helium weigh 4 times as much as 2 atoms of hydrogen (and, of course, 8 times as much as 1 atom of hydrogen)

1000 atoms of helium weigh 4 times as much as 1000 atoms of hydrogen

Providing equal numbers of atoms are considered, the helium atoms will always weigh four times as much as the hydrogen atoms.

The chemist's 'magic' number is called **Avogadro's number** (L) after a famous nineteenth-century chemist. It is approximately 600 000 000 000 000 000 000 000 or 6×10^{23}. The mass of 6×10^{23} atoms of hydrogen is 1 g. (**note:** this is the same as the relative atomic mass for hydrogen but has units of grams). It follows that if we weigh 6×10^{23} atoms of helium (we call this amount of helium 1 **mole** of helium atoms); they will weigh 4 g. If we weigh out 6×10^{23} atoms of any element the weight will be the same as the relative atomic mass of the element in grams.

It is hard for us to understand just how large Avogadro's number is. If the whole population of the world wished to count up to this number between them and they worked at counting without any breaks at all it would take six million years to finish. Alternatively a line 6×10^{23} mm long would stretch from the earth to the sun and back two million times.

The **mole** is defined as the amount of substance which contains as many elementary units as there are in 1 g of hydrogen (i.e. 6×10^{23} elementary units). In this definition an elementary unit can be considered as:

- **atoms**, such as He, C
- **molecules,** such as H_2O, CO_2
- **ions,** such as Cu^{2+}, Ag^+
- **specified formula units,** such as NaCl. (These, like NaCl, may not in fact exist as such but it is often helpful to use this idea.)

It is important to state clearly the particles considered in each case. For example:

1 mole of hydrogen atoms (H) has a mass of 1 g.
1 mole of hydrogen molecules (H_2) has a mass of 2 g.

In other books other terms may be seen.

The mass of 1 mole of atoms may be called 1 gram atom.
The mass of 1 mole of molecules may be called 1 gram molecule.
The mass of 1 mole of ions may be called 1 gram ion.
The mass of 1 mole of formula units may be called 1 gram formula.

Approximate relative atomic masses

H = 1	He = 4	C = 12
N = 14	O = 16	Na = 23
Mg = 24	Al = 27	P = 31
S = 32	Cl = 35.5	K = 39
Ca = 40	Fe = 56	Ni = 59
Cu = 64	Br = 80	Ag = 108
Sn = 118	Hg = 200	Pb = 207

1 mole of molecules of any gas has a volume of 24 dm^3 (24 000 cm^3) at room temperature and pressure.

Calculation examples

1 mole of sodium atoms (Na) has a mass of 23 g.
1 mole of oxygen molecules (O_2) has a mass of 32 g.
1 mole of methane molecules (CH_4) has a mass of 16 g.
1 mole of sodium ions (Na^+) has a mass of 23 g.
1 mole of sodium chloride (NaCl) has a mass of 58.5 g.
2 moles of nitrogen molecules (N_2) has a mass of 56 g (that is 2×28 g).
$\frac{1}{2}$ mole of calcium oxide (CaO) has a mass of 28 g (that is $\frac{1}{2} \times 56$ g).

Type 1: Calculate the mass of 1 mole of ethanol molecules (C_2H_5OH)
Mass of 1 mole of ethanol molecules $= (2 \times 12) + (6 \times 1) + (16 \times 1)$
$$= 46 \text{ g.}$$

Type 2: Calculate the number of moles of atoms present in 4 g of oxygen.

$$\text{Number of moles of atoms} = \frac{\text{mass of oxygen}}{\text{mass of 1 mole of oxygen atoms}}$$
$$= \frac{4}{16}$$
$$= \frac{1}{4}$$

Type 3: Calculate the number of moles of molecules present in 4 g of oxygen (O_2).

$$\text{Number of moles of } O_2 \text{ molecules} = \frac{\text{mass of oxygen}}{\text{mass of 1 mole of oxygen molecules}}$$
$$= \frac{4}{32}$$
$$= \frac{1}{8}$$

Approximate relative atomic masses

H = 1	He = 4	C = 12
N = 14	O = 16	Na = 23
Mg = 24	Al = 27	P = 31
S = 32	Cl = 35.5	K = 39
Ca = 40	Fe = 56	Ni = 59
Cu = 64	Br = 80	Ag = 108
Sn = 118	Hg = 200	Pb = 207

1 mole of molecules of any gas has a volume of 24 dm^3 (24 000 cm^3) at room temperature and pressure.

something to think about . . .

1 How many times heavier is:

   a one atom of carbon than 1 atom of hydrogen?
   b one atom of magnesium than 1 atom of carbon?
   c one atom of sulphur than 2 atoms of helium?

2 Work out the mass of:

   a 6×10^{23} atoms of silver (Ag)
   b 1 mole of potassium atoms (K)
   c 1 mole of nitrogen atoms (N)
   d 1 mole of nitrogen molecules (N_2)
   e Half a mole of calcium atoms (Ca)
   f 2 moles of carbon atoms (C)
   g 0.1 moles of bromine atoms (Br)
   h 0.1 moles of bromine molecules (Br_2)
   i One-third of a mole of aluminium ions (Al^{3+})
   j 0.1 mole of copper(II) carbonate ($CuCO_3$).

3 Work out how many moles of atoms each of these masses contain:
   a 200 g of mercury (Hg)
   b 64 g of sulphur (S)
   c 71 g of chlorine (Cl)
   d 5.6 g of iron (Fe)
   e 0.108 g of silver (Ag).

4 Work out how many moles of formula units each of these masses contain:
   a 40 g of sodium hydroxide (NaOH)
   b 74 g of calcium hydroxide $Ca(OH)_2$
   c 16 g of anhydrous copper(II) sulphate ($CuSO_4$)
   d 10.2 g of aluminium oxide (Al_2O_3)
   e 27.6 g of potassium carbonate (K_2CO_3).

5 Which of the following pairs contain the same number of atoms? (There may be more than one)
   a 1 g of hydrogen (H) and 1 g of oxygen (O);
   b 16 g of hydrogen (H) and 16 g of oxygen (O);
   c 0.1 g of hydrogen (H) and 1.6 g of oxygen (O);
   d 3.2 g of sulphur (S) and 1.6 g of oxygen (O).

6 Calculate the mass of 1 mole of each of the following:
   a carbon dioxide molecules (CO_2)
   b ammonia molecules (NH_3)
   c sulphuric acid (H_2SO_4)
   d hydrochloric acid (HCl)
   e phosphorus atoms (P)
   f phosphorus molecules (P_4).

Volume of one mole of atoms

One mole of atoms of different elements contain the same number of atoms (Avogadro's number) but the volume of 1 mole of atoms of different elements varies greatly.

The volume of 1 mole of atoms of an element depends upon:
- the different sizes of the atoms of different elements,
- the different arrangements of the atoms.

Figure A.4.1 shows a simple two-dimensional representation of the volume of 1 mole of atoms of different elements.

Notice that while there is no simple relationship between the volumes of 1 mole of atoms of solids and liquids, the volume of 1 mole of atoms of the different gases is either 12 dm³ or 24 dm³.

The volume of 1 mole of a substance is called the molar volume.

Molar volumes of gases

One mole of molecules of any gas occupies a volume of 24 dm³ (24 000 cm³) at room temperature and pressure.

A cube of side 29 cm (0.29 m) has a volume of approximately 24 dm³.

One mole of hydrogen **molecules** (6×10^{23} molecules) has a volume of 24 dm³ at room temperature and pressure. One mole of hydrogen **atoms** (6×10^{23} atoms) has a volume of 12 dm³ at room temperature and pressure. It follows that each **hydrogen molecule** is made up from **two hydrogen atoms**. The number of atoms in one molecule of a gas is called the **atomicity**.

Table A.4.1 explains the use of H_2, O_2, Cl_2 and N_2 in chemical equations.

Approximate relative atomic masses

H = 1	He = 4	C = 12
N = 14	O = 16	Na = 23
Mg = 24	Al = 27	P = 31
S = 32	Cl = 35.5	K = 39
Ca = 40	Fe = 56	Ni = 59
Cu = 64	Br = 80	Ag = 108
Sn = 118	Hg = 200	Pb = 207

1 mole of molecules of any gas has a volume of 24 dm³ (24 000 cm³) at room temperature and pressure.

Table A.4.1 The atomicity of gases.

Gas	Volume of 1 mole of atoms (dm³)	Volume of 1 mole of molecules (dm³)	Number of atoms in 1 molecule of gas (atomicity)
Hydrogen	12	24	2
Helium	24	24	1
Oxygen	12	24	2
Ozone (a form of oxygen).	8	24	3
Chlorine	12	24	2
Nitrogen	12	24	2

Examples

Type 4: Calculate the volume at room temperature and pressure of 0.1 moles of carbon dioxide molecules.

One mole of carbon dioxide molecules has a volume of 24 dm³ at room temperature and pressure.

0.1 moles of carbon dioxide at room temperature and pressure would have a volume of $24 \div 10$ dm³, that is, 2.4 dm³.

It follows that equal volumes of different gases contain equal numbers of molecules providing the temperature and pressure are the same. This is called **Avogadro's Hypothesis**.

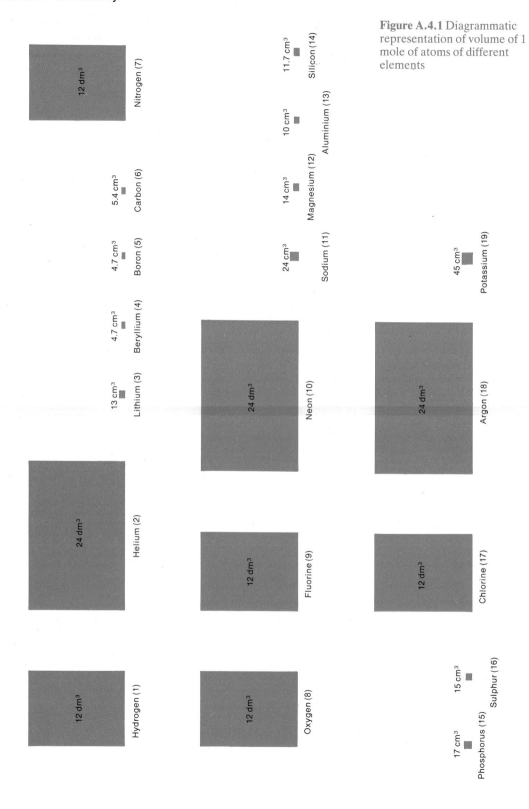

Figure A.4.1 Diagrammatic representation of volume of 1 mole of atoms of different elements

something to think about . . .

1 Work out the volume at room temperature and pressure of:
   a 1 mole of oxygen molecules,
   b 2 moles of chlorine molecules,
   c 0.2 moles of hydrogen molecules,
   d a mixture of 0.1 moles of hydrogen molecules and 0.1 moles of oxygen molecules.

Give your answers in both dm^3 and cm^3.

2 Work out how many moles of molecules each of the following gas samples contain:
   a 12 dm^3 of nitrogen (N_2)
   b 1.2 dm^3 of ammonia (NH_3)
   c 200 cm^3 of oxygen (O_2)
   d 250 cm^3 of nitrogen monoxide (NO).
All volumes are measured at room temperature and pressure.

3 In an experiment to find the mass of 1 mole of sulphur dioxide (SO_2) gas, a corked glass round bottom flask was used. The results are shown below.
Mass of corked flask filled with dry air = 190.85 g
Mass of corked flask evacuated   = 190.25 g
(i.e. no gas in the flask)
Mass of corked flask filled with sulphur dioxide = 191.58 g
a What was the mass of dry air filling the flask?
b If 1000 cm^3 of dry air has a mass of 1.20 g, what is the volume of the flask?
c What was the mass of sulphur dioxide filling the flask?
d What would be the mass of 1 dm^3 of sulphur dioxide?
e What would be the mass of 24 dm^3 of sulphur dioxide?
f What would be the mass of 1 mole of sulphur dioxide molecules?
g How does the experimental result for the mass of 1 mole of molecules for sulphur dioxide compare with the value you work out with relative atomic masses? Can you suggest any reason for the difference.

4 The following question refers to information in figure A.4.1.
   Compare the volume of 1 mole of atoms of the noble gases (helium, neon and argon). Predict the value for the volume of 1 mole of atoms of krypton and xenon (also noble gases).
   Compare the volume of 1 mole of atoms of the alkali metals (lithium, sodium and potassium). Predict the volume of 1 mole of atoms of rubidium.

Approximate relative atomic masses

H = 1	He = 4	C = 12
N = 14	O = 16	Na = 23
Mg = 24	Al = 27	P = 31
S = 32	Cl = 35.5	K = 39
Ca = 40	Fe = 56	Ni = 59
Cu = 64	Br = 80	Ag = 108
Sn = 118	Hg = 200	Pb = 207

1 mole of molecules of any gas has a volume of 24 dm^3 (24 000 cm^3) at room temperature and pressure.

Working out the formula of a compound

It is possible to work out the formula of a compound from the results of an experiment. Two examples are given below.

1 Magnesium oxide
The formula of magnesium oxide can be found by burning a known mass of magnesium ribbon in a crucible.

Approximate relative atomic masses

H = 1	He = 4	C = 12
N = 14	O = 16	Na = 23
Mg = 24	Al = 27	P = 31
S = 32	Cl = 35.5	K = 39
Ca = 40	Fe = 56	Ni = 59
Cu = 64	Br = 80	Ag = 108
Sn = 118	Hg = 200	Pb = 207

1 mole of molecules of any gas has a volume of 24 dm³ (24 000 cm³) at room temperature and pressure.

Sample results might be:

a Mass of crucible + lid	= 25.15 g
b Mass of crucible, lid and magnesium	= 25.27 g
Mass of magnesium **b–a**	= 0.12 g
c Mass of crucible, lid and magnesium oxide formed	= 25.35 g
∴ Mass of magnesium oxide **c–a**	= 0.20 g

From these results
0.12 g of magnesium combines with (0.20–0.12) g of oxygen to form 0.20 g of magnesium oxide.
0.12 g of magnesium combines with 0.08 g of oxygen.
Using the type 2 calculation (page 171):
$\dfrac{0.12}{24}$ moles of magnesium atoms combine with $\dfrac{0.08}{16}$ moles of oxygen atoms.
$\dfrac{1}{200}$ mole of magnesium atoms combine with $\dfrac{1}{200}$ mole of oxygen atoms.
($\dfrac{1}{200}$ mole of magnesium atoms contains the same number of atoms as $\dfrac{1}{200}$ mole of oxygen atoms).
The simplest formula is, therefore, MgO.

Good results can be obtained by doing a series of experiments with different masses of magnesium ribbon and recording the results on a graph (figure A.4.2).
This procedure reduces the inaccuracy of individual experiments.

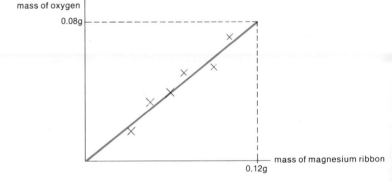

Figure A.4.2 Reaction of magnesium ribbon with oxygen

2 Copper(II) oxide

A known mass of copper(II) oxide is reduced to copper using hydrogen in apparatus shown in figure 6.7.
Sample results might be:

a Mass of combustion boat	= 12.20 g
b Mass of boat + copper(II) oxide	= 13.80 g
∴ Mass of copper(II) oxide **b–a**	= 1.60 g
c Mass of boat + copper after reduction	= 13.48 g
∴ Mass of copper **c–a**	= 1.28 g

1.28 g of copper combines with (1.60–1.28) g oxygen to form 1.60 g of copper(II) oxide.
1.28 g of copper combines with 0.32 g of oxygen.
$\dfrac{1.28}{64}$ moles of copper atoms combine with $\dfrac{0.32}{16}$ moles of oxygen atoms.
0.02 moles of copper atoms combine with 0.02 moles of oxygen atoms.
∴ Simplest formula is CuO.

Calculation examples

Type 5: 0.9 g of hydrogen combine with 4.2 g of nitrogen to form 5.1 g of ammonia. What is the simplest formula for ammonia?

$\frac{0.9}{1}$ moles of hydrogen atoms combine with $\frac{4.2}{14}$ moles of nitrogen atoms.

0.9 moles of hydrogen atoms combine with 0.3 moles of nitrogen atoms. (There are 3 times as many hydrogen atoms as nitrogen atoms)

∴ Simplest formula is NH_3.

something to think about . . .

1 Calculate the simplest formulae from the following data:
a 6 g of carbon combine with 1 g of hydrogen,
b 0.7 g of nitrogen combines to form 1.5 g of nitrogen oxide,
c 4.14 g of lead combines with 0.64 g of oxygen to form a lead oxide,
d 0.02 g of hydrogen combines with 0.32 g of oxygen to form a hydrogen oxide,
e 1.12 g of iron combines with oxygen to form 1.60 g of iron oxide.

2 Having found the simplest formula what has to be done to find the actual formula?

To calculate the simplest formula of a compound from its percentage composition

This is a variation of the type 5 above. For example:

Type 6: A compound contains 75 per cent carbon and 25 per cent hydrogen, Calculate the simplest formula of this hydrocarbon.

	C	**H**
a Percentage	75	25
b Mass of 1 mole of atoms	12	1
a ÷ b	$\frac{75}{12} = 6.25$	$\frac{25}{1} = 25$
÷ by the smallest i.e. 6.25	$\frac{6.25}{6.25} = 1$	$\frac{25}{6.25} = 4$

Simplest formula = **CH_4**

To calculate the percentage of an element in a compound

This is the reverse of Type 6. It is useful, for example, when comparing two fertilisers to find which one contains the larger amount of the 'active' ingredient.

Type 7: Calculate the percentage of nitrogen in ammonium nitrate (NH_4NO_3).

Mass of 1 mole of ammonium nitrate = $(2 \times 14) + (4 \times 1) + (3 \times 16)$ g
(Type 1)   = 80 g

1 mole of ammonium nitrate contains 2 moles of nitrogen atoms, that is 28 g.

Percentage of nitrogen in ammonium nitrate = $\frac{28}{80} \times 100$
                                                                   = 35%

Approximate relative atomic masses

H = 1	He = 4	C = 12
N = 14	O = 16	Na = 23
Mg = 24	Al = 27	P = 31
S = 32	Cl = 35.5	K = 39
Ca = 40	Fe = 56	Ni = 59
Cu = 64	Br = 80	Ag = 108
Sn = 118	Hg = 200	Pb = 207

1 mole of molecules of any gas has a volume of 24 dm³ (24 000 cm³) at room temperature and pressure.

Approximate relative atomic masses

H = 1	He = 4	C = 12
N = 14	O = 16	Na = 23
Mg = 24	Al = 27	P = 31
S = 32	Cl = 35.5	K = 39
Ca = 40	Fe = 56	Ni = 59
Cu = 64	Br = 80	Ag = 108
Sn = 118	Hg = 200	Pb = 207

1 mole of molecules of any gas has a volume of 24 dm³ (24 000 cm³) at room temperature and pressure.

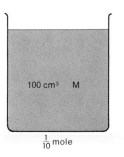

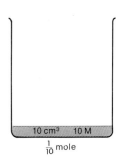

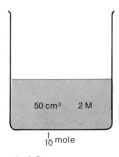

Figure A.4.3

Calculate the percentage of nitrogen in urea $CO(NH_2)_2$.
Mass of 1 mole of urea = 60 g
Percentage of nitrogen in urea $= \frac{28}{60} \times 100 = 46.6\%$
   Urea contains a larger percentage of nitrogen than ammonium nitrate. Because nitrogen enriches the soil and benefits plants, it would be expected that urea is a better fertiliser than ammonium nitrate. However, the solubility and price of the two compounds has to be considered before a 'best buy' can be decided.

something to think about . . .

1 In each case, calculate the simplest formula from the percentages given. (Type 6.)

a   Sulphur 50%, oxygen 50%.
b   Sulphur 40%, oxygen 60%.
c   Carbon 84%, hydrogen 16%.
d   Carbon 40%, hydrogen $6\frac{2}{3}\%$, oxygen $53\frac{1}{3}\%$.
e   Iron (Fe) 28%, sulphur 24%, oxygen 48%.

(In **d** and **e** you will need three columns in the calculations.)

2 Type 7 calculations. Calculate the percentage of:
a   carbon in calcium carbonate $CaCO_3$.
b   magnesium in magnesium sulphate $MgSO_4$.
c   magnesium in magnesium oxide MgO.
d   calcium in calcium bromide $CaBr_2$.
e   oxygen in tin(IV) oxide SnO_2.

Molar solutions

A molar solution is a solution containing 1 mole of a substance made up to 1 dm³ of solution.
For example, a molar solution (M) of sodium hydroxide (NaOH) contains 1 mole of sodium hydroxide in 1 dm³ of solution.
   The molarity of a solution may also be expressed as concentration in moles dm⁻³.
In general, the molarity of the solution can be found using the equation:

$$\text{molarity} = \frac{\text{number of g of solute dissolving to form 1 dm}^3 \text{ of solution}}{\text{mass of 1 mole of solute}}$$

Calculation examples are:
Type 8: Calculate the molarity of a sulphuric acid solution (H_2SO_4) containing 9.8 g of sulphuric acid in 100 cm³ of solution.

$$\text{molarity} = \frac{\text{grams of sulphuric acid in 1 dm}^3}{\text{mass of 1 mole of sulphuric acid (Type 1)}}$$
$$= \frac{9.8 \times 10}{98} \text{ M}$$
$$= 1 \text{ M}$$

From the definition of a molar solution, it follows that 1 dm³ (1000 cm³) of a 1 M solution contains 1 mole of solute particles dissolved.
All three solutions in figure A.4.3 differ in concentration but all contain the same quantity of solute dissolved.

$$\text{Number of moles present} = \text{molarity} \times \frac{\text{volume in cm}^3}{1000}$$

An example of the calculation:

Type 9: How many moles of sodium hydroxide (NaOH) are present in 100 cm^3 of 2M solution?

Number of moles of NaOH present $= 2 \times \dfrac{100}{1000}$

$= 0.2$ moles

Using calculation type 1, the mass of sodium hydroxide $= 8$ g.

Approximate relative atomic masses

H = 1	He = 4	C = 12
N = 14	O = 16	Na = 23
Mg = 24	Al = 27	P = 31
S = 32	Cl = 35.5	K = 39
Ca = 40	Fe = 56	Ni = 59
Cu = 64	Br = 80	Ag = 108
Sn = 118	Hg = 200	Pb = 207

1 mole of molecules of any gas has a volume of 24 dm^3 (24 000 cm^3) at room temperature and pressure.

something to think about . . .

1 Calculate the molarity of the following solutions:
   a 56 g of potassium hydroxide KOH in 1 dm^3 of solution.
   b 53 g of sodium carbonate Na_2CO_3 in 250 cm^3 of solution.
   c 73 g of hydrochloric acid HCl in 500 cm^3 of solution.
   d 17 g of silver nitrate $AgNO_3$ in 10 dm^3 of solution.
   e 21 g of calcium nitrate $Ca(NO_3)_2$ in 250 cm^3 of solution.

2 Work out how many moles of hydrochloric acid are present in:
   a 500 cm^3 of 2 M solution.
   b 5000 cm^3 of 0.2 M solution.
   c 1 cm^3 of M solution.
   d 100 cm^3 of 5 M solution.

3 Work out how many g of solute must be dissolved in water to make:
   a 1 dm^3 of M nitric acid HNO_3.
   b 100 cm^3 of M sodium hydroxide NaOH.
   c 250 cm^3 of 2 M ammonium hydroxide NH_4OH.
   d 100 cm^3 of 0.02 M sodium carbonate Na_2CO_3.
   e 10 dm^3 of 0.1 M sodium chloride NaCl.

Calculations from equations

Calculation examples are:

Type 10

Magnesium reacts with hydrochloric acid according to the equation:

$$Mg(s) + 2HCl(aq) \rightarrow MgCl_2(aq) + H_2(g)$$

From the equation you can see that 1 mole of magnesium atoms (24 g) reacts with two moles of hydrochloric acid.

What volume of 2 M hydrochloric acid exactly reacts with 0.1 moles of magnesium atoms?

0.1 moles of magnesium atoms reacts with 0.2 moles of hydrochloric acid. 1000 cm^3 of 2 M hydrochloric acid contains 2 moles of hydrochloric acid. 100 cm^3 of 2 M hydrochloric acid contains 0.2 moles of hydrochloric acid. $\therefore$ 100 cm^3 of 2 M hydrochloric acid reacts with 0.1 moles of magnesium atoms.

What mass of hydrogen is produced when 0.1 moles of magnesium reacts with excess acid?

From the equation,

Approximate relative atomic masses

H = 1	He = 4	C = 12
N = 14	O = 16	Na = 23
Mg = 24	Al = 27	P = 31
S = 32	Cl = 35.5	K = 39
Ca = 40	Fe = 56	Ni = 59
Cu = 64	Br = 80	Ag = 108
Sn = 118	Hg = 200	Pb = 207

1 mole of molecules of any gas has a volume of 24 dm^3 (24 000 cm^3) at room temperature and pressure.

1 mole of magnesium atoms reacts to produce 1 mole of hydrogen molecules,
0.1 moles of magnesium atoms react to produce 0.1 moles of hydrogen molecules,
Mass of 1 mole of hydrogen molecules (H$_2$) = 2 g,
∴ Mass of hydrogen produced = 0.2 g.

What volume of hydrogen measured at room temperature and pressure would be produced when 0.1 moles of magnesium atoms reacts with excess acid?

From the equation,
1 mole of magnesium atoms reacts to produce 1 mole of hydrogen molecules,
0.1 moles of magnesium atoms react to produce 0.1 mole of hydrogen molecules,
1 mole of hydrogen molecules occupies 24 dm^3 at room temperature and pressure,
∴ Volume of hydrogen produced = $24 \times \frac{1}{10} = 2.4$ dm^3.

Note: in all these calculations the use at some stage of a correctly balanced equation is essential.

something to think about . . .

1 $CaCO_3(s) + 2HCl(aq) \rightarrow CaCl_2(aq) + CO_2(g) + H_2O(l)$
a How many moles of hydrochloric acid would react with 1 mole of calcium carbonate?
b How many moles of hydrochloric acid would react with 0.1 moles of calcium carbonate?
c What volume of M hydrochloric acid would contain 2 moles of hydrochloric acid?
d What volume of M hydrochloric acid would react exactly with 0.1 moles of calcium carbonate?
e How many moles of carbon dioxide would be produced when 0.1 moles of calcium carbonate completely react?
f What volume of carbon dioxide at room temperature and pressure would be produced when 0.1 moles of calcium carbonate completely react?

2 $2NaOH(aq) + H_2SO_4(aq) \rightarrow Na_2SO_4(aq) + 2H_2O(l)$
a From the equation, how many moles of sodium hydroxide completely react with 1 mole of sulphuric acid?
b How many moles of sodium hydroxide are present in 50 cm^3 of 2 M solution?
c How many moles of sulphuric acid would react with 50 cm^3 of 2 M sodium hydroxide solution?
d What volume of 2 M sulphuric acid reacts completely with 50 cm^3 of 2 M sodium hydroxide solution?

Reacting volumes of gases

These are similar to previous examples but both reacting substances and products are gases.
When carbon monoxide burns in oxygen, carbon dioxide is produced.

$$2CO(g) + O_2(g) \rightarrow 2CO_2(g)$$

According to the equation, two moles of carbon monoxide molecules react with 1 mole of oxygen molecules to produce two moles of carbon dioxide molecules. One mole of molecules of any gas occupies 24 dm³ at room temperature and pressure. So, 48 dm³ of carbon monoxide gas reacts with 24 dm³ of oxygen to produce 48 dm³ of carbon dioxide.

In other words, the volume of carbon dioxide produced is twice the volume of oxygen required. Also, the volume of carbon monoxide used is the same as the volume of carbon dioxide produced.

If 20 cm³ of carbon monoxide and 10 cm³ oxygen are exploded together, 20 cm³ of carbon dioxide are produced. (All volumes measured at the same temperature and pressure.)

something to think about . . .

1 $2NO(g) + O_2(g) \rightarrow 2NO_2(g)$
   If 40 cm³ of oxygen and 40 cm³ of nitrogen monoxide are allowed to react what will be the:
   a volume of oxygen reacting with 40 cm³ of nitrogen monoxide?
   b volume of oxygen unused?
   c volume of nitrogen dioxide produced?
   d final volume of the gas mixture?

2 $2H_2(g) + O_2(g) \rightarrow 2H_2O(l)$
Note: the water produced is a liquid at room temperature and pressure and, therefore, has negligible volume.
   If 20 cm³ of hydrogen and 20 cm³ of oxygen are exploded together, what will be the volume of:
   a oxygen reacting with 20 cm³ of hydrogen?
   b oxygen unused after explosion?
   c gases left after explosion?

Approximate relative atomic masses

H = 1	He = 4	C = 12
N = 14	O = 16	Na = 23
Mg = 24	Al = 27	P = 31
S = 32	Cl = 35.5	K = 39
Ca = 40	Fe = 56	Ni = 59
Cu = 64	Br = 80	Ag = 108
Sn = 118	Hg = 200	Pb = 207

1 mole of molecules of any gas has a volume of 24 dm³ (24 000 cm³) at room temperature and pressure.

Electrolysis calculations

In an electrolysis experiment the amounts of substances produced at the positive and negative electrodes depends on the quantity of electricity that has flowed.

If a current of 4 A flows for 5 minutes (300 seconds), the quantity of electricity that has flowed can be calculated.

quantity of electricity = current (A) × time in seconds
                        = 4 × 300 coulombs
                        = 1200 coulombs.

When Avogadro's number of electrons has flowed through the wire (1 mole of electrons), 1 Faraday (F) is said to have passed.

1 Faraday = 96 500 coulombs

$$\text{quantity of electricity} = \frac{\text{current in A} \times \text{time in seconds}}{96\,500} F$$

Table A.4.2 shows the quantity of electricity required to produce 1 mole of atoms of different elements.

Approximate relative atomic masses

H = 1	He = 4	C = 12
N = 14	O = 16	Na = 23
Mg = 24	Al = 27	P = 31
S = 32	Cl = 35.5	K = 39
Ca = 40	Fe = 56	Ni = 59
Cu = 64	Br = 80	Ag = 108
Sn = 118	Hg = 200	Pb = 207

1 mole of molecules of any gas has a volume of 24 dm^3 (24 000 cm^3) at room temperature and pressure.

Table A.4.2 **Quantity of electricity required to discharge 1 mole of atoms.**

Ion being discharged	No. of Faradays to discharge 1 mole of atoms
Na^+	1
Ca^{2+}	2
Cu^{2+}	2
Al^{3+}	3
Cl^-	1
O^{2-}	2

If the ions being discharged at the positive and negative electrodes have a single charge (positive or negative), 1 Faraday of electricity will discharge 1 mole of atoms.

If the ions have a double charge, 2 Faradays will discharge 1 mole of atoms. Similarly, if the ions have a triple charge, 3 Faradays will discharge 1 mole of atoms.

It is possible to find the charge on nickel ions, for instance, by finding out how many Faradays of electricity are required to liberate 1 mole of nickel atoms. If the element is produced at the negative electrode, the ions being discharged are positively charged.

Calculation examples

Type 11: In the electrolysis of molten calcium bromide ($CaBr_2$), a current of 5 A flows for 193 seconds.

 a How many coulombs of electricity have passed?
  Quantity of electricity passed = current × time
            = 193 × 5 coulombs
            = 965 coulombs
 b How many Faradays of electricity have passed?
  No. of Faradays passed = $\frac{965}{96500}$ Faradays
           = $\frac{1}{100}$ Faraday

 c Calcium is produced at the negative electrode by the discharge of Ca^{2+} ions. How many moles of calcium atoms were produced at the negative electrode?
 2 Faradays of electricity produce 1 mole on calcium atoms (because calcium ions have a 2+ charge)
 $\frac{1}{100}$ Faraday of electricity produces $\frac{1}{200}$ mole of calcium atoms.

 d Bromine is produced at the positive electrode by the discharge of Br^- ions. How many moles of bromine atoms were produced at the positive electrode?
 1 Faraday of electricity produces 1 mole of bromine atoms (because bromide ions have a single negative charge)
 $\frac{1}{100}$ Faraday of electricity produces $\frac{1}{100}$ mole of bromine atoms.

something to think about . . .

1 Calculate the number of coulombs that have passed when
  a 5 A flows for 40 seconds.
  b 3 A flows for 1 hour.
  c 4 A flows for 3 minutes.

2 In the nickel plating of a metal object, the object is made the negative electrode in the electrolysis of nickel(II) sulphate solution. A current of 19.3 A flowed for 100 seconds.
  a How many coulombs of electricity had passed?
  b How many Faradays of electricity had passed?
  c How many moles of nickel atoms should have been deposited on the electrode by the passage of electricity?
  (Remember that nickel ions are Ni^{2+})
  d What change of mass of the metal object takes place during this process?
  e The change of mass expected was greater than the change of mass found in experimental conditions. Explain.

Energy calculations

In a heat of combustion experiment, a known mass of a substance is completely burned in oxygen. The heat produced is used to raise the temperature of water in a metal can.

Calculation examples

Type 12:

Mass of sulphur burnt   = 0.5 g
Mass of metal can   = 65.0 g
Mass of water in the can = 100 g

Temperature of water at the beginning of the experiment = 20°C
Temperature of water at the end of the experiment   = 30°C
$\therefore$ Temperature rise = 10°C
Heat required to raise the temperature of 100 g of water 10°C
= mass of water × temperature rise × specific heat capacity of water.
(specific heat capacity of water is the heat required to raise the temperature of 1 kg of water by 1°C. It is 4.2 kJ kg^{-1} deg^{-1})
= $\frac{100}{1000}$ × 10 × 4.2 kJ
= 4.2 kJ
Heat required to raise the temperature of 65 g of metal (the can) by 10°C
= mass × specific heat capacity × temperature rise
= $\frac{65}{1000}$ × 0.42 × 10 kJ
= 0.27 kJ
(specific heat capacity of the metal is 0.42 kJ kg^{-1} deg^{-1})
The heat required to raise the temperature of water and can
= 4.2 + 0.27 kJ
= 4.47 kJ
This heat came from the combustion of 0.5 g of sulphur. The heat produced when 1 mole of sulphur atoms (32 g) is completely burned will be 4.47 × 64 = 286 kJ
   The experimental result obtained is always low because energy evolved on combustion of the sulphur is lost to the surroundings.

Approximate relative atomic masses

H = 1	He = 4	C = 12
N = 14	O = 16	Na = 23
Mg = 24	Al = 27	P = 31
S = 32	Cl = 35.5	K = 39
Ca = 40	Fe = 56	Ni = 59
Cu = 64	Br = 80	Ag = 108
Sn = 118	Hg = 200	Pb = 207

1 mole of molecules of any gas has a volume of 24 dm^3 (24 000 cm^3) at room temperature and pressure.

Approximate relative atomic masses

H = 1	He = 4	C = 12
N = 14	O = 16	Na = 23
Mg = 24	Al = 27	P = 31
S = 32	Cl = 35.5	K = 39
Ca = 40	Fe = 56	Ni = 59
Cu = 64	Br = 80	Ag = 108
Sn = 118	Hg = 200	Pb = 207

1 mole of molecules of any gas has a volume of 24 dm^3 (24 000 cm^3) at room temperature and pressure.

Another slightly different calculation involves the reaction between two solutions. The heat evolved or absorbed by the reacting substances comes from or goes to the solution. By measuring the rise or fall in temperature, the heat change can be calculated.

Calculation examples

Type 13: Calculate the heat produced when 50 cm^3 of 2 M sodium hydroxide and 50 cm^3 of 2 M hydrochloric acid are mixed in a plastic beaker. The temperature rise is 13°C.

Mass of solution formed on mixing is approximately 100 g or $\frac{1}{10}$ kg. Specific heat capacity of these dilute solutions can be taken as 4.2 kJ kg^{-1} deg^{-1}.

Heat produced = $\frac{1}{10}$ × 4.2 × 13 kJ
= 5.46 kJ

The equation for the reaction is:

$$NaOH(aq) + HCl(aq) \rightarrow NaCl(aq) + H_2O(l)$$

In the experiment 0.1 moles of sodium hydroxide and 0.1 moles of hydrochloric acid react to evolve 5.46 kJ.

The heat of neutralisation is the heat produced when 1 mole of sodium hydroxide and 1 mole of hydrochloric acid react. The heat of neutralisation from this experiment will be 5.46 × 10 kJ, i.e. 54.6 kJ.

It is important to realise that the temperature rise would be the same if other volumes of these solutions were mixed providing the two volumes are the same.

something to think about . . .

1 How much heat is required to heat:
   a 100 cm^3 of water from 10°C to 20°C?
   b 2 dm^3 of dilute sodium hydroxide from 20°C to 40°C?
   c a kettle full of water (1500 cm^3) from room temperature (20°C) to 100°C?

2 Calculate the heat of combustion of carbon from the results below.
   0.42 g of carbon is completely burned in oxygen and the heat produced raises the temperature of water (320 g) by 10°C.
   (specific heat capacity of water = 4.2 kJ kg^{-1} deg^{-1})

Applications of chemical calculations

In industry chemical calculations help the manufacturer to work out costs. Here are a couple of simple examples.

1 In the production of aluminium by electrolysis, 3 Faradays of electricity are required to produce 1 mole of aluminium atoms (27 g) because aluminium ions have three positive charges. It is possible to work out the quantity of electricity and the cost to produce 1 tonne of aluminium.

2 If ethanol is being prepared by the addition of water to ethene, the manufacturer can work out how much ethene would be required to produce a given quantity of ethanol.

$$C_2H_4(g) + H_2O(l) \rightarrow C_2H_5OH(l)$$

From the equation, 1 mole of ethene molecules (28 g) produces 1 mole of ethanol molecules (46 g). By calculation it can be shown that 1 tonne of ethanol requires 0.6 tonnes of ethene.

This calculation assumes that all the ethene used is converted to ethanol (i.e. 100% yield). In practice some ethene will be wasted. The manufacturer, from experience, can estimate how much ethene is likely to be wasted.

something to think about . . .

There are two chlorides of mercury. One of these mercury chlorides was reduced to mercury in an experiment using hypophosphorous acid.

>Mass of beaker = 45.23 g
>Mass of beaker + mercury chloride = 47.94 g
>Mass of beaker + mercury produced = 47.23 g

a From these results calculate the masses of:
   (i) mercury chloride used.
   (ii) mercury produced.
b Complete the following:
   __ g of mercury combines with __ g of chlorine to produce __ g mercury chloride.
c How many moles of mercury atoms were produced in this experiment? (Hg = 200)
d How many moles of chlorine atoms were combined with mercury in the sample of mercury chloride? (Cl = 35.5)
e How many moles of chlorine atoms would combine with 1 mole of mercury atoms?
f What is the formula of the mercury chloride used?
                    (*Southern Regional Examinations Board CSE*)

Appendix 5. The elements

Atomic number	Element	Symbol	Approximate relative atomic mass	Melting point °C	Boiling point °C	Density g cm^{-3}	Date of discovery
1	Hydrogen	H	1	−259	−253	0.00008	1766
2	Helium	He	4	−270	−269	0.00017	1868
3	Lithium	Li	7	180	1330	0.53	1817
4	Beryllium	Be	9	1280	2700	1.9	1827
5	Boron	B	11	2000	3000	2.3	1808
6	Carbon	C	12		4200	2.2	*
7	Nitrogen	N	14	−210	−196	0.00117	1772
8	Oxygen	O	16.	−219	−183	0.00132	1774
9	Fluorine	F	19	−220	−188	0.0016	1886
10	Neon	Ne	20	−249	−246	0.0008	1898
11	Sodium	Na	23	98	890	0.97	1807
12	Magnesium	Mg	24	650	1110	1.7	1808
13	Aluminium	Al	27	660	2060	2.7	1825
14	Silicon	Si	28	1410	2700	2.4	1823
15	Phosphorus	P	31	44	280	1.8	1669
16	Sulphur	S	32	119	445	2.1	*
17	Chlorine	Cl	35.5	−101	−35	0.003	1774
18	Argon	Ar	40	−189	−189	0.0017	1894
19	Potassium	K	39	64	760	0.86	1807
20	Calcium	Ca	40	850	1440	1.6	1808
21	Scandium	Sc	45	1400	2500	3.1	1879
22	Titanium	Ti	48	1670	3300	4.5	1789
23	Vanadium	V	51	1900	3400	6.0	1801
24	Chromium	Cr	52	1900	2500	7.2	1797
25	Manganese	Mn	55	1250	2000	7.4	1774
26	Iron	Fe	56	1540	3000	7.9	*
27	Cobalt	Co	59	1490	2900	8.9	1735
28	Nickel	Ni	59	1450	2800	8.9	1751
29	Copper	Cu	63.5	1080	2500	9.0	*
30	Zinc	Zn	65.5	419	910	7.1	17th Century
31	Gallium	Ga	70	30	2200	5.9	1875
32	Germanium	Ge	72.5	950	2800	5.4	1886
33	Arsenic	As	75		615	5.7	13th Century
34	Selenium	Se	79	217	690	4.8	1817
35	Bromine	Br	80	−7	58	3.1	1826
36	Krypton	Kr	84	−157	−153	0.0035	1898
37	Rubidium	Rb	85.5	39	700	1.5	1861
38	Strontium	Sr	88	770	1380	2.6	1808
39	Yttrium	Y	89	1500	3000	4.5	1794
40	Zirconium	Zr	91	1900	4000	6.5	1789
41	Niobium	Nb	93	2500	4800	8.5	1801
42	Molybdenum	Mo	96	2620	5000	10.2	1782
43	Technetium	Tc	99	2200	4600	11.5	1937
44	Ruthenium	Ru	101	2500	4000	12.2	1845
45	Rhodium	Rh	103	1960	3700	12.4	1803

*These elements have been known for thousands of years.

Atomic number	Element	Symbol	Approximate relative atomic mass	Melting point °C	Boiling point °C	Density g cm⁻³	Date of discovery
46	Palladium	Pd	106	1550	3000	12.0	1803
47	Silver	Ag	108	961	2200	10.5	*
48	Cadmium	Cd	112	320	765	8.7	1817
49	Indium	In	115	156	2000	7.3	1861
50	Tin	Sn	119	232	2600	7.3	*
51	Antimony	Sb	122	630	1400	6.6	*
52	Tellurium	Te	128	450	990	6.2	1782
53	Iodine	I	127	114	183	4.9	1811
54	Xenon	Xe	131	−112	−108	0.005	1898
55	Caesium	Cs	133	29	680	1.9	1861
56	Barium	Ba	137	710	1600	3.5	1805
57	Lanthanum	La	139	920	3500	6.2	1839
58	Cerium	Ce	140	800	3000	6.7	1803
59	Praseodymium	Pr	141	935	3100	6.8	1885
60	Neodymium	Nd	144	1020	3100	7.0	1885
61	Promethium	Pm	147	1030	2700		1945
62	Samarium	Sm	150	1080	1600	7.6	1879
63	Europium	Eu	152	830	1430	5.3	1901
64	Gadolinium	Gd	157	1320	3000	7.9	1886
65	Terbium	Tb	159	1400	2600	8.3	1843
66	Dysprosium	Dy	162.5	1500	2400	8.5	1886
67	Holmium	Ho	165	1500	2500	8.8	1879
68	Erbium	Er	167	1500	2700	9.0	1843
69	Thulium	Tm	169	1550	2000	9.3	1879
70	Ytterbium	Yb	173	824	1500	7.0	1878
71	Lutetium	Lu	175	1700	3330	9.9	1907
72	Hafnium	Hf	179	2000	5000	13.1	1923
73	Tantalum	Ta	181	3000	5400	16.6	1802
74	Tungsten	W	184	3400	6000	19.3	1789
75	Rhenium	Re	186	3200	5630	21.0	1925
76	Osmium	Os	190	2700	5000	22.6	1804
77	Iridium	Ir	192	2440	5300	22.5	1804
78	Platinum	Pt	195	1770	4000	21.4	1735
79	Gold	Au	197	1060	2700	19.3	*
80	Mercury	Hg	200	−39	357	13.6	*
81	Thallium	Tl	204	300	1460	11.8	1861
82	Lead	Pb	207	327	1744	11.3	*
83	Bismuth	Bi	209	270	1560	9.8	16th Century
84	Polonium	Po	210	254	1000	9.3	1898
85	Astatine	At	210	302			1940
86	Radon	Rn	222	−71	−62	0.009	1900
87	Francium	Fr	223	30	650		1936
88	Radium	Ra	226	700	1500	5.0	1898
89	Actinium	Ac	227	1050	3000		1899
90	Thorium	Th	232	1700	4000	11.6	1829
91	Protactinium	Pa	231	1200	4000	15.4	1917
92	Uranium	U	238	1130	3800	19.0	1789
93	Neptunium	Np	237	640		19.5	1940
94	Plutonium	Pu	242	640	3200	19.6	1940
95	Americium	Am	243	1200	2600	11.7	1944

Atomic number	Element	Symbol	Approximate relative atomic mass	Melting point °C	Boiling point °C	Density g cm^{-3}	Date of discovery
96	Curium	Cm	247				1944
97	Berkelium	Bk	247				1949
98	Californium	Cf	251				1950
99	Einsteinium	Es	254				1952
100	Fermium	Fm	253				1953
101	Mendelevium	Md	256				1955
102	Nobelium	No	254				1958
103	Lawrencium	Lw	257				1961
104	Kurchatovium	Ku					1969
105	Hahnium						1970

something to think about . . .

1 Name the element which has the
  a highest density
  b highest melting point
  c lowest melting point
  d lowest boiling point

2 List the elements named after
  a famous scientists
  b countries or places.

3 Decide whether each of these statements is true or false
  a all elements ending in -ium were discovered after 1800
  b no new element that is a gas at room temperature has been discovered since 1900
  c all elements known before 1700 are solids at room temperature and pressure
  d antimony would melt in a hot burner flame
  e beryllium was discovered before any other element in Group 2 of the periodic table.

4 The elements in the list are arranged in order of increasing atomic number. They are also arranged in order of increasing relative atomic mass but there are a few elements out of order. Which elements are out order?

Index